Yankee
FOR LIFE

Yankee
FOR LIFE

My 40-Year Journey in Pinstripes

BOBBY MURCER

with Glen Waggoner

HARPER

An Imprint of HarperCollins*Publishers*

To Kay

My wife, my friend, my confidante . . . the mother of my two wonderful children, Tori and Todd . . . and a great Lali to our five grandchildren.

Thank you for being both Mom *and* Dad during all those years I followed my dream, playing baseball, and for building such a strong, loving family.

Thank you for being so brave these past 18 months, when we have had to cope together with a new and daunting challenge.

How can a man be so lucky as to find a woman so beautiful on the outside and even more beautiful on the inside?

God truly blessed me when He gave me you.

I love you with all my heart.

HarperCollins books may be purchased for educational, business, or sales promotional use. For information, please write: Special Markets Department, HarperCollins Publishers, 10 East 53rd Street, New York, NY 10022.

FIRST EDITION

Library of Congress Cataloging-in-Publication Data is available upon request.

ISBN: 978-0-06-147341-8

08 09 10 11 12   OV/RRD   10 9 8 7 6 5 4 3 2 1

Acknowledgments

This past year and a half, Kay and I have focused on the complicated task of managing my cancer rehab. But during that time we also took a crash course in Memoirs 101. Little did we know that it would take a team of talented professionals and an army of willing friends to get us across the plate. I thank you for helping make it happen.

Leading off, I would like to give Glen Waggoner my enormous thanks for helping to process, polish, and produce a story that Kay and I are so very pleased to share. We became friends during this dance, and only stepped on each other's toes a couple of times. We appreciate your abilities, Glen, especially your knack for bringing all the humor to our tale. You nailed it! A tip of my Yankee cap to you, pal.

The Hall of Famers at HarperCollins, David Hirshey and Kate Hamill, along with Kathy Schneider and Campbell Wharton, initiated us into the publishing world with welcoming hearts and invaluable insights. Thanks for your careful guidance at every turn.

A great double-play combination brought us all together: Robert Wilson and Marty Appel. Rob, it's been a pleasure to work with you. Thanks for your patience with a couple of green rookies. And, Marty, your love and friendship go back to my earliest days with the Yankees. Thanks for saving me from a bunch of E-Murcers.

Special thanks also to Jared Salvato, Jim Martin, and all my friends and colleagues at the YES Network and within the New York Yankees family.

A squad of Oklahoma buddies rallied to our side right from the start: Dr. Hanna and Judy Saadah; Kay Oliver; Mary and Gary England; James and Judy Cail; Linda Tapp; Bill and Larry Mathis; David and Tim Aduddell; Dee and Dick Dugan; and Lynn McMillon.

We received constant boosts of inspiration from many old

friends, some of whom have been with us since the 1960s: Bobby Kelmenson; Arnold and Barbara Cohen; Al and Carole Schragis; Eileen Goudge and Sandy Kenyon; Steve Lefkowitz; Mike and Bobby Lancelotti; Andrew and Shirley Rosen; Sharon Halper; Adrianna and Larry Sarapochillo; Yogi and Carmen Berra; Joe Torre; Mel and Jean Stottlemyre; Gretchen and Willie Randolph, Anita and Lou Piniella; Bruce and Nancy Moran; Michele Magee; Suzy Hart; Steve and Debbie Thompson; Lon and Sue Zimolzak; and, of course, my other brother, Jimmy Lindstrom.

We also drew strength from new friends along the way: Aaron Gaberman and his family; Colonel Doug Wheelock; and Mark Hunert and the staff at the Marriott Medical Center Hotel.

We had our very own Club Med at M. D. Anderson Cancer Center in Houston: Dr. Jeff Weinberg; Dr. Sam and Rhonda Hassenbusch; Dr. Mark Gilbert; Dr. Amy Heimberger; Dr. Chris Pelloski; Lamonne Krutcher, Georganne Mansour; Lacy Perry; Toranio Oliver (a.k.a T.O.); Debbie Cohen; and Krista McAlee. Guys, words can't express our appreciation for your professionalism, kindness, and friendship.

We enjoyed the love and support from members of the Palm Desert, Manhattan, First Colony, and Memorial Road Churches of Christ, who have continued to buoy our spirits every step of the way. We are so thankful for all of your prayers. Keep it up, please.

My heart is full of love for all those we've come to know this past year who share my cancer struggles—too many to mention by name, but you know who you are, and how you've touched our lives. Keep up the good fight.

Let's have a standing O, please, for the Starting Lineup of the Murcer All-Star Team: Tori, Todd, David, Lynne, Sara, Lloyd, Dwaine, Phyllis, Cindy, Calvin, Randy, and Dana. We could never have maintained our strength without your love and encouragement. Big hugs and eternal thanks to you all!

Finally, our Pee-Wee Squad, the little loves of our lives: Sophie, Jack, Knox, Holden, and Ava. If ever Bobby Pops is having a rough day, all I have to do is pull out my photo album and see your faces. I just adore you all.

Contents

FOREWORD: A TRUE YANKEE

Yogi Berra

---

*I*f you don't know Bobby Murcer, that's too bad. I don't know too many people I'd rather know even if I already know them.

Bobby's a wonderful person. He's a class act with a big heart. He's been a great friend all these years, a true Yankee.

When he first came to the Yankees for a cup of coffee in 1965, I was gone. But I remember meeting him a year earlier when I was a rookie manager, and we were in Kansas City.

Tom Greenwade, the Yankees scout who ended up signing Bobby, brought Bobby up from Oklahoma City to Municipal Stadium before our game, to meet the guys and put on a Yankee uniform and take some batting practice. Heck, he was a nervous kid, only 18 years old, just out of high school. We had a veteran team, and we were in the middle of a pennant race. In fact, I yelled to him that he better not get too comfortable in the cage, that my players needed the swings.

I was just kidding, but maybe it unsettled him a bit, I don't know.

From the day he got to Yankee Stadium, people started talking about how Bobby was a big deal, how he was going to be the "next Mantle." Nobody needed that kind of pressure or hype. Still, all you heard was how Mickey had been his idol growing up, how both came from Oklahoma, how both came up as shortstops, how both were recruited and signed by the same scout.

What I do know is that when Bobby made it to the majors to stay in 1969 he always gave his all, and he became one heck of a player. Early on he made a bunch of errors at shortstop and then third, at least that's what they said. But when he shifted to the outfield, he was one of the best. Bobby took enormous pride in being a Yankee, even when the teams weren't good—and most of his years in New York, they weren't.

When he returned to the Yankees in 1979, after spending four seasons and change with the Giants and the Cubs, I was a coach. He was an older player then, and he'd missed on those back-to-back championship teams in 1977 and 1978—just lousy timing. I'd kid him he was really brought back to help us out on Old-Timers' Day.

Bobby was way more, though. He was clutch. He helped a lot of fellows, especially young guys. He raised everyone's spirits. And he was a great team guy. On the field and in the booth, he's forever a Yankee, just like his book tells you.

With all that, Bobby is also the face of courage. Few things are more powerful in an individual than courage and optimism. Couple that with integrity and loyalty, and you've got the full package.

They just don't make better people than Bobby Murcer.

INTRODUCTION: A DREAM COME TRUE

Derek Jeter

*M*y dream from the time I was a little boy was very specific: to play shortstop for the New York Yankees when I grew up.

Not just play baseball, not just any position, but *shortstop*.

And not just for any team, but for the *Yankees*.

The first part of my dream is easy to explain: my dad had played shortstop, and I wanted to be like him. I thought shortstop was the coolest position on the field. Still do.

The second part of my dream needs a little explaining. I was born in New Jersey, but my family moved to Kalamazoo, Michigan, when I was four. But I spent much of every summer with my grandparents back in West Milford, New Jersey, so the Yankees were always *my* team.

The first big league baseball game I ever saw was in—you guessed it—Yankee Stadium. I was six or seven, and we sat up so high in the upper deck that the players looked like ants. I don't remember who the Yankees were playing that day, and I don't know whether they won or lost. But I do remember Yankee Stadium.

Yankee Stadium! It was enormous, bigger than anything on TV had prepared me for. The infield, so perfect. The outfield, spreading out as far as I could see. The huge crowd, more people in one place than I had ever seen in my life. And when I think of the sound of all those people cheering when the National Anthem was over . . . well, it still gives me goose bumps.

That was the day I knew with all my heart what I wanted to be when I grew up: a New York Yankee.

So I can absolutely relate to the title of this book, *Yankee for Life*. That's all I can ever remember wanting to be.

And I also can absolutely relate to Bobby Murcer, who in his heart has been a Yankee for life.

I never saw Bobby play ball—he was already up in the broadcast booth by the time I was learning to read a box score. My first encounter with him came in spring training in 1996, just before my rookie season. He went out of his way to introduce himself and wish me well. I learned then that he had worn number 2 before me, and a month later when we got up to Yankee Stadium, I learned that he had once used the locker that was now assigned to me.

From day one, Bobby was very supportive, very upbeat, very encouraging. You could tell that he wasn't just going through the motions, that in fact he was genuinely interested in seeing a young player develop.

The one characteristic about Bobby that shines out to me is his positive attitude. He's always a lot of fun to be around. He makes young players feel comfortable, at ease.

To me, that all adds up to one thing: Bobby Murcer is a true Yankee for life.

PREFACE: YANKEE FOR LIFE

*I*f it's true that "all the world's a stage"—and who am I to argue with Mr. William Shakespeare?—then my stage has been a grassy baseball diamond.

From the time I knew to run from home to first, I've spent most of my summer days on one baseball field or another. Baseball has been my life, my passion, from daybreak till dark. And from just about the time I could hold a bat, I dreamed of one day stepping up to the plate in a Yankee uniform at Yankee Stadium.

Hey, the Yankees were winning all those championships with a guy from Oklahoma leading the way. Surely they could win a few more after I got up there.

I'd tell myself that if I worked really hard at playing the game I loved, someday I might get a shot at wearing those pinstripes and calling Yankee Stadium home.

Bingo! At the age of 19, I walked out onto the grass at Yankee Stadium, a bona fide member of the New York Yankees. I just knew I was the luckiest kid ever! One year out of high school, and here I was rubbing elbows with Mickey Mantle and Roger Maris and Elston Howard and Whitey Ford and Bobby Richardson and . . .

Man, I was livin' the dream!

Sure, I would need to put some time in down in the minors, but New York was still holding its doors wide open for me when I was ready to return. How can you not love a city that welcomes you with open arms? As they say, it's a town so nice they named it twice: New York, New York.

Many of you know that I got to live out most of my playing career (17 seasons) in New York. There *were* a couple of short stints in two other cities on the major league map: San Francisco (1975–1976) and Chicago (1977–1978, plus half of 1979). Both were very exciting places to visit, but neither held a candle(stick) to my beloved New York.

In 1979, when the Cubs traded me back to the Yankees in mid-season, I wanted to kiss every fan in Yankee Stadium during my first game back.

Believe me, pinstripes have always been, and will always be, my favorite attire! One of the best things about Old-Timers' Day, almost as good as hanging out with the fellows I used to play with, is putting those pinstripes back on once again. In fact, that's my real incentive for staying in decent shape after all these years: that uniform deserves *respect*.

Hanging up that uniform for the last time as an active player in 1983 was tough, really tough.

So now, on August 3, 1983, there I was, a 37-year-old ex-ballplayer getting ready for the second phase of his baseball career. The Yankees had given me a big sendoff during the pregame ceremonies that afternoon, and then just 30 minutes later . . . "Ta-da! Live from the broadcast booth in New York, it's Bobby Murcer!"

Suddenly I was stepping onto a whole different stage, an unfamiliar one without grass. But believing I was the "can-do" kid again, I learned to romance the camera, and I fell right in with the veterans at my side: Scooter, Frank Messer, Bill White. They were the first 3 of the eventual *31* broadcast partners I would have during the past 24 years as one of the voices of the Yankees.

Tell you what, I'll send you a bottle of my brother's "Uncle Randy's" award-winning barbecue sauce if you can name every broadcast partner I've had over the years. I'm betting that even the most hard-core Yankee fan is going to come up five or six short. (See chapter 11.)

I've been witness to many great games and many great moments during my tenure in the booth: George Brett and the Pine Tar Incident; David Cone's perfect game; the return of the Yankees' reign of supremacy that began during the 1996 World Series—events that remain indelible not only in my memory but probably in many of yours as well.

———

If you know your Shakespeare—and I don't, but I looked it up—there's a line after the "all the world's a stage" business that goes like this: "And one man in his time plays many parts."

Well, let me tell you that I wouldn't have been able to handle my next part, which came along just a few years later, if it hadn't been for Kay.

Diana Kay Rhodes Murcer, my now-and-forever high school sweetheart, my bride for 41 years, has always been my sounding board, with heavy emphasis on the word "sound." She is rock-solid, the most centered person I know, and not the least bit shy about telling you what she thinks.

In fact, from time to time in the pages that follow, she *will* tell you what she thinks; I couldn't imagine doing anything—even writing a book—without including Kay's two (okay, maybe like four or five) cents.

Throughout our lives, whatever we might be facing, Kay has always made me believe it would be just fine. It was for a purpose. It was something that we could handle—together.

And this brings me to Christmas Eve 2006, when the "stocking stuffer" I received was a diagnosis of a brain tumor.

That's right: I got the news on Christmas Eve.

And I learned four days later that it was the worst kind of malignant brain tumor you can have.

Now, I've had a few punk Christmases in my day, but this one was the topper. Shock and disbelief, followed immediately by surgery and chemotherapy and radiation, followed by uncertainty about what lay ahead. Everything from that Christmas Eve on has happened in rapid succession.

Not even a Nolan Ryan fastball inside and high had ever knocked me back as hard as the words "You . . . have . . . *brain . . . cancer.*"

But here's the payoff pitch: within days, miraculously, I was enveloped by a calming sense of peace, acceptance, and trust.

Peace. Acceptance. Trust.

Those three words sustained me until I could regain my footing, and they have been with me ever since.

Kay and I asked for prayers from every source available, and we were flooded with an outpouring of them—and they worked! Little "miracles" started to arrive on our doorstep, just like the morning papers, and that's when we realized we had our answer to "What's next?"

———

My story hasn't ended yet. In fact, I believe I'm exactly where God intended for me to be all along. He just needed to set the stage for me so none of you would miss hearing all of this. If I hadn't become a New York Yankee, and then a Yankee broadcaster, and consequently somebody you knew on a first-name basis—or, as in the case of Phil Rizzuto, a last-name basis ("Hey, Murcer! How about that Mattingly!")—then my story would never have gotten beyond my family. And I think it's important that it has.

My Christmas Eve "gift" has been like one of those special stacking wooden boxes. You know, you open the biggest one and there's another hidden inside, then another, and soon there are 11 of them.

Cancer has opened me up to more blessings than I could ever have imagined, and it has let me look at my life as one gigantic jigsaw puzzle. Guess what? All the pieces fit!

So now I may not know what lies ahead, but I'm just trying my best to live and love every single hour of every single day, with the words of one of my most lovable, caring, and insightful friends ringing in my ears:

"It ain't over till it's over."

A MAJOR LEAGUE HEADACHE

*D*uring the summer of 2006, I began getting a lot of headaches. No big deal. More annoying than anything else. I figured they were just sinus headaches. As a Yankee TV broadcaster, I put in a lot of hours in the air, at least six or seven flights a month. All that going in and out of pressurized cabins can really mess with your sinuses. Ask people who travel a lot; that's what they'll tell you.

I've never been big on pills, and the few aspirin I took didn't do any good, which just confirmed my thinking on the subject. The headaches would stop when they were good and ready: end of story.

But after a while, maybe a month or so, they started getting worse and more frequent.

So finally, at Kay's urging, I went to an ear, nose, and throat specialist. Mind you, I still figured the headaches would go away sooner or later; worst case when the season was over and I stopped all that air travel. Heck, they were just sinus headaches.

Well, the ENT, a good friend and old high school classmate of ours named Dr. Ronnie Wright, checked me out and said, "You may have an infection in there. For us to figure out if it's a deep infection, let's do a CT scan on you." (That's what they used to call a CAT scan, which is a three-dimensional, high-tech X-ray.) So at the end of July I had a CT scan performed at Mercy Hospital in Oklahoma City.

After the exam, Ronnie came back in to go over the results. He'd read them, the other radiologists there at Mercy read them, and they all came up with the same conclusion: nothing.

By "nothing," of course, they meant no infection, nothing abnormal in my sinuses. So Ronnie didn't give me any special medications. Just "Tylenol as needed." That's basically what it came down to.

But the headaches continued. And they got progressively worse over August and early September. They weren't migraines. I didn't get nauseous or anything. They just hurt enough to be annoying. And they weren't on just one side, the way I understand a lot of migraines are. They were mostly in the front of my head and every now and then in the back of my head as well. Nothing I couldn't manage, mind you, but by the end of the summer they were coming more often.

Then, in October and November, the pain cranked up a notch or two. But that wasn't the worst part. The worst part was the fatigue factor that kicked in, big-time. For no good reason, I found myself getting tired, really exhausted.

That, more than the headaches, got my attention.

═══════

Okay, there's a little break in the action, and I'd like to introduce my longtime playing partner, someone I've known since I was 11 years old. Diana Kay Rhodes Murcer and I have been finishing each other's sentences for more than four decades. Her wise counsel and enduring love lurk behind every word in the book, so I think it's only fitting that you should hear from her directly from time to time as this story unfolds.

After all, in every possible sense, it's *our* story.

Now Coming to the Plate . . .

Kay Murcer

W hat got my attention besides the fatigue during the second half of 2006 were the changes in Bobby's personality.

I remember telling my sister, Cindy, in early December 2006 that there were times that Bobby seemed like he was in some kind of stupor. It started with little things, like not closing the garage door down when he left to go somewhere.

Very un-Bobby-like behavior.

And then there was his office at home. Bobby has always been super meticulous about keeping papers filed and bills paid and letters answered, everything neat and orderly. Okay, he was a neat freak. But in December his desk suddenly became cluttered with unfinished business. Almost overnight. After a couple of days, I said to him, "What's going on in there in your office? What's wrong?" And he said, "I don't know, I just don't seem to care about it."

That wasn't the Bobby I'd known for nearly 50 years. And it was very, very disturbing.

But the scariest thing came two weeks before Christmas. We were driving down to Dallas with my parents to be with our son, Todd, and his wife, Lynne, who was expecting twins in January; our daughter, Tori, and her husband, David; all the grandkids; and Tori's in-laws for a big family Christmas.

We were celebrating Christmas early because Bobby and I were flying out on Christmas Eve to go to our California home in La Quinta for the winter.

At least that was the plan.

On the drive down, with our car all loaded up with Christmas presents, and with my parents trailing us in their car, we stopped at this restaurant we all like in Ardmore, Oklahoma, to have lunch. We were there for an hour, maybe an hour and a half, and as we left the restaurant, Bobby discovered that he couldn't find his car keys.

You have to understand that in all the time I've known him, from the time he first got his driver's license, I don't recall his once misplacing his car keys. Not once. And he was acting very befuddled. I mean, he really was not himself at all. It crossed my mind at the time—and I learned later that my parents had the same thought—that Bobby'd had a mild stroke or something. That's how odd he was acting.

I had my keys, so we headed back out to the car, where we found Bobby's. He'd left them in the ignition, with the car doors unlocked.

All the gifts and luggage and everything were still there, so we all tried to laugh it off. But I think this was a huge sign to all of us—to my parents and me, and to Bobby as well—that something was definitely not right.

Bobby was not who he'd always been, not the person we all knew. He had become a different person.

Later, when we found out what had been causing all this mess and set about fixing it, I asked Kay what it had felt like for that crazy Christmas season, living with an alien. And she just said, "Very unsettling."

I knew immediately what she meant. Not knowing what's wrong with you can sometimes be worse than knowing, even when what's wrong with you turns out to be brain cancer.

———

A few weeks earlier, when the headaches had come back with a vengeance, and the fatigue was laying me low, leaving me without the strength to play golf or do any of my usual physical activities, I had called our family physician, Dr. Hanna Saadah, and told him, "I think there's something wrong with my blood, and that's what's causing this doggone fatigue. I need to come and see you." So he brought me in and ran blood tests, which all came back negative.

So much for my brilliant self-diagnosis.

Dr. Saadah did think he had just the ticket for the headaches, though. "Here's what I'm going to do," he said. "I'm going to give you a couple of shots in your sinuses, and that'll relieve your headaches, believe me." So that's what he did: two injections on each side of my nose. They hurt like the dickens, and for the first couple of days, they seemed to give me some relief.

But then the headaches came back, and they wouldn't go away.

Finally Kay, God bless her, got up the morning of the 23rd and called Dr. Saadah at home. I guess the anxiety and worry had gotten to her. Thank goodness it had. That call might have saved my life.

Kay

*B*obby knew that there was something out of the ordinary going on with his health, and—knowing him—I'm sure he wanted to start eliminating things, like diabetes and other blood disorders.

He never said—he never would say—that he was afraid it might be some form of cancer, but we both knew that with his family history, it was possible.

So the day before Christmas Eve, I called Dr. Saadah at home and I asked him, "Look, I know it's a Saturday, and the holidays are just getting ready to begin, but can Bobby possibly come in and see you right now, today?"

The night before, I'd gotten on the Internet and Googled "stroke" and "dementia" and "depression" and just about everything else I could find that might explain Bobby's symptoms.

Strangely enough, I told Dr. Saadah, the condition that seemed to line up best with Bobby's symptoms was depression.

"Does he have anything to be depressed about?" Dr. Saadah asked, and I said that sure, he had the fatigue and the headaches to be depressed about. "But I gave him those shots for the headaches," he said. "I think it'd do you both good to go on out to California."

Bobby and I were . . . well, we were a little bit disappointed at that advice. I knew Dr. Saadah was going on vacation Christmas Day, and

> that he wouldn't be able to see us next week, so he's telling us to go to California—a change of scenery, great weather, play some golf (which Bobby couldn't do because of the way he felt).

Kay had already rebooked our flight to California for the following week; neither one of us was in any mood for travel. We were both feeling pretty let down that we'd have to wait for Dr. Saadah to return from his vacation before I could see him, so we decided, the heck with it, let's just go to a movie. I mean, we were so frustrated, so unsettled—there's that word again—that we'd just go to a movie and chill out. But the movie we chose had just the reverse effect: *The Good Shepherd* was bleak and depressing and nearly three hours long. (It only seemed longer.)

But the minute we walked out of the movie theater, I saw I had missed a call on my cell from Dr. Saadah. I called him back, and he said, "Bobby, I went into the office, and I looked at your records. Let's give you an MRI first thing tomorrow morning. I really don't like the fact you still have your headache."

God bless Dr. Saadah! Here he was getting ready to leave on his own vacation, and yet he went to his office right before Christmas Eve to check my records.

"I know tomorrow's Christmas Eve, and it's Sunday morning," he said, "but I'm going to schedule you for an MRI at 8 A.M. Can you do that?"

You bet I can!

It sounds a little strange, I guess, being excited about going into the hospital to have an MRI on Christmas Eve, but the mere act of *doing something* made us both *feel* a whole lot better.

All of a sudden we were pretty upbeat, certainly compared to earlier. I'm not the kind of person who stews about things. If I have a problem, I like to fix it, then and there, and move on. So now we had ourselves a plan: on Christmas Eve morning, we would drive straight to the hospital for an MRI.

What did it mean? What *might* it mean? Didn't know. Didn't want to go there. Just take it one step at a time. Don't overreact. Don't speculate. We'd find out soon enough, because we had a *plan*.

Sunday morning, 8 sharp, we reported to the Radiology Clinic at Mercy Hospital in Oklahoma City for my MRI. I'm never late for anything, and this sure wasn't something I was going to be late for. The whole deal took 45 minutes, tops. MRI stands for "magnetic resonance imaging," which meant they took an up-close-and-personal picture of my brain. Dr. Saadah needed a little time to review the results, and then we'd have our answer and could get started fixing whatever was broke. Sounded easy at the time.

Afterward, it being Sunday and all, Kay and I went to church, and then we drove over to meet her parents and her brother and his wife at one of our favorite restaurants for lunch. Pretty ordinary Sunday drill for us, except that we'd been to the hospital three hours earlier for me to get an MRI.

But then things got different real fast. We'd just gotten out of our car and were heading into the restaurant when I got a call on my cell. It was Dr. Saadah. I clicked the speakerphone on so Kay could hear, too. Knowing me as well as he does, Dr. Saadah didn't beat around the bush:

"Bobby, you have a brain tumor."

———

Let me tell you, nothing in my life ever got my attention quicker than those six words.

"Bobby, you have a brain tumor."

I was in shock.

We were in shock.

Utter and complete and total shock.

Kay and I just stood there, pretty much dumbstruck, trying to process what he was telling me. I had to have him repeat everything, because I was only absorbing about every third word. Really only hearing the same two, over and over: *brain tumor*.

"You have a lot of edema," he said at one point. "That's what's been causing your strange behavior. We've got to reduce the edema immediately."

(*Edema?* My mind was racing at warp speed, and I'm thinking, I've got an edema, too?)

"The fluid is causing swelling in your brain," Dr. Saadah said, explaining to me what edema is. "That's why you're having the headaches, and that's why you're acting the way you have been. Let's get you on a steroid immediately." He said that he'd call in a prescription to our local pharmacy, and that we could pick it up in 15 minutes or so. He told me to take it at once, right there.

About that time my brother-in-law, Dwaine, walked out into the parking lot from the restaurant. His wife, Phyllis, and Kay's folks, Lloyd and Sara Rhodes, were inside already. He saw us and walked over.

We were just so totally stunned. We were standing by our car, speechless, which for me and Kay is rare. My brother-in-law said, "I'm going to our car to get some gifts." Then he looked back over his shoulder, and he said, "We saw you on the phone. Were you talking to the kids?"

Kay said, "No, that was Dr. Saadah, Bobby's got a brain tumor . . ."

And she started bawling.

It took Dwaine a second for Kay's words to sink in, and then he started to cry. After a minute, he went back inside the restaurant and brought out the rest of the family. They all came outside, and there we were, all congregated by our car, crying away like crazy.

My mind roller-coastered from numb to this-can't-be-happening-to-me and back again about a dozen times in the space of a minute. Finally, I said, "C'mon, let's all go back over to our house." So we left.

Fortunately, it dawned on somebody that we were going to be getting hungry pretty soon. So we pulled into a Sonic drive-in and got a big carryout order. Sonic's an Oklahoma City–based company, and we know the CEO, Cliff Hudson. Great guy. We laughed about how Cliff would have loved knowing that we were ordering our holiday lunch at a Sonic, right after receiving this life-changing news.

Not exactly what we'd planned, but we weren't about to let a little thing like a brain tumor keep us from eating. So we spent the next couple of hours at our dining room table, trying to digest what we'd just learned, trying to figure out what to do next, trying to avoid talking about what was on everybody's mind.

After all, what's the very next word that comes to mind when you hear the two words "brain" and "tumor"? I'll give you a hint: it starts with the letter C.

But for now, we were sticking with only those first two words.

"Brain tumor."

Not good, but something we could fix. Something we were *going* to fix.

We'd just take that sucker out and move on.

BOOMER SOONER

I'm a Boomer Sooner Baby Boomer.

(Try saying that three times, fast.)

I was born in Oklahoma City in 1946, the year after World War II ended, which makes me a Baby Boomer. And I spent the first 19 years of my life in Oklahoma City living and breathing University of Oklahoma football, which makes me a Boomer Sooner.

As a kid, baseball was my first love, but we didn't have major league baseball in Oklahoma City. The nearest big league city was St. Louis, with the Cardinals and the Browns. No kid in his right mind could root for the Browns, and the Cardinals were in the wrong league, because they never played my Yankees.

Oklahoma City's minor league team, the Indians, was a Cleveland farm club in the Texas League, Class AA. That was a pretty good class of ball, and back then an AA team would have a fair share of career minor leaguers who developed ties to the local community. But for a kid who might never have learned to read if it hadn't been for *The Sporting News*, it was still minor league.

The Yankees, of course, were a whole different deal. They dominated the sports pages because they dominated baseball. They had guys like Yogi Berra and Phil Rizzuto and Bobby Richardson and Whitey Ford and—oh yeah, almost forgot him—a guy from my home state named Mickey Mantle. They were my baseball heroes.

But New York was a long way away. Exactly how far and where, I wasn't all that sure, because my family never did a lot of traveling, and certainly never to anyplace as strange and different and far away as New York. But Norman, Oklahoma, the home of the University of Oklahoma Sooners, was only about 20 miles south of us, and my dad would take me down there to watch my Sooners play a couple of times a year. One of my biggest thrills growing up was running on the field after a game—they let you do that back then—and having one of my heroes, Clendon Thomas, give me his sweaty chinstrap.

The University of Oklahoma Sooners were *definitely* big league. Heck, for a while there, I thought all my Sooners knew how to do was win. Between 1953 and 1957, from the time I was 7 until I was 11, the Sooners ran off a 47-game winning streak. That's right, *47 straight wins*, a college football record that will, I guarantee it, last forever. Let me tell you, something like that catches the attention of your average sports-crazy kid. As for me, from the ripe old age of 7, I was head-over-heels in love.

My football heroes as a boy were guys like Billy Vessel and Tommy McDonald and Clendon Thomas and Prentice Gautt, all great running backs on great Sooner teams. My major goal in life was to grow up and play halfback in Bud Wilkinson's split-T offense. My dream was to score the winning touchdown in the Oklahoma-Texas game, the annual face-off between the Sooners and the Longhorns in the Cotton Bowl—we called it OU-Texas, folks south of the Red River called it TU-OU because they didn't know any better. Back when I was growing up, the OU-Texas weekend was bigger than the Fourth of July and Thanksgiving and Christmas combined.

The marketers have long since taken the game over, as they have just about everything else in sports, and now it's called the

Red River Classic. That's fine, but for me that annual throwdown in the old Cotton Bowl at the Texas State Fairgrounds (now the SBC Cotton Bowl, of course) will always be simply "the Texas game."

For as long as I can remember, I listened to the game on the radio or watched it on TV, but the first time I ever saw the Texas game in person was in 1963 when I was 17. The Friday night before, Southeast High played our homecoming game. I was the captain of the football team, so it was my job to crown our homecoming queen at halftime. That involved kissing Miss Suzy Lusk. Kay remembers her as "a petite little cutie pie who was very popular with everyone," so it can't have been exactly a tough assignment. Then, after playing a pretty good second half in a game that we won going away, I jumped into the car with Kay and her parents, and we made the four-hour drive to Dallas. We left that night rather than wait until the next morning because OU-Texas always takes place during the Texas State Fair, and we wanted to hit the midway before the big game. After the game, it was back to the fair, and then back again the next morning, before driving home Sunday afternoon.

You have to understand that the Texas State Fair was the biggest thing in our part of the world. It had been going strong for more than six decades when Disneyland came on the scene in 1955. Heck, it was the place where the corny dog ("corn dog" outside the Southwest) first saw the light of day—or so Texans will tell you. The fairgrounds had a great midway and the biggest, scariest rides a kid could imagine and (so I'm told) some great museums and, of course, the Cotton Bowl. A little bit of heaven, only in the wrong state.

The only downside to a really great, glorious weekend was the game itself. It was a thrill just to walk into the stadium and be jammed in with 68,000 other football fanatics, most of them showing off their loyalties with a crimson and cream scarf or an orange and white cap or something. And it was great to watch Oklahoma run out onto the field for the first time. We'd come there hoping for an upset. Maybe, just maybe . . . But no. The Longhorns, on their way to a national championship, beat my Sooners, 28–7.

Whoa, there. You've probably read this far because you're a New York Yankee fan or a baseball fan in general, and I've always believed in the old adage, "You ought to dance with them what brung you." So let me shift away from my football dreams and get back to how I ended up on a major league baseball diamond.

My family was about as Middle America as you could get, long before people started using that term. We lived on the South Side of Oklahoma City. South of the tracks, people on the North Side used to say. There's no question that ours was the lower income side of town. And believe me, the snooty kids on the other side of the tracks made sure we didn't forget it. But we never felt we were poor or anything. Growing up, I always felt like we had plenty.

My father was a mix of French/German stock. His given name was Robert, but I wasn't named after him. Fact is, I never was any kind of Robert. I was named after a friend of Dad's from his merchant marine days. On my birth certificate it's Bobby Ray.

Dad was a jeweler. At one time he owned four jewelry stores in Oklahoma. This wasn't a Tiffany's deal. They were small jewelry stores that he and my mom operated in branches of a big, Oklahoma City–based chain of five-and-dime stores called TG&Y, the initials of the chain's founders. (The operation's nicknames, Turtles, Girdles, and Yo-Yos; and Toys, Games, and Yo-Yos, give you a pretty good idea of the range of products.)

My mother had a great old Southern name: Maybelle. She was about 5-foot-7, with high cheekbones that I attribute to the fact that she was part Native American. (The rest was Native Okie.) She was a good-looking woman (as her son, I'm perfectly objective) and outgoing.

She was a terrific cook who specialized in good old-fashioned Southern cooking. Mom always made big suppers for the four men in the family: pot roast, fried chicken, meat loaf, pinto beans, and fried potatoes. (Her fried potatoes were the best I've ever had.)

Mom was a housewife, but she also worked in the jewelry stores at various times when the three Murcer boys went off to school.

Fact is, we all worked in the jewelry stores at one time or another. Getting a part-time job for a little extra money before Christmas was never a problem.

I had two brothers: DeWayne, who was five years older than me, and Randy, who's eight years younger.

Because of the big gaps in our ages, my brothers and I weren't terribly close when I was growing up. Oh, we loved each other and all that, but when I was just starting grade school, DeWayne was going into junior high, and Randy was two years away from being born. I mean, we didn't grow up playing ball with each other or anything. If I'd tried to play catch with DeWayne, he'd have beaned me for sure. And by the time Randy was old enough for a serious catch, I was being looked at by big league scouts.

My father grew up during the Depression when playing ball pretty much ended when you got old enough to hold down a job. He liked to bowl, but I don't remember him ever talking about playing any other sport. He played some catch now and then with DeWayne when I was too little to do anything but watch, and later with me, and later still with Randy, and he was a regular at our football and baseball games. He always made sure we had whatever sports equipment we needed; there were times when money was a little tight that he traded jewelry for whatever new gear the season called for.

Mom was the extrovert of the family; Dad was much more reserved. She loved being around people and pretty much drove the family social life, what was left of it after our sports. They had lots of friends, including some regular canasta partners.

Dad was the disciplinarian. There'd be some misunderstanding at school, or I'd be unfairly accused of violating this or that family rule, and I'd be told to go to my room and wait for what I had coming to me. I'd wait, and I'd wait, and I'd wait a little while longer, and Dad would finally show up and s-l-o-w-l-y take off his belt and snap it a couple of times. Then he'd say, "Do you promise never to do that again?" And after he heard the words, "Yes, Daddy, I promise," he'd s-l-o-w-l-y put his belt back on and assure me that the next time he'd use it. I don't recall that he ever did, but he didn't have to: the long wait was punishment enough.

Mom and Dad didn't go to church much. She was a Nazarene, and he was a Baptist, and I'm guessing they avoided any doctrinal disputes by sleeping in on Sundays.

From the time I was seven or eight, Grandmother Sadie Murcer took me and my cousins to her Baptist church. We always sat in the front row when we went to church with Grandmother Sadie. She wasn't about to allow any of the sort of back-row nonsense that kids employed to make the sermon move faster.

My religious training wasn't what you'd call deep.

My older brother, DeWayne, was a great high school athlete, but he had a lot of major health problems in his life. He had polio when he was a kid, and that set him back awhile. People today, they don't even know what polio is, but back then, it was every parent's greatest fear that their son or daughter would get polio.

Polio left DeWayne with one leg shorter than the other. And then, when he was about 15 or 16, he got even sicker.

Our family dog, one of the few dogs we ever had as a family, got real sick, and the vet thought he had rabies. As a precaution, the whole family had to take rabies shots. Man, that was something. The doctor came to the house every day for 21 days and gave every member of the family a big, painful injection in the stomach. Well, it turns out that DeWayne was allergic to the horse serum they used to make up the rabies vaccine back then. He ended up with something called encephalitis because of that, and darn near died. Fever, headaches, seizures—he was really, really sick for months. Ended up, he missed a year of school.

The disease messed up his nervous system, so he was never the same. I think he probably would have gone on to play baseball if he hadn't come down with that terrible sickness.

My younger brother, Randy, played baseball in high school, but that was it. He was interested in sports, but more in being a fan than actually playing. Like me, Randy's always been a huge Yankees fan, but we're split on our football loyalties. I mean, there's a *big* family rivalry there. He's Oklahoma State orange all the way, and I bleed Sooner red. But that's okay—he's still my kid brother.

Truth is, so much emphasis in our family was placed on me and my career—by the time he got into middle school in September 1965, I had just been called up by the Yankees—that I think Randy just focused on other things. That's kind of natural, I guess.

Even so, the summer before Randy's senior year in high school, my father started pressuring me to get my all-time favorite manager, Ralph Houk, to give Randy a tryout, take a look at him throw, see what was there. I kept trying to tell Dad that if Randy wasn't being scouted down there at home, and he wasn't, then his chances were somewhere between slim and none. The scouts knew pretty much all the good ball players around; they didn't let too many people slip through the cracks.

Of course, there was no way for me to know for sure. I was in New York playing baseball by then, and I'd never seen my younger brother play any sports, to tell you the truth. So finally I said, "Okay, Dad, I'll ask Ralph to take a look at him." You know, what could I do? Randy was my brother, and maybe he'd been overlooked or something.

Well, we were going to Texas for a series with the Rangers, and Ralph said, "Okay, bring him down, and let me take a look at him. We'll have some other Yankee people take a look at him, too. We'll have him throw in the bullpen before the game."

That was nice of Ralph. He didn't have to do it. But he did, because that's the kind of guy he is, and it got my dad off my back. Ralph and some other Yankee people watched Randy throw, and they determined that he wasn't a prospect. That had to hurt Randy some, but all along I thought it was Dad's dream more than it was his.

Dad died of a heart attack in 1980 at the age of 57. He had been suffering from heart disease for a long time. In fact, there's a lot of heart disease on my dad's side.

DeWayne died in 1989 at the age of 47. DeWayne was a heavy

smoker, and he was a fireman. He retired from the fire department after 27 years when he got lung cancer. He suffered greatly before he passed away.

Mom died in 1995 at the age of 72. The cause of death: lung cancer. She also was a heavy smoker.

Randy and I are the only ones left. He lives with his wife, Dana, in Moore, Oklahoma, a suburb of Oklahoma City. (They have three grown-up kids: Zane, Ashley, and Levi.) An electrician by trade, Randy loves to cook, and about six years ago he submitted one of his smoked hams to David Rosengarten, a hall-of-fame foodie who at the time had a very popular show on the Food Network. Randy's ham was selected as the best in the country. Now Randy has his own Web site and sells his barbecue (including a *great* BBQ sauce) all over the country.

No, I do not get a commission for sending friends and readers to his Web site. But yes, Kay and I do get a free smoked ham or smoked turkey every now and then.

My teenage years were pretty ordinary: play ball (whatever was in season); go to school (I was an average student, good enough to stay eligible but never a threat to make the National Honor Society); court Kay (a full-time job); and work at a slew of part-time jobs.

For me and all my friends, work was a given. It was simple: you wanted spending money, you wanted to keep gas in your car, and you wanted to take your girlfriend to the movies, so you got a job. Or jobs. Here are a few of mine:

- Delivering furniture for Spivey's Furniture. (The best part: sleeping in the delivery truck.)

- Mucking out the barns at a dairy farm. (Hated it. Couldn't take the smell. Think I lasted two weeks, tops.)

- Clerking and sacking up and carrying bags out to cars and fronting the shelves and sweeping up and whatever else needed doing at Kay's father's grocery store. (The best part: fried bologna sandwiches and lemon-lime rickeys when I'd go over to her house for lunch.)

•   Mowing lawns. (In Oklahoma City, summer temperatures are always in the 90s, but the humidity makes them feel a lot worse. Need I say more about the joys of mowing lawns?)

•   Selling the Sunday edition of the *Oklahoman* on Saturday nights at the corner of 10th Street and North Walker. (Maybe my least favorite employment experience this side of Candlestick Park. High school kids cruising the streets thought I made a pretty good target for empty beer bottles. But I was 11–12 years old, and I desperately needed the money for baseball cards and football cards. A boy's got to do what a boy's got to do.)

•   Working in one of Dad's jewelry stores. (Low pay, but I liked the boss.)

My first car was a red and white 1953 Chevy that I bought in 1962 when I was 16 years old for $200, a huge amount of money that I'd been squirreling away for two years. I loved that car. It was clunky compared to the '55–'56–'57 series—back in the day, Detroit manufacturers trotted out their models in three-year cycles—but it was mine and it was sweet. Drove that puppy proudly for a year before trading up for a '57 hardtop (turquoise and white with killer tail fins) just before my senior year.

Having a car liberated me. Folks who grow up in New York and the few other big cities where public transportation gets you pretty much wherever you want to go can't imagine the effect of having your own wheels in a town like Oklahoma City. One day you're having your mom or dad drive you and your girlfriend to the movies. The next day you're driving yourself and your girlfriend to the movies. *Big* difference.

Remember the movie *American Graffiti?* If not, run out and rent it. That movie tells you all you need to know about the relationship between teenagers and their cars in the early 1960s.

Kay and I met when she was 9 and I was 11, when her brother,

Dwaine, and I were on the same Little League team for a tournament.

Among Kay's many fine attributes, one of the finest was that her father owned a grocery store. Lloyd (her dad) told me that he'd give me a steak for every home run I hit that day. He knew of me from the neighborhood, and I guess he figured that would be a pretty good incentive. It was. I hit three dingers that day and got me three steaks the next day.

Call it a case of love at first bite.

You have to understand that once I got to know Kay, I'd have hung out over at her house as much as I could anyhow. But an added plus was all the great food I could count on there. I loved all the stuff that they try to scare you to death about today: chicken-fried steak with cream gravy, fried okra, fried potatoes, fried pies. Country food like cornbread and pinto beans and lima beans and black-eyed peas.

Before becoming a cheerleader her senior year, Kay was a member of the Spartans Pep Club. I remember kidding her once: "Let's see, this week you'll be cheering at basketball games and football games, but I don't remember seeing you cheering for me last spring at my baseball games. What are you, some kind of front-runner?"

Baseball in high school didn't hold a candle to football or basketball, leastways not in Oklahoma. If the pep squad had bothered to pay a courtesy call at our games, most of the time they'd have outnumbered our fans.

Kay and I loved music. Still do, but my taste in music today is not exactly what you would call contemporary. My all-time favorite is Ray Charles. And right behind him come Tony Bennett, Billy Joel, Rod Stewart, Frank Sinatra, and Barbra Streisand. Don't go asking me about rap and hip-hop.

Today I also listen to what I'd call your country classics: Merle Haggard, Johnny Cash, Hank Williams, Garth Brooks, Vince Gill, Reba McEntire, George Strait, and, especially, Willie Nelson. I love Willie, I really do. I've played golf with him many times at various charity events. That man loves golf almost as much as I love listening to him make music.

When the world and I were a whole lot younger, back when I was in high school, the music I listened to seemed to be speaking directly to me. If I was in my car, the radio was on. If I was in my room, the radio was on. If I'd had my way, the radio would've been on in classrooms at school. (Who knows? Maybe I'd have been a better student.) My first love as a teenager was R&B. For just driving around, I liked upbeat stuff: Elvis, Chuck Berry, Bo Diddley, and anything (fast or slow) by my man, Ray Charles.

For the sock hops in the gym Kay and I went to after football and basketball games, I leaned toward the slower songs—Sam Cook's "You Send Me" was a biggie, and anything by Jimmy Reed—because they meant slow dancing, *close* dancing. Every steady couple had "their" song. Ours—mine and Kay's—was "I Can't Stop Loving You" by Ray Charles.

Ray Charles was my guy:

> *I got a woman*
> *Way over town*
> *She's good to me*
> *Oh-oh yeah!*

That would be Kay that Ray was singing about, only she lived on the same side of town as me.

I saw Ray perform for the first time back in the mid-1960s, when I was in high school. He was appearing at this supper club on the East Side of town, which was a mostly black neighborhood. I just had to see my man, Ray Charles.

I was underage and definitely looked it, but I managed to talk my way in. I was the only white guy there. Kay's mother would never have let her go to a nightclub then, so I went solo. (I didn't tell my parents where I was going that night.) And Mr. Ray Charles put on some kind of show. I'll never forget it. Maybe the best music show I've ever seen. Ray moving around behind that piano. People off their feet, moving to the beat.

Later on, Kay and I would go see Ray wherever we were, when-ever we found out that he was around. Ray and Aretha Franklin, that album they made together, *The King and Queen of Soul?* Music doesn't get better than that.

As to me being the only white person in the audience at that first Ray Charles concert I ever went to, you have to remember that the Oklahoma City I grew up in back in the 1950s and early 1960s was pretty much completely segregated. Whites lived in one part of town, blacks in the other. Separate schools, separate churches, separate restaurants, separate lives.

I remember that when Prentice Gautt, who would become one of my Sooner sports heroes, became the first black football player at the University of Oklahoma in 1956, it was a huge deal. Bud Wilkinson had been pressured into not giving Gautt a football scholarship, even though on the basis of his high school record he clearly deserved one. Then a group of prominent leaders in Oklahoma's black community gave him money to attend the school.

A year later, the university gave Gautt his football scholarship, and the money that had been donated for his education was given to another black student. Gautt went on to become a two-time All–Big Eight player and the MVP of the 1959 Orange Bowl. After a seven-season NFL career with the Cleveland Browns and the St. Louis Cardinals, he got a Ph.D. in psychology at the University of Missouri, then went into athletics administration in the Big Eight and Big Twelve conferences. He died in 2005 at age 67.

I had the privilege of meeting him and shaking his hand when he was the guest speaker at a sports banquet when I was a teenager. He was friendly and kind and obviously talented. So why did it have to be such a big deal just to give him a chance?

Sometimes, when I hear a person go on and on about the "good old days," I think that in some cases, for some people, those times weren't so good at all.

━━━━━

For me, though, they were.

My last two years in high school were a blur of pretty much year-round sports—in addition to baseball and football, I played basketball, turned myself into a pretty good bowler, ran track, and spent whatever spare daylight hours I could find on the golf course. Back in those days, especially in the South, being a high school sports star made you a BMOC, and I ate that up.

I had a loving, supportive family.

And I had Kay.

What more could a high school kid ask for?

BOUND FOR GLORY . . .

 idway through my junior year in high school, when we started gearing up for baseball season that spring, I began to realize that my dream was getting ready to come true.

I was going to get a shot at the big leagues.

That spring major league scouts started coming to my high school games, talking to my coaches, making a point of introducing themselves to my parents, and stopping by our practices, stopwatches and clipboards in hand. This was before the major league draft, and there weren't any restrictions regarding big league teams making contact with high school players, so if they were looking at you, you knew it.

I gotta tell, it was pretty easy for that sort of thing to go to a kid's head. I know it did to mine. I mean, to be 16 years old and have major league scouts talking to you like you were a grown-up, talking to your coach and telling him what a fine ballplayer you were, and going on and on to your parents about what a first-rate organization they had and how well you'd fit in. I'm telling you, it's hard to keep things in perspective when that sort of thing's going on around you. Shoot, I didn't even try—I just lapped it up.

Then that fall, during football season of my senior year, college football scouts started sniffing around. That was pretty sweet, too. I was a good football player, All-State my senior year as a running back. I was also our kicker. I received letters expressing interest in me as a football prospect from about a dozen colleges. It soon became clear to me and my parents that if I wanted to, I was going to be able to go to college just about anywhere in the region on a football scholarship.

But baseball was my first love, and by the early spring of my senior year, when the new season rolled around again, I knew what I was going to do when I left school: play major league baseball.

The only question was with whom. The way it worked, "bird-dog scouts" would scour a region, going from ball game to ball game to ball game, looking for prospects. They'd send names of players they liked back to the mother organization, which would then send a regional scout out to have a look-see.

Scouts were always easy to spot. Unlike football and basketball, high school baseball games didn't draw big crowds in my neck of the woods, so any adult male who wasn't somebody's father or uncle was likely to be a scout. The dead giveaway? The clipboard he was carrying. Who takes a clipboard to a high school baseball game and sits up in the stands behind home plate but a scout?

That spring, a bunch of scouts from a bunch of teams visited me and watched me and talked to me. I don't remember the number exactly, but it was close to all of the 20 big league outfits at the time. They couldn't talk money, not until I graduated, but they all made it clear they were ready to do so the minute I got my diploma.

As you can imagine, I was flattered, but only two teams really mattered to me: the Yankees and the Dodgers.

Back then, the Yankees were the Oklahoma Sooners of base-ball, which was the highest compliment a kid from the South Side of Oklahoma City could pay. Between 1956, when I was 10, and 1964, the year I graduated from high school and signed with them, they won seven American League pennants and four World Championships. And they won the pennant again the summer I signed.

The Dodgers became my second favorite team after a family vacation to California when I was 14. My father's sister, Dorothy, was married to the country & western singer and songwriter Johnny Bond, who was pretty big back in those days, and who was great friends with Gene Autry and Tex Ritter and all the other big C&W stars. Anyway, he and Aunt Dorothy lived in Burbank, and we drove out there to visit them. We stayed at their house, saw the Pacific Ocean, visited Knott's Berry Farm, heard Uncle Johnny perform with Tex Ritter and Jimmy Wakeley at some honky-tonk—and went to a Dodgers game at the L.A. Coliseum.

My first major league game!

I don't remember the final score, but I do remember that they beat the Cubs, and that Pee Wee Reese hit a homer. And I also remember the Coliseum, which could seat 100,000 or so for football, as the weirdest setting for a baseball game I have ever seen. It was something like 250 feet in straightaway left, so they had to put up a 40-foot screen to prevent "cheap" homers. That meant you could hit a 280-foot pop-up and touch 'em all. Or you could hit a long drive that would be out of most parks and be lucky to leg out a double off the screen. The walls in right and center? Not more than a quarter mile away.

The idea of playing ball on either coast seemed pretty exciting to a certain wide-eyed kid from Oklahoma who'd only been out of the state a few times to visit kinfolk in Texas and California. And the way things were set up in baseball at the time, the choice was going to be mine.

Before Major League Baseball instituted the player draft in 1965, all prospects my age were free agents. We could sign with anybody, go with whatever team we wanted. Whereas when the player draft went into effect a year later, you could only sign with the team that drafted you. I was lucky; I came in just under the wire before that new system was imposed.

The night of my high school graduation, a dozen or so scouts that we'd invited to come around gathered in our front yard to make one last pitch to me and my folks. Each made a presentation about why I should sign with this or that team, and then each made a formal offer. To every single one of them, our response was "Thank you. We'll get back to you."

Fact is, the only two offers that I really cared about came from the Dodgers and the Yankees.

The Dodgers' offer was huge: a $20,000 signing bonus, plus they'd pay for me to go to college in the off-season. Pretty dog-gone good, considering that you could get a brand-new Corvette at the time for a little over $4,000. Shoot, I'm pretty sure my dad didn't clear that in a year, and he'd been working more than 20 years. And getting my college paid for, that meant an awful lot to my parents.

The Yankees' offer? Exactly half what the Dodgers put on the table: a $10,000 bonus, plus the college money.

So naturally I was leaning toward the Yankees.

Don't get the idea that money didn't matter or that I was a little slow in math. I thought about it long and hard, and talked it over with my parents, and what I figured was that I would make up the difference—or for sure close the gap—with all the postseason pay I could count on with the Yankees. That looked like a pretty safe assumption: after all, a World Series share for each player on the winning team back then ranged from about $6,500 to $7,500.

Pretty good logic, don't you think? Play for my favorite team for a little less—okay, half as much—money than my second favorite team was offering, but easily make up for it in postseason money and incalculable glory?

It made a lot of sense at the time.

That night in our front yard after my graduation, Mr. Tom Greenwade of the Yankees had played his Mickey Mantle card. He offered to take me up to Kansas City, where the Yankees were playing the Athletics, and introduce me around.

Can we leave tonight?

Not quite, but we drove up to KC a couple of days later. The first of my boyhood heroes I met was Yogi Berra, just into his second month as Yankee manager. I don't remember exactly what he said—I was so awestruck, it was all I could do to remember my own name—but the *feeling* I remember was all warmth and welcome.

Then I met Mickey. He had that big grin, and he told me what a great guy Tom Greenwade was, and with his familiar accent, he made me feel right at home.

Next I got to take BP—*in a Yankee uniform.*

The money Mr. Greenwade offered on behalf of the Yankees was more than I could even have imagined just a couple of years before: $10,000!

The Dodgers and their $20,000? They'd been history from the minute Yogi said, "Hello" and Mickey said, "Hey."

The next week after I got back home from Kansas City, a momentous event took place at our kitchen table. My mom and dad, Mr. Howard Parkey (the bird-dog scout who'd sniffed me out for the Yankees), and Mr. Greenwade looked on, all smiles, as I signed my lifelong dream into reality.

I was a New York Yankee.

. . . BUT A WAYS TO GO

My first stop in professional baseball wasn't quite what I had in mind: Johnson City, Tennessee (pop. 30,000).

Now, when you think professional baseball—at least when *I* thought professional baseball back then, when I was fresh out of high school—it was all "Bright Lights, Big City." Like the old Jimmy Reed song, know what I mean? Of course, I knew I wouldn't start off in Yankee Stadium, and I knew I wouldn't be visiting places like Boston and Chicago and Baltimore right off the bat. I knew I'd begin in the minors, but I didn't have much of an idea what that meant. I knew that Oklahoma City had a team in the minor leagues, in AA ball. So did other big places like Dallas and Tulsa and Houston, all in the Texas League. That was about all I knew about minor league baseball.

None of it prepared me for Johnson City in the Appalachian League, where I would spend the first 60 days of my professional baseball career playing rookie league ball.

I got a big send-off from Oklahoma City in June. My folks, my brother Randy, Kay and her family, and a wonderful older family friend of ours, Maurice Katz, all came out to the airport that day to bid me adieu. As we were walking down the terminal corridor toward the boarding gates, Maurice, who was very excited for me, stopped at one of those flight insurance machines they used to have at airports and bought me a small policy, for just in case the plane went down. Since nobody in our crowd had done much flying before, his generous gesture was a little scary, but that emotion got swept up in the general excitement of the moment.

Even though I was only going to be away for the remainder of the summer, and my destination was only about a two-day drive, you'd have thought I was heading out for a two-year hitch of overseas duty. I mean, the love and support and happiness were just pouring out. That's the great thing about close families—those goodbye hugs can sustain you a long, long time no matter how far you go.

I knew I'd miss them all, especially Kay, but I couldn't wait to play ball.

Farewell, Oklahoma City.

Hello, Johnson City.

———

Today, Johnson City has about 60,000 people, but back then it was a *small* town. Located in beautiful, hilly country in northeast Tennessee, about 20 miles from the Virginia border, Johnson City was a pretty place, but it wasn't all that easy to get to. And I almost didn't.

By then, see, I thought I knew all there was to know about travel and visiting new places and whatnot. Why? Because I'd been recruited heavily by some pretty big colleges to play football, and I figured I knew the drill. You fly into someplace. A guy with your name on a signboard greets you as you come off the plane. You hop into the backseat of a limo. And he drives you to your hotel, gets you checked in, and makes sure you're squared away. Depending on what time you arrive, there might be somebody at the hotel to greet you, too.

Not a bad way to travel, if you think about it. And by now I was an old veteran of that sort of thing, so I figured I knew what to expect in Johnson City.

I wasn't close.

For starters, when I flew into Johnson City, I didn't land at the Johnson City airport, because there wasn't one. We touched down at the Tri-Cities Airport, the transportation hub of northeastern Tennessee, which serves Bristol, Kingsport, and Johnson City.

We landed at 7:30 in the evening, and there was nobody there to meet me. No sign with my name on it. No limo. I stood outside on the sidewalk and waited, and waited—still nobody. Then they started shutting off the lights; the airport was closing.

About that time the cook at the grill where I'd bought a sandwich earlier walked by, heading for the exit. I told him there must have been some sort of mix-up, and I asked where I could get a taxi. He gave me a look like I'd just dropped in from outer space and told me there wasn't any taxi service this time of night. Then, seeing my face drop, he asked me where I was going.

Johnson City, I said.

C'mon, he said. That's where I'm headed.

Welcome to the pros, kid.

Oh, by the way, here's lesson number one: you're on your own.

Rookie ball back then was sort of like it is in *Bull Durham*—only without Susan Sarandon. (Though Kay says to this day that one of my teammates, Davey Truelock, was almost as cute as Kevin Costner.)

A blur of games in tiny little ballparks, usually before no more than a few hundred fans. The endless "special promotions"—sack races and whatnot—a lot bigger draws than anything we were doing on the field. A bunch of just-out-of-high-school kids looking like they belonged back in high school. Girls in those small towns getting all goo-goo-eyed over us "professional baseball players"—and Kay turning up at just enough games with her parents or my parents to make sure everybody knew I was spoken for.

How tough was the competition? Well, keep in mind that

everybody in rookie ball had recently been a high school star somewhere, and we were all fighting hard for our big chance. But this was the level where the weeding-out process was harsh. Organizations didn't want to waste time and money on kids who didn't have the tools and makeup they were looking for. A guy might put up decent numbers, but the organization would spot a flaw that the rest of us didn't see, and that would be it, goodbye, hope you enjoyed your summer.

That summer, 1965, I was the only guy on the Johnson City team to get promoted to the Yankee A ball franchise in Greensboro, North Carolina, the following spring. I had hit .365, so I figured I deserved it, but I was a little surprised to be the *only* one to get promoted. In fact, to my recollection, I was the only guy from our entire rookie league that year ever to go on and make a 25-man-roster in the majors.

I had a good first month at Johnson City, and I was named Topps Player of the Month. Kay, who keeps everything, has the certificate to this day. Probably also came with a year's supply of bubble gum or something, long since chewed.

What stands out most in my mind about my season in rookie league ball is that it was the first—and just about the only—time I ever got hurt in baseball. In the first game of a doubleheader in Bluefield, West Virginia, I slid home hard and jammed my right leg against the catcher's shin guard. I didn't even know I was hurt at the time, but my knee swelled up pretty good, and later that night the pain got so severe that I finally called my manager, Lamar North, at about 1 A.M. About an hour later, Lamar, our trainer, and I were cabbing it over to the nearest hospital.

I'll always remember the name: the Bluefield Sanitarium. My first thought was, Hey, guys, it's my knee, not my head.

The preliminary diagnosis: spinal meningitis! Well, needless to say, that scared the you-know-what out of me, and when I called home to tell the folks, Mom flipped out. But the next day, it was something else: hepatitis! My knee was still swollen and hurting, so they put me in an ankle-to-hip cast, and then—after some blood tests, I guess—they came up with a new idea: mononucleosis!

The team left Bluefield to go back to Johnson City, but I stayed at the hospital "for observation." Lamar left behind a pitcher who wasn't scheduled to work for a few days to keep me company. We spent the next three or four days racing up and down the hallways in wheelchairs with a couple of interns pushing us. Hey, it wasn't baseball, but it was competition.

Finally they sent me back to Johnson City, swollen knee and all. I was lucky to get out of there before the sanitarium people conjured up something else I didn't have. Since there'd been no improvement in my knee, Lamar and the Yankee brass decided to fly me up to New York to see Dr. Sidney Gaynor, the longtime Yankee team physician.

Unfortunately, my plane landed at Newark, and no one had bothered to tell me how to get to New York City. I was just a country boy from Oklahoma, remember? But I finally figured it out and made my way into the Big Apple. The Yankees had booked me into a down-at-the-heels hotel in Times Square, which was not a very good neighborhood at the time, but it was still in New York, and I was pretty psyched—even if I couldn't exactly go out and see the sights, what with my knee all ballooned up like it was.

The next morning I went straight to Doc Gaynor's office. Turned out the doc came from the rub-some-dirt-on-it-and-you'll-be-just-fine school of medicine. His philosophy was to let young, healthy athletes heal themselves. That was just fine by me; I hated the very thought of cortisone shots. (In my whole 17-year big league career, I was on the DL only once—in 1965, during my September cup-of-coffee call-up.)

Doc Gaynor determined that amputation would not be necessary, and that I didn't have some mysterious "itis" or "osis" or anything. He said that I had busted a bursa sac under my kneecap, whatever that was, and that in time the swelling would go down, and pretty soon I'd be as good as new. (It did, and I was.)

I turned around and flew back to Johnson City the same day. The Yankees were on the road, and I never even got a peek at Yankee Stadium.

Wait till next year!

"Next year" came for me the following March, when I reported to the Yankee minor league camp in Hollywood, Florida.

Based on my rookie league season—or half season, since they held me out after the knee injury as a precautionary measure—I was assigned to Greensboro in the Carolina League. That was a great sign, because the Carolina League was what was (then) called "high Class A." That's where teams put their top prospects. Lamar North, my manager in Johnson City, was going up to Greensboro, too. I was feeling pretty good about my chances.

Greensboro was another one of your classic minor league towns. Ten guys—all about the same age, all at the same place in our careers—lived in a rooming house right across the street from the ballpark. When it was time to go to work, we just walked across the street to an old wooden structure with a tin roof and an infield with some fair-size boulders. We'd see fans around town. By the end of the season, we knew a lot of them by name. Most important, we played, talked, and dreamed baseball 24/7—though nobody used that term back then.

Today, with all the big money being thrown around and the hovering agents and the organizations taking such an active role in bringing players along and minor league ball being such big business, it's really hard to imagine young players having the kind of *baseball* experience we did.

I had a great year in Greensboro: hit .322, won a shiny new Bulova watch for being named Topps Player of the Year in the Carolina League, got named team MVP. But the high point for me came on September 1.

My call-up.

═══════

September 1 is a magical date for young players in the minor leagues dreaming of playing in the majors. September 1 is when major league teams can expand their rosters from 25 to 40.

Teams in contention use the opportunity to bring guys off the DL without having to send anybody down, and especially to bring up guys from the minors who might help them down the stretch.

A lefty spot reliever, or a speedy outfielder who can be used to pinch-run in a tight ball game, or an infielder with great hands who can go in as a defensive replacement.

Teams not in contention expand their rosters to have a look at minor leaguers in their systems whom they think could play a role in the future. Getting called up in September is like a cross between an audition and a reward for having a good season. I had hit .322 at Greensboro in A ball, so I fit into this latter category.

You can imagine how I felt when Lamar called me into his office at the end of August and told me that the Yankees wanted me to come up and spend the last month of the season with the big club: like I had died and gone to heaven.

Here I was, less than two years out of high school, packing my bags and heading north to put on pinstripes for the first time. I was going to be a New York Yankee.

The Yankees put me and other September call-ups in the fabled Concourse Plaza Hotel, located on the Grand Concourse (at 161st Street) in the Bronx. The Grand Concourse was at one time one of the city's grandest boulevards. It had been the centerpiece of a thriving nightclub and restaurant scene from the 1930s into the 1950s. President Truman stayed at the Concourse Plaza. John F. Kennedy gave his last big speech of the 1960 campaign there. The Yankees stayed there as a team after night games. More important, Babe Ruth and Lou Gehrig had both lived there for a while!

The Concourse Plaza had definitely seen grander days by the time I checked in—18 years later it was closed down and turned into an old folks home; after that it was converted to condos—but I couldn't have cared less. They could have handed me a sleeping bag and pointed me toward the nearest parking lot. All that mattered was that I was soon going to be playing on my very own personal field of dreams.

I arrived at the hotel around 6 in the afternoon, threw my suitcase in my room, and walked straight down to Yankee Stadium a couple of blocks away. The Yankees were on a road trip and wouldn't be back until the following day, so I couldn't get in. Instead I did the next best thing: I walked around the place three times.

Yankee Stadium!

That first morning of the rest of my life I got up early, bolted down breakfast in the hotel coffee shop, and walked—okay, semi-ran—the few blocks to the ballpark and . . . how do I get in?

I didn't exactly expect a big "Welcome, Bobby Murcer!" banner, the way I had back in Johnson City a year before. But I was a New York Yankee, doggone it, and I couldn't figure out how to get into the Stadium, much less into my own clubhouse.

That time of morning, the Stadium was sealed up tight and there was nobody to ask, so I walked halfway around the place—a trek I already knew by heart—then all the way back, my heart pounding like a conga drum: *Where's the front door?*

Finally I spotted a sign that said, in big letters, a beautiful word: "PLAYERS." I walked up to a security guard whom I had also somehow missed the first time around, and asked him, in the deepest, most Oklahoma accent–free voice I could muster, if I might enter.

Bill Burbidge, a great guy who is still with the Yankees 43 years later, eyed me up and down, decided I might be some crazed teenage autograph seeker at this time of the morning, and suggested firmly that I run along.

But sir, I said, I'm a ballplayer, a New York Yankee. Yeah, right, and I'm Babe Ruth. He didn't say that in so many words, but I could tell it was what he was thinking. But he took my name, made a couple of phone calls, finally got the green light, and gave me a big smile: "Welcome to Yankee Stadium."

To this day, Bill kids me that if it hadn't been for him, I might still be walking around Yankee Stadium, looking for a way to get inside without a ticket.

———

What followed was the best month of my life up to that point.

My first game in a Yankee uniform felt like it was going to be my last, my heart was pumping so hard. Like Phil Rizzuto and Tony Kubek before me, I was the starting shortstop for the *New . . . York . . . Yankees*!

Right after infield warm-ups in the first inning, third baseman Clete Boyer draped an arm around my shoulder and steered me over toward second base. He was telling me to relax and have fun, but I couldn't process his exact words because I was so thrilled that a great veteran Yankee like Clete Boyer was going out of his way to make a 19-year-old rookie feel comfortable.

Finally, about 10 feet away from second, Clete stopped and drew a line in the dirt with his toe. "Everything from here," he said, nodding toward the second-base bag, "is yours." Then he went on: "And everything from here to back over there"—he nodded his head back to third—"is mine."

Yes, sir!

I got my first major league hit on September 14: a two-run, game-winning home run off Jim Duckworth of the Washington Senators.

That's right, a *home run*!

Hey, this was going to be a piece of cake.

Little could I have known at the time that my next homer in the majors wouldn't come until almost four years later, after another season in the minors and two years in the army. But I was on my way!

True, I didn't exactly tear up the league or anything in my short visit that September: .243, 1 HR, 4 RBIs in 37 AB in 11 games at shortstop. But I certainly didn't humiliate myself, and I pretty much locked up an invitation to the Yankee major league camp the following spring.

Plus Kay said I looked good in pinstripes.

WELCOME TO THE BIG LEAGUES, KID

My first Opening Day in a New York Yankees uniform was April 12, 1966. The September call-up the year before had been just a taste. This was the real thing.

My promotion to the Opening Day roster came the usual way: a position needed to be filled. Tony Kubek had retired. He'd had a neck injury earlier in his career, and there was a chance that if he continued playing, he could suffer permanent damage. I guess the Yankees didn't have a shortstop in the system that they were considering as a prospect other than me. I'd played only the one full season in Greensboro in Class A ball, and I got into only a few games the previous September after my call-up and, honestly, didn't do a whole lot. But they must have liked what they saw enough to give me a chance to win the job down in Florida in 1966.

Spring training that year was a blur. Still is, when I think back on it. I mean, I knew they were counting on me to take over the job at short, but I still had to win it. Strange, though, I didn't feel any special pressure. I was just doing what I loved to do: playing baseball. "Confident but not cocky," that's how I'd describe the way I felt, with maybe a little "unconscious" thrown in for good measure.

Right out of the box, I got saddled with a nickname. Sometimes a player's nickname sticks: Babe Ruth, Scooter Rizzuto, Pudge Fisk, Catfish Hunter, Whitey Ford, and so on. Other times, a player gets assigned a nickname by his mates in the clubhouse and it pretty much stays there. That happened to me in Fort Lauderdale in 1966 when Fritz Peterson took one look at me and decided I was "Lemon." What was odd was that Fritz was a rookie, just like me, and here he was passing out nicknames, usually a prerogative reserved for veterans. (It was the least odd of the many odd things about Fritz, as I would discover over the years.)

So, Lemon, where'd that come from? Certainly not from any sour disposition, because I've never had one. Maybe it was because of the shape of my face, coupled with my sunny glow, plus my . . . Honestly, I had no idea then, and I have no idea now.

But Lemon I was all through spring training, and into the first month of the season. Then I was sent down to Toledo for most of the rest of the summer so I could play every day, and in 1967 and 1968 I was serving Uncle Sam. By the time I came back in 1969, Lemon was just a memory.

Too bad, in a way. I'd never had a nickname before, and have never had one since, except when Scooter called me Huckleberry, but at one time or another he called just about everybody that, with the possible exception of his beloved wife, Cora.

Back in those days, a rookie tried to be seen on the field but not heard in the clubhouse. Speak when spoken to. Laugh at jokes, funny or not. Go about your business and try not to attract any attention anywhere except between the foul lines. The clubhouse belonged to the veterans, and you were just visiting—until you made the 25-man-roster.

If you had a sore arm, and a veteran saw you going to the trainer's room, he'd likely get on a rookie's case about being a softy and a sissy, only he'd put it in stronger words: "Hey, kid, how come you're moaning about a sore arm? How's it possible that you could be so weak? I'm the one who's supposed to have a sore arm. What does a young kid like you even know about having a sore arm?"

I caught on fast enough so that if something was bothering me, I went to the trainer's room either before anybody got to the clubhouse or after everyone had left.

Most of the hazing was good-natured, like, "Go back into the clubhouse and bring a bat" and "Shut up, rook, who cares what you think?" when you started to answer a question you'd just been asked. Veterans (some of them with only a couple of years under their belt) made fun of a rookie's accent, his haircut, his taste in clothes, just about anything. Certain things make you a bit squeamish? Keep them to yourself if you're a rookie. Afraid of spiders? Don't let on or you can count on finding fake tarantulas lurking in your locker until the toy shop runs out.

All good-natured, as I said, all in good fun, so long as the rookie doesn't get his back up and let on that it's really bothering him. If that happens, it just becomes relentless.

My hazing, mild to begin with, came to a screeching halt about midway through camp. After practice one day, Mickey stopped me in the middle of the locker room, put his arm around my shoulder, and stood there talking with me for a couple of minutes. Right then and there everybody—I mean *everybody*—stopped razzing me. Mick had decided I belonged.

Mick didn't say anything special at the time, and he never mentioned it later, not even when we got to know each other pretty well. I learned later that Tom Greenwade, the veteran Yankee scout who had signed both of us, had said something to Mickey like, "Hey, when this kid gets there, you take care of him." Tom was the number one scout for the Yankees back then. A very gentle man from Missouri, a dapper guy who always wore a hat. But I also think Mickey recalled what it was like being a teenager and being in the New York Yankees locker room for his first spring training.

Another thing that made me feel accepted, made me feel like part of the team that first spring training, was when Clete Boyer and Roger Maris took me out to dinner one night. I had played ball with Clete's little brother, Ronnie Boyer, in Greensboro, and he was at the Yankee minor league camp there in Hollywood.

(Quite a baseball family, the Boyers. Three Boyer brothers—Ken, Clete, and Cloyd—played in the majors. Ronnie and two others played in the minors. Eight more siblings pursued other interests.)

Anyway, Clete and Roger took me and Ronnie to this famous, fancy Polynesian restaurant in Fort Lauderdale named Mai Kai—my first introduction to Polynesian food, and, more important, my first introduction to mai tais. And I have to tell you, I got to know them pretty well that night. Roger drove us back to the hotel after dinner, and all I can say is that it was a good thing that *anybody* but me was driving.

My roommate in spring training was Steve Hamilton. Remember big Hambone Hamilton out of Kentucky? He was also an NBA basketball player. And a really great guy.

Well, when I got back to our room, I told Hambone I was sick as a dog, only I wouldn't wish how I felt on a dog. I'd already barfed all over the side of the car while we were driving back. I was sick all night long, throwing up, dry heaves, the whole bit.

The next day, when I woke up, I felt awful. Oh, I had drunk a little beer back in high school—most everybody did—but this was my first major league hangover.

I can't make it, I told Hambone. I'm too sick. I'll be throwing up all over everybody. And he said, I'll tell you what we'll do. I'll tell Joe Soares—he was our head trainer—that you've got the flu and that you're throwing up and see what he wants to do. So the next thing you know, Soares gives me a call in my room, and I tell him I'm sick. And he says, You got any fever? I said, I don't think so, just nauseated, and I really don't feel good. And he says, Well, okay, you just stay there, and after practice today, I'll come by and check on you.

Great! I'd dodged that bullet. Man, was I relieved. But that feeling didn't last long.

About 25 minutes after that, I get another call, this time from traveling secretary Bruce Henry, saying that Johnny Keane (our manager) wanted me to come out to the ballpark to be checked out. So I had no choice. I had to go to the ballpark. And I was nervous—no, borderline terrified—that I'd get there and everybody would find out that I wasn't really sick, that I was just a rookie at the drinking game.

Now, in Fort Lauderdale at the Yankee camp, when you walked through the outside door there was a wall in front you had to walk around to get into the clubhouse proper.

Well, there was a team meeting going on (that I was late for!), but once I opened the door, I couldn't just close the door and leave, because everybody had heard the door open. So I thought, Well, what I'll do is, I'll walk directly to the trainer's room, which I did. But when I started in, Boyer and Maris began clapping, and pretty soon everybody was applauding and cheering.

What had happened, although I didn't know it the time, was that Boyer and Maris had told Keane that I'd gotten drunk and was hung over. The joke, clearly, was on me.

But I went on in and climbed up on the training table. The trainer checked my temperature, and they checked this and that, when really everybody knew that I was just suffering from a severe case of mai tai–itis.

Keane walked into the trainer's room and said to me that since I didn't have a fever or anything, I was going to hit for all the pitchers in the intrasquad game that afternoon. The thought of standing in against major league pitching after a night of mai tais makes my stomach turn to this day, but fortunately I had a surprise supporter: Elston Howard.

Ellie was catching on the other side that day, and every time I came to the plate, he told me what was coming on every pitch. I guess he was afraid I might get hurt up there in my condition. Thanks to Ellie, I got three hits.

Let me assure you, that helped my case. Three hits in a game, even an intrasquad game, was certainly a big boost to a rookie trying to make the club. And Elston Howard helped me do it.

Later on, Ellie also went to bat for me with Vern "Radar" Benson, our pitching coach. A former pitcher for the Philadelphia Athletics and the Cardinals in the 1950s and 1960s, Benson had come over from St. Louis with Keane, and he was called Radar because anything you said in his earshot would be sure to get back to Johnny.

Once I was standing next to the batting cage alongside Radar waiting to take my cuts in BP, and he started ragging me—ragging me *hard*—about my fielding. "You've got, without doubt, the *worst* hands I've ever seen on a ballplayer," constructive stuff like that. Well, Ellie was standing nearby, and he heard this, and the next thing I know he's in Radar's face: "If I ever hear you to speak to a rookie like that again," he said in his strong but quiet voice, "I am going to kick your ass. Do . . . you . . . understand . . . me?"

And he walked away, not bothering to wait for Radar's response.

Ellie Howard—what a sweet, gentle bear of a man. The Yankees traded him to the Red Sox near the end of the 1967 season, when I was in the army, but I got to know him when he came back to the Yankees as a coach in 1969. He used to kid me that I owed him my major league career for tipping pitches to me back in spring training in 1966. Ellie died of a heart ailment at the very young age of 51 in 1980. I remember Red Barber saying at the time, "The Yankees lost more class on the weekend than George Steinbrenner could buy in 10 years."

To show our respect for Ellie, we all wore black armbands on our sleeves during the 1981 season. Three years later, the Yankees retired his uniform number 32 and installed a plaque in his honor in Monument Park at Yankee Stadium. The plaque describes Ellie as "A man of great gentleness and dignity."

Truer words were never written.

———

Thanks, in part, to Elston Howard . . . *I was a New York Yankee.*

That's right: near the end of spring training, Johnny Keane called me into his office and told me I was on the 28-man Opening Day roster. (Back then, they didn't cut back to 25 until May 1.) Before that fact had a chance to sink in, it was April and we had left Florida and were in New York for Opening Day against the Tigers.

I was a New York Yankee.

There I was, on April 12, 1966, my first Opening Day in

Yankee Stadium, lined up with all the guys out there on the field between first and second, my first time ever being introduced by the legendary Bob Sheppard as a New York Yankee.

Was I psyched? A 19-year-old kid from Oklahoma standing out on the field wearing pinstripes in front of 65,000 fans standing and singing the National Anthem? Hey, is the Grand Canyon deep?

The only downside: my number one fan, Kay, wasn't there to cheer me on. She was back in Oklahoma City doing her homework, living on her laurels as Basketball Queen at Southeast High School, and getting ready for her senior prom. (No, she did *not* have another date; she and three of her female friends got all glammed up and went as a posse.)

Personally, I've always wondered why she didn't drop all that and hustle up to New York for Opening Day.

I think it was pretty clear to everybody in the Yankees organization by then that if it turned out I could hit, my future with the club was in the outfield, not at shortstop. See, I had a strong arm, but . . . I think they were worried about the fans in the first-base boxes if I stayed too long at short. I was a bit, er, erratic. Just a bit.

But that likely shift was down the road a bit. I started the 1966 season as a shortstop because that other fellow from Oklahoma was still the Yankee center fielder.

As the Yankees were introduced, one by one, by Bob Sheppard's incredibly rich, sonorous voice, all the veterans got huge ovations. The biggest, naturally, went to Mickey Mantle.

I got only a little polite applause, of course, but that sounded pretty good to me. I mean, those other guys were household names to all the people in the stands that day. This kid Murcer, nobody knew who he was. (But pretty soon they'd find out that as shortstop, he'd make a pretty good outfielder.)

That historic day, however, I didn't play.

A couple of weeks earlier, a few days before we broke camp and headed north, Johnny Keane had sat me down and told me he was going to break me in slowly. We had another shortstop on the roster, Ruben Amaro, a veteran who knew his way around the horn, a solid glove man. Keane said he didn't want to put all the pressure on me of having to come in and take over at short-stop from Kubek, who'd been there for years and had a handful of championship rings to prove it. Keane said he was going to play me against right-handers and Ruben against left-handers at first, and then somewhere down the line, maybe I'd take over full-time.

Fine. Okay. Play against right-handed pitchers only. I could live with that. I had to, after all: he was the manager. But then, in that three-game series against Detroit that opened the season, we faced right-handed starters every day, and I didn't play at all. Not an inning. That was puzzling, considering what Johnny had told me. I sure didn't say anything about it to him; a rookie just doesn't do that. So I tried to look on the bright side: at least I had a good seat for the ball games.

Then, after that series against the Tigers, we traveled down to Baltimore for three games against the Orioles. That's where I got my first start—and it was against a right-hander, Wally Bunker. I went 0-for-3 against him and Moe Drabowsky. Not what I'd hoped, of course, but this was at least the way it was supposed to be: me against right-handers, Ruben against lefties, until I could get established and comfortable.

Only it didn't work out that way. The next day, the Orioles started Dave McNally, one of the toughest lefties in the American League. (He won 13 games with a 3.17 ERA that year.) That meant I was back on the bench. But in the second inning, Ruben collided with left fielder Tom Tresh chasing a blooper down the left-field line. Ruben tore up his knee and was pretty much done for the season. So I replaced him at short and went 0-for-3 against McNally. The next game, I was at short again and went 0-for-4 against Steve Barber, another tough lefty (15 wins, 2.69 ERA), and a couple of relievers.

Not exactly a barn-buster start for the Oklahoma Kid: 0-for-10.

Suddenly I felt like I was looking at either a very long season or a very short career.

I finally got a hit a couple of games later against the Indians—a home run! That lifted my spirits at the time, but I soon filed that first dinger under the heading "Too Little, Too Late."

=======

We got off to a terrible start in 1966. Early on, Johnny Keane called a clubhouse meeting and really ripped into us. Can't blame him, really, we were playing awful baseball, all of us, from Mickey, Roger, Ellie, all the veterans, right on down to the bottom of the roster.

But the two guys he singled out for the most heat were me and Joe Pepitone, who was just entering his fifth year as our first base-man (and who would go on to lead the club in homers that season with 31). I'm telling you, he let us have it. If there'd been a hole in the middle of the clubhouse floor, I think I'd have tried to crawl into it. He was right about my play—I was hitting a buck-thirty-something, and I'd launched some satellites from short.

But Joe and I weren't the only reasons we were a couple of zip codes the wrong side of .500. I guess Johnny felt more comfortable ripping into young players than taking on the veterans.

I didn't care much. I was too excited about wearing that Yankee uniform to get bent out of shape by anything Keane or anybody else said.

After all, the Yankee fans loved me. I could tell they did. Every time I'd walk from the on-deck circle to the batting box at Yankee Stadium, I'd hear this great roar from the stands. (I was hitting second, and it didn't dawn on me until later that the cheers were for the guy coming out of the dugout to take his place in the on-deck circle: Mickey Mantle.)

Shortly thereafter, the Yankees decided to send me down to Triple A, move Clete Boyer over to short, and bring Tresh in from left to play third, at least for the time being. Later, they used Horace Clarke some at short, and toward the end of the season they picked up Dick Schofield from the Cardinals.

Me?

Hey, kid, have you ever visited Toledo?

Sending me down was simply smart baseball. Clete was a terrific fielder, way better than I was at short. Tommy was a great young athlete who could handle third. And it was a whole lot better for me at the age of 19 to be playing every day in Triple A than sitting on the bench in the majors. At least that's what general manager Ralph Houk told me, and as much as I didn't like hearing that at the time, I know now in retrospect that he was right.

At Toledo, after I got my bearings, I played okay, but then I hit a little slump: 3-for-62. Heck, I could have done that against big league pitching.

Thing is, during that slump I was making good contact, hitting the ball hard, so I never got down on myself. Very few strikeouts. But no breaks. I couldn't buy a hit, not a blooper or a squibber or a broken-bat grounder that found a hole or anything. You hear ballplayers sometimes say they had a "good" 0-for-4? Well, I had a good 3-for-62. (That's .048, if you're scoring at home.)

Any way you look at it, it was a pretty nasty slump, by far the worst of my career—maybe of anybody's career, for that matter. But at least it came in the minors, not the majors. And when I broke out of it, I broke out pretty good: in back-to-back games, I hit four consecutive home runs.

Later in the summer, I was called back up to the big club, but I didn't make much noise. Even if I had, it wouldn't have made any difference. See, 1966 was the season that—for the first time since 1912—the Yankees finished dead last in the American League, 26.5 games behind the pennant-winning Orioles, with a record of 70–89. At least we edged out the Mets (66–95) for the Championship of New York.

My line for my first season on the 25-man roster (not long, but I did start the year there): 21 games, 1 HR, 5 RBIs, .174 BA. Not too sparkling, and it certainly didn't put me in the race for Rookie of the Year.

But there was one super highlight in 1966, undoubtedly the best play of my life.

On October 14, I said "I do."

Kay

═══

*B*obby hasn't surprised me too many times. I guess that's a conse-quence of us knowing each other pretty well, since I was 9 and he was 11. But he got me good the year I graduated from high school.

He was playing in Toledo, and had three days off or something, and wanted to sneak home for a quick visit without me knowing. Everybody was in on his game plan—my mother included. One day during the last week of my senior year, I came home from school, headed into my bedroom, opened the bifold doors to my closet, and Bobby jumped out.

Surprise!

(He always said he did it because he knew I couldn't stand to be without him another day.)

We got engaged in Toledo in June of that year. I guess it didn't exactly come as a shock to anyone. We'd been going together since I was 14 and Bobby was 16. Oh, we would break up now and then for some silly reason or another, and then get back together right away.

Most people close to us thought it was about time when we finally got married.

Someone did ask me jokingly a lot of years later if that 3-for-62 slump of his had given me any second thoughts. Truth is, these days I couldn't for the life of me tell you whether our engagement came before, after, or during that monster slump. I do know that I never ever doubted for one minute that he was going to fulfill his dream.

Remember, Bobby had been a star for as long as I'd known him, since the day I first saw him.

No little 3-for-62 slump in Toledo was going to change my mind.

The proposal wasn't what you'd call Hollywood romantic. I mean, I didn't drop to one knee at home plate, turn to the stands, and ask her if she'd marry me. Nope, ever the practical ones, Kay and I discussed our engagement on the phone and decided to make it official when she and her parents drove up to Toledo for a vacation that summer. Both families knew it would happen on that trip, so my folks sent a few ring choices from their stock so we could select one together. (Kay, of course, had already picked out the ring she liked best.) We went out to dinner and I put the ring on her finger and that was that.

Our wedding, on October 14, 1966, was a whole different deal. We got hitched at the Louise Prichard Chapel of the First Baptist Church in Oklahoma City, with about 250 guests in attendance. Kay was the most beautiful bride that I had ever seen. Her father, who was an ordained minister, walked Kay down the aisle to the altar, and then stepped forward to preside over our exchange of vows. We picked him to marry us rather than some other preacher because we figured it was those three steaks he awarded me for my three homers nine years before that had set this whole thing in motion.

The Murcer honeymoon took place in two parts.

Part one was a two-day trip to Tulsa, where we stayed at the fabulous, brand-new Camelot Hotel. Built in the shape of a pink castle complete with a moat and a drawbridge, the Camelot was certainly the most luxurious edifice either one of us had ever seen. It was *the* place to be seen in Tulsa. President Nixon stayed there. Elvis stayed there. Mike Wallace stayed there. Anybody big visiting Tulsa stayed there.

But the Camelot's heyday didn't last long. It hit the skids in the 1980s, and by the mid-1990s it was closed up for all kinds of safety and health code violations. It's scheduled for demolition in 2008.

Part two of our honeymoon took place that December when we flew out to L.A. to visit my Aunt Dorothy and Uncle Johnny Bond and see the sights. That we did, under the able direction of my three cousins. We had a great time, despite a bumpy start. You see, on the flight out we'd been knocked about by a series of thunderstorms, and sharp shifts in the cabin's air pressure had caused Kay's ears to stay stuffed up the whole time we were in L.A. Rather than risk going through an encore on our return home, she suggested that we do something romantic: take a train.

Great! Only it wasn't, because the traveling secretary of our new team—yours truly—didn't think to book a sleeper. We sat up for two and a half days on a milk train that stopped at every junction along the railroad equivalent of Route 66. We finally arrived back home completely exhausted.

Kay became a big fan of air travel on the spot.

═══════

That fall, the new groom enrolled in some college classes, courtesy of my Yankee contract, at Central State in Edmond. (In 1991 Central State got promoted to the University of Central Oklahoma.) I took the courses mainly to keep my mind occupied so that I wouldn't spend every waking minute counting the hours until spring training. The winter crawled along, and crawled along, until finally it was time to pack up and head down to Fort Lauderdale. I got there a couple of days early to play in a golf tournament, have a little fun. Once spring training started, I knew it was going to be all business.

Let me tell you, I was one happy Yankee until, on the day I reported to camp, I got a telephone call from Kay.

"Honey," she said. "You've got your greetings."

I'd been drafted.

Ten-hut!

Son, you're in the army now.

My basic training was at Fort Bliss, Texas, near El Paso, which as anybody who's ever been to that part of the world can tell you, is not exactly blissful—especially for a kid from Oklahoma who thought he ought to be getting ready to move to New York.

My next stop was Fort Huachuca, Arizona, about 75 miles southeast of Tucson, 30 miles or so north of the Mexican border, and 310 miles farther away from New York. And even less blissful than Fort Bliss.

Now I don't want you to get the wrong idea. I wasn't exactly ecstatic to be spending two years 2,500 miles from Yankee Stadium. But I took my military training seriously; that's the way I was brought up. I was assigned to the radio corps. I was a good soldier. And I counted the minutes until my hitch was up.

I could have played some semipro ball during my off-duty time, but that would have required a 150-mile round-trip to Tucson, and it couldn't have been on a regular basis, so I decided against it.

Once I flew out to Anaheim for a Yankees-Angels game. It cost me $275 for the flight, which was about four months' pay for a buck private back then. But I got to say hello to Ralph and the guys, so it was worth it. I didn't want them to forget my face.

Looking back, I can say truthfully that military duty helped me grow as a ballplayer and as a man.

I put on 10–15 pounds, which gave me a big boost in power. I don't think the Yankees looked on me as a power hitter when they signed me; I know I didn't. But the extra muscle I returned to the game with helped make me a better run producer.

Even more important, I believe, was the maturity I developed in two years in the service. I went in as a kid; I believe I came out a man.

Three specific good things about those two years: I didn't have to go to Vietnam, like a lot of people I know did; our daughter, Tori, was born on July 29, 1968; and I was discharged from the army at the end of 1968, just in time to get down to Puerto Rico to play a little winter ball.

Just a few weeks later, I reported for reinduction into the New York Yankees. No Fort Bliss. No Fort Huachuca.

This time I was assigned to Fort Lauderdale.

THE GREAT DEPRESSION

*Y*ou've heard of the Great Depression, right? No, not the one my parents, and maybe your parents (or certainly your grandparents) lived through in the 1930s. I'm talking about the Great Depression that descended on Yankee fans from 1965 through 1975, when the Bronx Bombers were a bust, failing to make the postseason a *single* time.

It was supposed to be like it had been the preceding decade and a half: "Yankees Win the Pennant! Yankees Win the World Series! Yankees Win, Win, Win!"

It wasn't supposed to be like this: "Yankees Finish Last for the First Time Since 1912!" (That would be in 1966, the year of my first Opening Day in pinstripes.)

And it *really* wasn't supposed to be like this: "Yankees Fail to Make the Postseason, 1969–1974!" (That would be my first six seasons as a Yankee, after I got back from military service.)

What happened? A bunch of things, all at once.

For starters, the big Yankee stars who won all those pennants and World Championships in the 1950s and first half of the 1960s got old. (Make that "baseball old.") Mickey, Roger Maris, Whitey

Ford, Ellie Howard, Bobby Richardson, and Tony Kubek were all in their 30s in 1966, some of them (Mickey, Tony) so crippled up by old injuries that they were shadows of their former selves.

That's natural. It happens. One day you're a fire-eating rookie ready to run through outfield walls to get a fly ball. Next thing you know, you're a creaky veteran hoping your knees hold up as you chase down a ball hit into the gap. That's what a farm system is for, to have people ready to take over when your studs can't cut it anymore.

Back then, of course, 30 was considered borderline old by baseball management. You turned 30, the front office began sifting through its minor league system looking for your replacement. Most guys were edged out in their early 30s, gone almost for sure by the time they hit 35.

Some of it, I suppose, had something to do with conditioning. Players in my day weren't as super-fit as players are today. But mostly it was a matter of tradition and attitude: once a player turned 30, the front office considered him "old" and started moving to replace him. Minor league systems were much, much larger, so management was quicker to dip into the pool of available talent.

Today players keep on keeping on until well into their late 30s, some longer. Barry Bonds hit 28 homers in 2007 at the age of 42. Back in 2005, Roger Clemens was 13–8 with a 1.87 ERA—at the age of 42. Okay, both may have received a little extracurricular boost, but I think you get the point: in baseball today, 40 is the new 30.

But at the same time that the Yankee stars were getting "old," the Yankee farm system was drying up. Not a good combo.

To compound the Yankees' problem, their number one *unofficial* farm team, the Kansas City Athletics, stopped being a prime source for such hot young talent as Roger Maris, whom the Yankees got before the 1960 season for four guys they no longer had any need for.

Earlier, in 1955, the Athletics had signed Clete Boyer and given him a bonus that required them, under prevailing rules, to keep him on their major league roster before they could send him down for seasoning. Then, a couple of years later they sent him over to the Yankees as part of a multiplayer deal that obscured the fact that they had, as they later admitted, signed Boyer on the Yankees' behalf in the first place.

Confused? Yeah, me too, but the bottom line is that the Yankee farm system dried up just about the same time that Charlie Finley bought the Athletics and stopped feeding the Yankees good young talent.

The biggest blow to Yankee dominance, though, came with the institution of the First Year Player Draft in 1965. Prior to then, the Yankees, Dodgers, and Cardinals—baseball's three richest teams—could waltz in and skim the cream off the amateur crop every year. And they did.

The First Year Player Draft in 1965 put an end to that. Beginning that year, all amateur players were subject to a draft. The draft order was based on the previous season's standings, with the team that had the worst record getting the first pick, and so on.

To top things off, after the 1964 season, CBS purchased 80 percent of the Yankees from longtime owners Dan Topping and Del Webb for $11.2 million. (Within a year or so, CBS picked up the other 20 percent.) Yes, that's CBS as in Columbia Broadcasting System. The minute the deal went down, the jokes started popping up: Walter Cronkite was going to put on pinstripes, and over in the dugout, Yogi was going to slip into a pinstriped suit and anchor the *Evening News*.

Sort of funny, but CBS had the right idea—they were just a little premature. The CBS guys saw that baseball was going to flourish because of TV and all the doors it would open up, not because of sellout crowds. And they were right. Baseball represented programming, and programming meant advertising dollars.

The sale of the Yankees to CBS signaled a new era in corporate ownership of sports teams, but there was one small glitch: the Yankees started losing. In the 20 years that Topping and Webb owned the club, the Yankees had missed the World Series only five times and had gone 10–5 in the ones they went to. By contrast, in the eight years that CBS owned the club, the Yankees never played a single postseason game.

What's wrong with this picture?

None of that mattered a whit to Bobby Ray Murcer of Oklahoma City on Opening Day 1969.

I was out of the army.

I was a brand-new father: Tori had been born on July 29, 1968, at Fort Huachuca. And Kay was pregnant again: Todd would come along on September 2, 1969, while we were playing Seattle at home. I sent Kay a huge bouquet of roses with a bat in the middle and took the first flight out to be with them.

And I was the starting third baseman for the New York Yankees.

Play ball!

Our manager my "real" rookie season was Ralph Houk, who was entering the fourth season of his second go-round as Yankee field boss. Ralph had managed the Yankees in 1961, 1962, and 1963, and in those three seasons had won two World Championships and an American League pennant. Then he went into the front office, where he ran the show as GM until he fired Johnny Keane partway through 1966 and took over in the dugout.

If he was expecting to pick up where he'd left off three years earlier, Ralph got a rude awakening. Over the next seven-plus years the Major was in command, the best we could do was one second-place finish (1970).

Does that mean he did a lousy job? Absolutely not. In fact, I believe with all my heart that we'd have done worse under anybody else. Not for one game, one inning, did Ralph lose the team. Everybody played his heart out for him. The fact is, we just weren't that good.

Ask the Yankees who played under Ralph in that eight-year-span and for other managers before or after who their favorite was, and I *guarantee* that most of them will put the Major at the top of their list.

That's because, first and foremost, Ralph was a player's manager. He never said anything bad about anybody, and he never bad-mouthed any player to the press. (That, in my view, is the absolute worst thing a manager can do. And you'd be surprised how many do it, making it even worse by supposedly going "off the record.") Ralph always protected his players, not only on the field, but off the field as well.

He was an especially good manager for young ballplayers. When I broke in, Ralph gave me every opportunity in the world. We just seemed to hit it off together, and we're dear friends to this day.

Ralph and his wife, Betty, lived in Florida during the off-season when he was with the Yankees. Ralph loved to fish, and I remember they had this boat named *Thanks, Yanks.* I always thought that was cool, maybe because it's a sentiment that I share every single day.

A good manager is someone you can talk to about anything, not only about baseball, but also about your own personal life, your family life, whatever. You might not think that players need anyone like that, but they do. They need to have somebody they feel they can trust, and they need to know that a private conversation stays just that: private.

Ralph Houk was that guy for me.

═══════

By the way, the third-base experiment didn't last long. I didn't kill anybody in the first-base boxes in the 31 games I played before they moved me to center field, but I did make 14 errors. In one series in Oakland, I made four throwing errors in two games. After the first couple of moon shots, every time I fielded a grounder, I'd hear this fan in a third-base box holler out to the people behind first, "Watch out! He's got it again!"

What can I tell you? They moved Mickey out of the infield to center field, so I wasn't going to get my dobber down when they did it to me.

Regarding that little matter of my moving to the outfield, one side effect that I guess I ought to have anticipated but didn't was the buzz in the press that began about me being the "next Mickey Mantle," me being his successor, me being the guy who was going to "inherit his mantle of greatness."

After all, we were both from Oklahoma, we both came up as shortstops, we both got moved to center, we both . . .

Stop right there. That was sheer nonsense from the git-go. Sure, there were some obvious similarities in our backgrounds and in the circumstances that got us to Yankee Stadium.

But me being the next Mickey Mantle? Please. I had enough on my hands trying to be the first Bobby Murcer.

I figured it would all blow away.

Wrong.

Over the next couple of years, when the Yankees didn't return to their championship ways with the "New Mickey" in center field, it got worse.

I had a good year in 1969. In fact, at the risk of sounding immodest, let me say that I had a very good year. How good? Only the best year of any rookie position player in baseball: 26 HRs, 82 RBIs, .259. And, of course, that translated into American League Rookie of the Year honors, right? Wrong. Turned out I spent too many days on the roster in 1965 and 1966 combined to be considered a rookie in 1969.

And the guy who did get voted AL Rookie of the Year in 1969, despite having clearly inferior numbers (11, 68, .282)? A KC Royals outfielder, what was his name . . . oh, right: Lou Piniella.

Yes, as you can probably guess, the subject has popped up in conversation a few hundred times since Sweet Lou and I became teammates in 1974.

The most interesting character from that 1969 team was, hands down, Joe Pepitone. By 1969, Pepi had been a Yankee for seven seasons and had developed a reputation as an all-star "character." Legend has it that when he signed with the Yankees in 1958 he used his entire $25,000 signing bonus to buy a brand-new Thunderbird and a boat, which he hauled down to Fort Lauderdale for spring training. Born and raised in Brooklyn, Pepi evidently figured that he'd take advantage of the Florida weather and get in some fishing and do some cruising around in his T-Bird. I understand it didn't take Ralph Houk long to straighten him out on that score.

Except for his well-deserved rep as a solid fielder and a good hitter, Joe was probably best known within baseball circles as the first guy to use a hair dryer in the clubhouse. He used it to maintain his two hairpieces, one for street wear and one for under his baseball cap (his "gamer").

In *Ball Four*, maybe the funniest sports book of all time, Jim Bouton tells of a time when he and Fritz Peterson, semi-bored midway through a game in which the Yankees held a commanding lead, went back into the clubhouse in the sixth inning and loaded up Pepitone's hair dryer with talcum powder. A perfect stunt in the making, except that the Yankees lost the lead and then the game in extra innings, with Pepi striking out in the clutch. The mood back in the clubhouse afterward was foul, as it always is after a tough loss. Then Joe came out of the shower, dried off and dressed, donned his street lid, and fired up his hair dryer. Whoosh! A cloud of talcum powder everywhere. Bouton writes that Pepi looked like "an Italian George Washington wearing a powdered wig." The clubhouse went wild.

The great thing about Pepi is that he was—is—drop-dead funny. I swear, if he hadn't been a mighty fine baseball player, the man could have made a living as a stand-up comedian. Sometimes his humor was pretty "purple," but he always made you laugh. You need a guy like that in the clubhouse to loosen things up, especially when you're not doing so great on the field.

Joe was one of the two "power guys" on the team, though that's not saying much. I led the club with 27 homers, while he hit 26. Then it dropped off to part-timer Frank Fernandez (12); nobody else was in double digits. Pepi was third in RBIs (70) behind Roy White (74) and me (82).

As you may have guessed by now, we weren't exactly a big run-scoring machine. That year we finished next to last in the American League with 532 runs scored, several country miles behind the league-leading Twins (790). Helps explain why we finished fourth in the AL East, 28.5 games behind the Orioles.

So naturally our biggest off-season move was to trade away . . . Joe Pepitone?

Yep, Joe went to the Astros for Curt Blefary in what turned

out to be one of the worst deals—maybe *the* worst deal—in all the time I was with the club. The following year for us, Curt hit 9 HRs, drove in 37 runs, and batted .212 in 99 games. Meanwhile, Joe—who was traded by Houston to Chicago in mid-season—went 26, 79, .258 for the Astros and Cubs.

So why were the Yankees so anxious to get rid of Joe?

I heard from an authoritative source inside the Yankee front office that GM Lee MacPhail traded Pepi because the Yankees were afraid Pepi might become a bad influence on me. Similar to the reason, I'm told, that Billy Martin had been traded in the middle of the 1957 season, so that he wouldn't be a bad influence on Mickey Mantle.

If something like that really did drive the Pepitone-Blefary deal, it was just plain crazy thinking. I was spending all my spare time away from the ballpark with Kay and two new babies, and was happy as a clam to be doing so. I wouldn't have been available to be "influenced," even if Joe had tried to lead me into any kind of wild behavior—and he never did.

In 1970, we made a great leap forward as a team, going from 80–81 in 1969 to 93–69.

Too bad for us, though, that was the year that the Orioles obliterated everything in their sight. They won the AL East by *15 games*, swept the Twins in the playoffs to win the AL pennant, and blew away the Reds in the World Series, 4–1.

Talk about having the horses: the O's had three future Hall of Famers (Jim Palmer, Brooks Robinson, Frank Robinson), three 20-game winners (Palmer, Mike Cuellar, Dave McNally), and the AL MVP (Boog Powell).

But things were looking up for us—I thought.

Hey, second is just one rung away from the top, right?

One of our anchors that year, as he was his entire Yankee career, was Mel Stottlemyre.

Mel's record was 15–13, and at first glance, you might dismiss him as a middle-of-the-pack guy, no more. Wrong. Mel's ERA that year was 3.09. A pitcher with an ERA that sweet, you'd figure to be an 18-game winner, maybe better, if he got any support at all. But Mel didn't. Throughout his 11-season Yankee career, we were mostly a weak-hitting ball club.

Look at his career numbers: 2.97 ERA, 164 wins (sixth on the all-time Yankee list), three-time 20-game winner, and *40* shut-outs.

Pretty great, huh? But I know for a fact that Mel's favorite numbers all came on one day—September 26, 1964, at the Stadium against the Senators—when Mel went 5-for-5 and drove in two runs. Oh, and he also pitched a two-hit shutout.

Mel loves to fish. Really loves it. And since the Yankees spring training camp is in Florida, near some mighty fine Everglades bass fishing, he always made sure to be out on a boat just about every spare minute he had.

For several springs, before exhibition games kicked in, we had us a little fishing tournament, complete with teams. The one I remember best was me and Mickey, who was with the team several springs as a special coach, versus Mel and John Ellis, a big, strong catcher–first baseman. (John weighed in at 225, and he practically dared base runners coming into home to try to knock him over.)

The rules were pretty simple: everybody threw in a few bucks, and the team with the biggest catch *by weight* won it all. And you had to be at the dock and have your fish weighed by 5 sharp. One minute later and you were DQ'd.

Well, this one day it got close to 5, and Mickey and I knew that Mel and John were ahead of us in fish. We had a big one and a few small ones. Mel and John had seven or eight middle-size bass. Things weren't looking good for the home team.

But on the way in, Mickey had a genius idea: he took our big fish, and he stuffed a big sea weight—a two-pound hunk of lead, if memory serves—down the gullet of our lunker bass.

It worked! We won by a couple of ounces and took home all the money.

I finally remembered to confess to Mel many years later.

===

My second full season as a Yankee, I picked up pretty much where I left off in 1969: 23 homers, 78 ribbies, .251 BA.

My personal high point of the season came on June 24, 1970, in a doubleheader against Cleveland in Yankee Stadium, when I hit four homers in four consecutive at-bats. (Old hat for me, actually; I did it once before in Toledo back in 1966.)

In the fall of 2007, I ran into a fellow who caught one of those back-to-back-to-back-to-backers all those years ago. You may have heard of him—a guy named Bob Costas.

Bob told me he almost came away with another one of them, but lost it in a mad scrum in the aisle. When I graciously offered to sign the ball, Bob said he had lost track of the priceless souvenir, oh, some 36 years ago.

Can you believe it? And he calls himself a baseball fan!

===

My first All-Star Game was in Detroit in 1971.

A year or so before, a dear friend of ours named Carl Rosen, whom Kay and I had recently gotten to know down in Florida, told me, "Bobby, if you ever make the All-Star team, I'll rent you a jet and send you there, you and Kay, along with your family or any other friends you want to go along."

We met Carl and his wife, Shirley, one Christmas week through Al Schragis (he and his wife, Carole, had become good friends with Kay and me). At the time Carole's family owned what's now called the Doral Golf Resort and Spa in Miami, where Kay and I and the kids had spent a couple of Christmas seasons.

Golfers know Doral as the home of the Blue Monster, one of the longest and toughest stops on the PGA Tour for the last four decades. I'm a golf fanatic, and Al mentioned that there was this New York guy who was the first one off the tee every morning, and asked if I would like for him to arrange for me to play with him, You bet, I said, and that's how our friendship with Carl and Shirley Rosen began.

In addition to being a crazy-mad golfer like me, Carl was a prominent figure in the New York fashion trade. Over the decade or so that I knew him, he became my mentor and adviser in financial matters.

Carl, who died in 1983, was also a big man in Thoroughbred racing. He even named a colt after me, which was quite an honor. Unfortunately, Bobby Murcer could outrun Bobby Murcer, and the slower one never came close to breaking into the majors.

Even so, I got interested, and Carl let me buy into a few ponies. Boomer Sooner won a few small races in the minors, and at one time I was a part-owner of seven Thoroughbreds. Unfortunately, I kept buying the wrong part.

After a few years, and at considerable expense to the Murcer bank account, I hung up my saddle. They say horse racing is the sport of kings, but I was only a knight, so I figured it was time to get out. It was fun while it lasted, but if it had lasted much longer, I'd have had to get a second job.

Anyway, back in 1971 when I was elected to the All-Star team for the first time, Carl graciously reminded me of his promise and set about delivering on it.

CBS owned the Yankees at the time, and Michael Burke was the president of the club. The day before the All-Star Game, Mike called me and said, "I've got first-class tickets for you and Kay on American Airlines tomorrow. I'll go with you, if that's all right."

"Mike," I said, "I got us a better deal. I've got my own jet. Why don't you come fly with us?"

Kay

*M*ichael Burke was one of the loveliest people I've ever met in baseball. Many times, when Bobby would hit a game-winning home run or do something special in a game, I would get a beautiful bouquet of flowers the following day from Mike

I think he believed that the wife was the wind beneath the wings of the player, but also the one sitting home not getting the standing ovations.

People who saw the 1971 All-Star Game in person there in Tiger Stadium will tell you that Reggie Jackson hit a home run that *still* hasn't come down. But that wasn't the only segment on my own personal highlights film.

My first time up, I got a hit off Juan Marichal. I thought at the time, Great start! But I never got another hit in 12 All-Star at-bats. Matter of fact, I fear that I may be the all-time All-Star leader in hitting into double plays.

But my takeaway from my five All-Star appearances? I'm hitting 1.000 off Juan Marichal lifetime.

One other thing about the 1971 All-Star Game is the astonishing number of participants who are now in the Hall of Fame. It's gotta be an all-time record for Hall of Famers in two dugouts. Let me drop a few names:

Henry Aaron	Willie Mays
Johnny Bench	Willie McCovey
Lou Brock	Jim Palmer
Steve Carlton	Brooks Robinson
Roberto Clemente	Frank Robinson
Reggie Jackson	Tom Seaver
Harmon Killebrew	Willie Stargell
Juan Marichal (I own him.)	Carl Yastrzemski

Plus one guy who's not in the Hall but deserves to be there: Pete Rose.

My dear friend Joe Torre, who was with the Cardinals at the time, was the starting third baseman for the National League. Much later, after he'd become manager of the Yankees, Joe told me that I'd gotten him in big trouble with Willie McCovey in that game.

"You hit this monster pop-up in the infield"—*after* my hit off Juan Marichal, Joe forgot to add—"that kind of started over toward third base. But the wind was blowing so hard you'd have thought we were in Chicago. Anyway, I kept hollering, 'Mine! Mine!' and tracked it all the way across the field until I finally caught it over near first base. Willie gave me this hard look and said, 'Just what in the hell are you doing over here?'"

The All-Star Game was definitely the high point of the season for me. But while I took another step forward at the plate in 1971—25, 94, .331 (the highest BA of my career)—it didn't matter much, because we took a major step backward as a team, going 82–80 to finish fourth in the AL East, 18 games behind the Orioles.

━━━━

Just before the beginning of the 1972 season, we stole Sparky Lyle from the Red Sox in one of the all-time great Yankee trades. We gave up two decent utility players, outfielder Danny Cater and middle infielder Mario Guerrero. But what we got was the top closer of the era, a hard-nosed competitor who would go on to win the Cy Young award in 1977—and one of baseball's hall-of-fame pranksters.

Sparky did all sorts of wacky things to keep the clubhouse loose, some of them in the unprintable department, but his specialty was sitting bare-butted on birthday cakes. Anytime a player with a big following had a birthday, his fans would typically send birthday cakes, pies, cupcakes, that sort of thing down to the clubhouse. The more popular the player, the bigger the birthday spread. It was great, except for one thing. Unless the cakes and pies were placed under armored guard the minute they arrived, Sparky would drop trou and sit himself right down on top.

I can't tell you exactly how many cakes and pies Sparky squashed in the five seasons he was a Yankee, but it was a lot. Back then, they didn't keep stats on that sort of thing.

Now, longtime Yankee pitching coach Jim Turner, who was one of the best in the business and had seven World Championship rings dating back to the Casey Stengel era, absolutely loved chocolate cake. The Colonel—that was the nickname somebody hung on him when he went into coaching in the early 1950s—liked anything chocolate, but he positively adored chocolate cake.

So one time before a game, a clubhouse attendant came walking through the clubhouse door carrying this huge chocolate cake over his shoulder like a waiter. I don't remember who it was intended for, but you could see the Colonel eyeballing it. He *wanted* that cake.

But on the other side of the clubhouse, Sparky was already starting to drop his drawers so he could be on the spot as soon as that guy set the cake down on the table in the middle of the clubhouse. Next thing you know, bare-naked Sparky and the Colonel are converging on the table, the Colonel trying to grab off a handful—no time to slice it neatly!—before Sparky could flatten it.

Sparky won the race. He sat down, causing the cake to explode, with chocolate icing shooting off every which direction. As Sparky walked off toward the shower laughing his head off, his backside covered in black goop, you could see the Colonel's spirits sag at having come up empty-handed.

Pretty soon everybody started heading out to the field for pregame practice except the Colonel, who was hanging back a little bit. I had to go back to my locker to get something, and I caught him out of the corner of my eye. The clubhouse was empty now except for me and him, and he didn't see me as he circled the table a couple of times, hoping to ID a piece of cake that Sparky's posterior hadn't touched. He looked and looked and finally reached out and grabbed a big hunk off to the side that might—*might*—have escaped being butt-cheeked by Sparky. Or so he convinced himself. And, his cake in hand, the Colonel contentedly strutted out of the clubhouse.

Jim Turner died in 1998 at the ripe old age of 95, one of the oldest former Yankees in team history up to that point, and the club's all-time, number one chocoholic.

━━━

Sparky led the AL with 35 saves in 1972, I led the league with 102 runs, and we were in the race down the stretch until we faded in September. We finished fourth, but only 6.5 games back of the Tigers in the AL East.

Overall, it was the best year of my career: 33 homers and 96 ribbies, plus I batted .331, 50+ points over my career BA (.277). Funny, though, the thing I think I was proudest of that season was winning my first—and only—Gold Glove. I always took pride in my fielding, and I really worked at getting better.

(Glad they awarded them to outfielders without designating left, right, or center; otherwise I'd have been going head to head with Paul Blair, who that year won the fifth of the eight GGs he'd hang in his trophy case by the time he retired.)

If you're in a pennant race, you're having a good time by definition. And with the guys we had in our clubhouse, we were having an especially good time.

There was Thurman Munson, of course. He'd been Rookie of the Year in the AL in 1970, and even though he was only 25, he was clearly a leader on the rise. He wouldn't be named captain until 1976, but I think that was because the organization was reluctant to fill a job that had remained vacant since Lou Gehrig gave his farewell speech in 1939. I know this: if you look up "intensity" in the dictionary, you'll likely find a picture of my dear friend Thurman Lee Munson.

Then there was Ron "Bloomie" Blomberg, who would gain fame the following season as the first-ever designated hitter. (You can look it up: April 6, 1973. He drew a walk from Luís Tíant in Fenway Park.) But he was famous already in our clubhouse for coming out with all sorts of weird observations that left us scratching our heads. One of my favorites: "The sugar always rises to the top." I swear, the man never met a metaphor he couldn't mangle.

Bloomie's a great guy. Inducted into the National Jewish Hall of Fame in 2004, Bloomie went on to manage a team in the inaugural season of the Israel Baseball League in 2007. He and former Cubs and A's lefty Ken Holtzman were helping to get baseball going in Israel.

Gene "Stick" Michael was, for a pretty big dude (6-foot-2, 183), a real Punch-and-Judy hitter: .229 lifetime, 47 RBIs a career high, and just 15 HRs in 10 seasons. But Stick was a terrific fielder, a really smart baseball player—and an absolute master of the hidden ball trick. The guys who count such things claim he pulled it off five times in his career. I can't say otherwise, but it sure seemed like more, which is why it was such a weapon: Stick got such a rep for it that guys on second took to taking shorter leads, which meant a lot more of them stopping at third on hard-hit singles to the outfield.

Like a lot of guys who didn't hit too many home runs, Stick remembered every one of his with perfect recall.

Years after we'd both retired, we were having lunch one day in the Yankee clubhouse, and he asked me if I remembered "the time M and M and M went B to B to B?" Huh? What in the world is this man talking about? What language is he speaking?

"You know," he said. "The time Murcer and Munson and Michael went back to back to back."

The game did come back to me, but my question to Stick was, "What in the world were you doing hitting so close to me and Thurman in the lineup?"

Today, Stick's one of the top guys in the Yankee front office. Like I said, he always was a really smart baseball player.

———

Sometime in 1972, team president Mike Burke was authorized by CBS to go out and find some backers and put together a deal to try to buy the team. (The news didn't get out at the time: this was one of the best-kept secrets ever in a sport—and town—not noted for them.) Mike had been bitten by the baseball bug and wanted to stay in the game. We all liked Mike, so when he managed to pull together some investors out in Cleveland and create a limited partnership to take this pinstriped lemon off CBS's hands, we were happy for him and for us—insofar as we paid much attention to the transaction at all.

What I mean is that players play and owners own. We were a bunch of 20-year-olds trying to turn on hard sliders inside and shave corners outside and get on the good side of .500 and maybe, if we were good and lucky the same season, win a championship ring. That (and our families) were all that mattered. Playing baseball was our lives. Owning baseball teams? Somebody else's business.

The papers were signed and the sale announced on January 3, 1973. The purchase price was announced at $10 million (about what a decent number two starter would cost you these days). But that number included some nearby real estate; the actual price for the ball club was only $8.7 million. Seeing as that was $2.5 million or so less than CBS had paid for just 80 percent of the team a decade earlier, the consensus was that the Cleveland group got a bargain. In fact, it's the only time in major league history that a franchise was sold at a loss.

(Just in case you were wondering, *Forbes* magazine puts the value of the Yankee franchise today at $1.2 *billion*.)

Nobody knew anything much about the guy who put up most of the money except what we read in the papers, which was that he had made his money building ships. (The only thing that caused me to perk up my ears was that this George Steinbrenner fellow had once been an assistant under Woody Hayes at Ohio State.) But Mike Burke was going to be a limited partner in the new ownership group, and he was going to stay on as president of the ball club, so I figured nothing much was going to change.

I was only about 100 percent wrong.

―――――

The really big Yankee news coming out of spring training in 1973 figured to be the announcement that I had just signed a $100,000-a-year contract. At least *I* figured it would be the big news. It sure was big to me.

I remember talking with Mickey about my contract negotiations before going in to Yankee GM Lee MacPhail. Lee had a reputation as being pretty tight with a buck, and Mickey told me he would "never, ever, *ever* come up with that kind of money. That's the most *I* ever made."

"Well," I said, "I'm going to ask him for it anyway."

I'd put together another two straight strong years:

YR	G	AB	R	HR	RBI	SB	BA	SLG
1971	146	529	94	25	94	14	.331	.543
1972	153	585	102	33	96	11	.292	.537

Not Mickey Mantle numbers, maybe, but I'd made the All-Star

team both years, and I'd finished in the top 10 both years in the American League MVP race.

Much to Mickey's surprise—and to mine, I have to admit—Lee said okay. I got a one-year deal for $100,000. The only other Yankees to hit that mark? Mick and Joe DiMaggio.

I know that sounds a little quaint nowadays, what with the major league *minimum* salary in 2008 being $390,000. But in 1973, $100K was a big deal. In today's dollars, it amounted to about $450,000. Only a couple of dozen players in the majors had reached or crossed the $100K threshold, and I guess Yankee management realized that it was time to bring their star player up to that level.

Kay's always said, "You provide the nest egg, and I'll provide the nest." Well, this was the biggest nest egg I'd ever laid.

Back then, of course, every contract was a one-year deal. Players negotiated directly with teams. Nobody I knew had an agent. (Today, of course, even batboys have agents.) You went in to the GM, you made your best case, and then . . . well, if you didn't like what you were offered, you had two options: shut up and sign, or go coach high school baseball somewhere.

In other words, take it or leave it.

Let's say you had a "bad" year, dropped from 40 homers to 30. Management had the contractual right to cut your salary up to 20 percent the following season.

Again, take it or leave it.

There was a little give: teams didn't want a bunch of unhappy ballplayers, especially not their stars. A little give, but not much. This was before free agency, remember, and players had zero leverage.

(Speaking of free agency, I think Curt Flood deserves a special plaque in the Hall of Fame for having the guts to take on Major League Baseball—and give up a chunk of his own career—to win ballplayers the fundamental right to sell their services to the highest bidder. You know, as in the rest of America.)

A couple of reporters asked me later if I felt any additional pressure, now that I'd joined such an exclusive group.

"Not a bit," I said, and I meant it.

I believed in my heart that I *deserved* to be in the $100K club.

CHANGING TIMES

I was on top of the world.

Just before spring training opened in 1973, I had signed a contract making me only the second New York Yankee—after Mickey Mantle, of course—to earn $100,000 a year and the youngest member of the $100K club in American League history.

It's like Waite Hoyt, the Yankee Hall of Fame pitcher from the Babe Ruth era, once said: "It's great to be young and a Yankee."

But a funny thing happened on the way to the press conference where my new contract would be announced and I could bask in a little glory:

Two Yankee teammates announced that they had swapped families.

Let me back up here a little bit.

I'm no social historian, but you don't have to be one to know that American society was coming a little unglued in the 1970s. I guess it all started in the 1960s, when the Baby Boomers came of age and began challenging the American Establishment up one side and down the other.

But Kay and I hadn't gotten caught up in all that. (We grew up in Oklahoma City, remember?) And by the end of the decade, most of our attention and energy was focused on raising two little kids, not partying at Woodstock.

In the 1970s, especially in urban areas, there was an escalation of all types of extreme behavior from rampant drug use to all-night disco parties to swinging. And I'm not talking here about people taking more cuts at the plate . . . or that dance style from the 1930s.

You couldn't help but hear about "swingers" and "wife-swapping" and "free love" any more than you could fail to recognize the smell of marijuana smoke if you went into the men's room at a nightclub. That stuff was all around us, even closer than we realized, we soon found out.

Kay

A group of us who lived in New Jersey used to go out to dinner from time to time at a little Japanese hibachi steakhouse near Fort Lee. You could get a large group of people around one of their big tables, so it was perfect for four or five couples, even more.

One night when we'd finished dinner and were getting ready to leave, someone said, "How about everybody just throw your keys out into the middle of the table, and whoever's keys you pick up . . ."

Everybody laughed, but nobody threw in their keys, much less realized that two couples in the group had gone way beyond that joke already.

Turns out that swinging was more than just "in the air" for two of our starting pitchers, Fritz Peterson and Mike Kekich, who'd been best buddies in the four seasons since Mike had come over to the Yankees from the Dodgers in 1969.

Swinging was in their bedrooms.

It all started in the winter of 1972, everybody learned later, after a party Fritz and Mike and their spouses attended at the home of *New York Post* columnist Maury Allen. Seems they negotiated a trade in the driveway, each going home with the "other" spouse. But however it might have started out, this was no casual one-night stand. Not too long thereafter, they swapped *families*.

That's right: Fritz moved in with Susanne Kekich, and Mike moved in with Marilyn Peterson. They swapped wives, kids, dogs, parakeets, mailing addresses, cars, everything—lock, stock, and lawn mowers.

So now flash forward to spring training 1973, when Ralph Houk called a clubhouse meeting before practice the day before my new contract was going to be announced. We all gathered around, some guys in full uni, some in jocks and socks. None of us knew what was coming.

"We've got a little family matter that everybody needs to know about," Ralph said, after everybody quieted down. "You'll be reading about this in the papers sooner or later . . ."

And Ralph proceeded to break the news to us.

We sat there dumbfounded, in a state of shock. Nobody knew what to say, so nobody said much of anything. I never understood it, what they were doing. I never got it. But I figured it was their lives, and none of my business.

Look, to their credit, this wasn't something Fritz and Susanne and Mike and Marilyn were exactly hiding—they had neighbors, after all. And it wasn't something they were selling as a model for other people. It was just something they wanted to do, and so they did it.

(Postscript: Fritz and Susanne are still together. Mike and Marilyn broke up pretty soon after. I still to this day can't get my mind around the whole situation.)

The Yankees' family swap was front-page news in the *New York Post* and the *New York Daily News* for several days, but then faded away. The story really didn't have legs with the media, partly because after the initial flurry of articles there was nothing left to say. This was in the days before *People* magazine, before ESPN and CNN, before Oprah, before the Internet. In fact, portions of the New York press had at first agreed not to report it (on the quaint grounds that it was a "personal matter"), but then everybody jumped in when the *Post* broke the story.

Can you imagine what the media would do today with something like the Peterson-Kekich trade, especially if it came out of the Yankee clubhouse, which gets scrutinized more than any clubhouse in sports?

Talk about different times!

By the way, guess which story generated more ink after the press conference the following day, my new $100K contract or the Peterson-Kekich trade?

———

Now that I had joined baseball's financial elite, you might expect that my career took a turn toward the more sophisticated. But that's not how baseball works. Even though we were grown men with 5 o'clock shadows and five-figure (or, in my case, six-figure!) salaries, most of us were still boys at heart.

And that always seemed to be truest with left-handed pitchers: it's a proven scientific fact that they're a little bit off-center, if not borderline nuts.

I'm not talking here about the marital (re)arrangements that Fritz and Mike—both lefties—constructed for themselves. I'm referring to the stunts and pranks and generally weird things this terrible twosome pulled off, often in tandem, sometimes alone. A lot of the stuff they did is unsuitable for a family book, but let me give you a few examples of their capers so you'll get a sense of what I'm talking about.

- **RUN IT UP ON THE FLAGPOLE AND SEE WHO SALUTES.** Mike used to swipe articles of clothing from a teammate's locker and run it up on the center-field flagpole before a game—a raincoat, a pair of uniform pants, a jockstrap, whatever. Fortunately, the grounds crew always got it down before it was time to run up the American flag.

• **WHERE'S MY STUFF?** Back then we flew commercially on road trips, of course, so the luggage had to be properly tagged so it could get to our destination. But once in a while, Fritz and Mike would manage to get their hands on some bag tags—maybe they bribed a skycap or something; I don't know. Anyway, if we were going off on a 10–12 day road trip to the West Coast, say, they'd retag somebody's luggage and route it to Bogotá or Anchorage or someplace far, far away. They'd hang on to the tag numbers so the stuff could eventually be tracked and claimed, but they wouldn't give them to the traveling secretary until near the end of the trip. Meanwhile, the poor guy whose gear was waiting in baggage claim a thousand miles away would have to go out and buy new gear to get him through the trip.

• **YOU'VE GOT MAIL.** And then there was . . . well, there was this other crazy thing Fritz used to do that's so disgusting I'm going have to have Kay tell you about it.

Kay

One winter day in Oklahoma, I went out to get the mail, and among all the usual bills and letters and magazines and stuff, there was this one envelope, addressed to Bobby. It was in such a crudely penciled scrawl that I assumed it was a piece of fan mail from a fourth grader or some such.

Well, when I got back in the house, I opened it up—I handled a lot of Bobby's fan mail—and there was this single piece of paper with something Scotch-taped to the middle of it.

I couldn't figure out what it was. It was about the size of a fingernail but it looked like a bloody scab. Really icky. So I showed it to Bobby—and he practically gagged. (He's a pretty fastidious fellow, my husband.)

"Oh, it's that crazy Fritz Peterson," Bobby explained. "He chews the skin off of the inside of his mouth and collects it and tapes it to a piece of paper and leaves it my locker because he knows it grosses me out so bad."

We got a few more letters like that from Fritz from time to time during the off-season. But I learned to recognize the handwriting on the envelopes, and so I would just toss them.

As a player, I always tried to be a good citizen. Not some kind of Mr. Goody-Two-Shoes, but a player who concentrated on playing, not trying to run his team or the game of baseball.

For instance, I never took public potshots at ownership or management of the teams I played for. Sure, I felt like saying something from time to time—like, when the front office made what I thought was a dumb trade (or, more often, when it didn't make a move that might have helped us out). But my theory was that it isn't smart to bite the hand of the guy signing my paycheck, at least not in public.

And I never made any public pronouncements about how I thought Major League Baseball ought to be run. I was too busy trying to pick up the movement on hard sliders from tough lefties.

But I did cross that self-imposed good citizen line once—quite openly and quite publicly and quite explicitly—when I called the Commissioner of Baseball and the president of the American League "gutless" for not dealing with a certain issue that I felt strongly about.

The issue was Gaylord Perry's spitter, the commissioner was Bowie Kuhn, the AL president was Joe Cronin, and I said straight up to several newspaper guys in 1973 that I thought the latter two of them were just plain gutless for not doing something about the first.

The spitball, of course, is as old as baseball. Back in the day, the guys who *didn't* mess with the ball were probably in a minority. And most of the time a "spitball" didn't have anything to do with spit, except maybe back when a lot of guys chewed tobacco. Oh, I suppose a "spitball" pitcher in modern baseball will occasionally doctor a ball with saliva, but most prefer to cut it, scuff it, or smear something greasy on it. Whatever it takes to make what starts out like an ordinary fastball dance and dart like a jitterbug.

The best at doing this in my playing era—and maybe the best of all time—was Gaylord Perry. One of the great pitchers of his era, Gaylord never tried to hide the fact that he was a natural-born genius at doctoring the ball. In fact, in 1974, midway through his career, he wrote a book called *Me and the Spitter: An Autobiographical Confession.*

Only it wasn't exactly a confession: all he owned up to was instilling the belief in a batter that he was throwing a wet one on every pitch. That, he said, was enough to keep the batter off guard.

That was genius. You get inside a guy's head that way, you've got him half licked (pun intended) even before you let the ball go.

But Perry was a genius at doctoring the ball in such a way that he wouldn't get caught. I bet he had more balls checked by umpires than all the other pitchers combined in the majors most years. But somehow Perry didn't get himself kicked out of a game for throwing an illegal pitch until 1982, his next-to-last season in baseball.

(Gaylord must have laughed all the way to the dugout the day he got the thumb, wondering how in the world it took 'em so long.)

Once when Gaylord was with Cleveland and the Indians came to the Stadium, I had a clubhouse boy take a big can of lard over to the Indians' clubhouse and leave it in his locker.

Gaylord got me back pretty good soon after that. He had a mutual acquaintance grease up his hand and come up to me and shake hands, saying, "Gaylord says hello." The name of that mutual acquaintance shall go undisclosed in order not to incriminate the guilty.

As you may have suspected, I couldn't hit a lick off Perry. (Pun intended again.) If I batted a buck-thirty off him over the years, I'd be startled. Matter of fact, I don't want some stat hound running to his data bank to find out what I hit off Perry lifetime, because I don't want to know. It was that bad.

Finally, after a game in which I had four particularly ugly at-bats against him in Cleveland late in the summer of 1973, I decided I'd had enough. I told some reporters that AL President Joe Cronin and Commissioner Bowie Kuhn were just flat-out gutless for not doing anything about Gaylord Perry throwing an illegal pitch.

Well, the next day, the spit hit the fan. My comment was all over the newspapers, in big headlines: "Murcer Calls Commish Gutless!" Someone from the Commissioner's Office called and said that Mr. Kuhn wanted to see me in his office as soon as we got back to New York.

Great. I said those things to get the commissioner's attention so that he would *do something*. By speaking out, I thought I was being a *good* baseball citizen. And now I was going to get face time with the commissioner. So far, so good.

But the first office I visited when we got back to New York was that of Yankee GM Lee MacPhail. Lee had our manager, Ralph Houk, join us there for a little summit talk on how I should handle myself when I went to see Commissioner Kuhn. We were in a pennant race, and they didn't want me to fly off the handle and get suspended.

"Now, look," Lee said, "don't carry this thing too far. Everybody knows Gaylord doctors the ball. But we can't have you go crazy when you see Bowie."

Made sense. Lee was trying to soften my attitude before I sat down with the commissioner.

He needn't have bothered, because I never even got a chance to sit down.

The minute I set foot in his office, Bowie stood up from his desk—he was something like 6 foot 4—and said, "I'll tell you who's gutless—a guy who talks to the press instead of the person he has a complaint with. If you want to call me gutless, you call me gutless to my face."

And he added: "If you call me gutless one more time, I'm going to throw you out of that window over there."

On the spot, I clammed right up, not because I was scared of being thrown out of any windows, but because I was so mad that I decided I couldn't trust myself not to say something I'd later regret.

In fact, the only thing I ever *liked* about Bowie Kuhn was that he *didn't* throw me out that window. He was the owners' man, all the way, on every issue; and I was just a player. He demanded that I make a public apology for my remarks.

No way.

Meeting adjourned.

On June 30 the Commissioner's Office announced that I had been fined $250 for my effort to protect the integrity of the game. (The press release may not have put it quite that way.) That night, I hit a two-run homer off Perry as we beat the Indians 7–2. After the game, I told reporters that "I hit a hanging spitter."

The following year, Lee MacPhail was named president of the American League. Remember, Lee had been our GM when all this went down, and he'd said in our meeting before I saw Kuhn that everybody knew Gaylord threw an illegal pitch. So I sent Lee a little congratulatory note, and I added, "We all know that *you* know that Perry throws that illegal pitch, so we'll be waiting to see what you do about stopping him."

I got no reply.

Know what I think now? I think I was right to speak up back in 1973.

Gaylord Perry won 314 games in a career that spanned 22 seasons. He was the first pitcher to win Cy Young awards in both leagues (Cleveland, 1972; San Diego, 1978). He had a lifetime 3.11 ERA. And he was elected to the Hall of Fame in 1991.

Great accomplishments, but I say that he racked them up by throwing an illegal pitch. By cheating. And that's a fact.

Gene Mauch once said that Gaylord Perry "should be in the Hall of Fame with a tube of K-Y jelly attached to his plaque."

Not a bad idea. That and an asterisk.

Down the road, Perry and I actually shared dugout space in 1980 when the Yankees picked him up from the Rangers in a late-season trade. The earlier business between me and Kuhn never came up. In fact, I'm not sure Perry and I ever exchanged a word.

But on days he was pitching, when we were at bat, I watched him like a hawk, strictly out of professional interest. Sitting there in the dugout, I saw him squeeze something from a tube onto the inside bill of his cap, the left side of his uniform top down by his ribs, and the right-hand side of his pants on his upper thigh. You know, places a pitcher might naturally touch while out on the mound.

He was getting all ready to doctor the ball, right there, in our dugout. I knew it. Everybody knew it.

I didn't say anything, though, not to him or anyone else. Gaylord Perry was no longer my problem.

———

Family swapping and broadsides against the Commissioner of Baseball behind us, the Yankees were definitely on the move in 1974. I could feel it. In March we picked up Elliot Maddox from the Rangers. (Elliot would go on to hit .303 for us that year.) Early in the season, we made a great trade with Cleveland that brought us Chris Chambliss, Dick "Dirt" Tidrow, and Cecil Upshaw. In June we bought Rudy May from the Angels. (He went 8–4 for us with a 2.28 ERA that summer.)

Oh, and the previous winter we picked up that guy from KC who stole the Rookie of Year award from me back in 1969 on a technicality: Lou Piniella.

For Mr. Steinbrenner, though, it was a pretty bumpy summer. On the eve of Opening Day, he was indicted in federal court on 15 criminal counts related to campaign financing shenanigans in the Nixon reelection campaign in 1972, the operation that introduced America to the word "Watergate." Mr. Steinbrenner's legal troubles commanded oceans of ink over that summer in the New York press, and the flood only increased when on August 23 he pleaded guilty to making illegal contributions to the Nixon campaign and obstructing justice. Three months later, he was suspended from baseball for two years by Commissioner Kuhn.

Strangely enough, his troubles didn't percolate down into the clubhouse. All we knew was what we read in the papers, and I know that I tuned it all out early on. This was complicated legal stuff, and we were ballplayers, not lawyers.

Anyway, it wasn't as if Mr. Steinbrenner was so preoccupied with all his personal stuff that he couldn't pay attention to what was happening on the field. We learned that early in the season, when we came in one afternoon before a game and discovered that a clubhouse meeting had been called before BP. At the appointed hour, our new manager, Bill Virdon, walked in, placed a tape recorder on a stool, told everybody to listen up, hit the play button, and walked out without saying a word.

Next thing you know, we heard Mr. Steinbrenner's voice: "Okay, men, we're in a pennant race"—it was late April, if memory serves—"and I want to talk to you about a few things."

Then, because he was only beginning his second season of ownership and didn't know everybody by name yet, he started addressing us by numbers: "Number 53, lose the muttonchops"—I'm making up the numbers to protect the guilty—"Number 23, you were slow backing up third in Cleveland the other night, and when the ball got away it could have cost us a run . . . Number 16, the team rule is no hair below the collar line . . . Number 19, you looked pathetic against that lefthander in Boston. Take some extra BP . . . Number 36, you need to drop about 10 pounds . . ."

And so on, for about 10 minutes.

We sat there, stupefied. Nobody in the room had ever heard of anything like this before. At least no one could say that our owner wasn't engaged.

Our big problem that season obviously wasn't lack of attention from the top. Our big problem was that that we didn't play a single game at home. Not one. Yankee Stadium closed for renovations at the end of the 1973 season—with yours truly making the last out there—so we played all our 81 "home" games in 1974 in Shea Stadium.

No offense intended to Mets fans, but I *hated* Shea Stadium from the first pitch. Still do.

I have mixed feelings about Yankee Stadium being replaced by the new ballpark that will open for play in 2009. But I think that when Shea is reduced to rubble after the 2008 season, to be replaced by Citi Field in 2009, the baseball world will be a far, far better place.

Besides having our ears assaulted by airplanes taking off from and landing at LaGuardia Airport (a long fly ball west of the left-field fence), the thing that made me hate hitting at Shea Stadium can be summed up in two sets of numbers:

- At Yankee Stadium, it was 296 feet down the right-field line and 344 to straightaway right, to the edge of the bullpen. (As a lefty pull hitter, I hit most of my home runs between those two points.)

- At Shea Stadium, it was 338 feet down the line in right and 371 in the RF power alley.

Get the picture?

Mickey kidded me that I led the AL in warning track shots that year. Only I don't think he was really kidding.

———

Another problem was that I lost my job.

On Tuesday, May 28, 1974, I got an ugly surprise when I showed up for work: I wasn't the New York Yankees' center fielder anymore.

Managers post the lineup in the clubhouse before games, and players always check it when they come in or as they go out to warm up. The utility players look to see if they've been penciled in for duty because somebody's in a slump or nursing a minor injury. The regulars glance at it just out of habit, even though they know, say, that they're playing center field and batting third, the way they've been doing for almost four seasons.

This day I looked at the card as a matter of routine, and what I saw stopped me in my tracks: "3. Murcer RF." And two slots up: "1. Maddox CF."

Say what?

Since Opening Day, Maddox and I had both been in the starting lineup together only a handful of times. (A part-time player for the Tigers, Senators, and Rangers before coming to the Yankees, so far Maddox had been our fourth outfielder.) And when we were in the starting lineup together, I had always played center field (*my* position) and Maddox had been right.

I turned on my heel and walked into the manager's office to find out what was going on.

Let me give you a little Bill Virdon background.

Hired away from the Pirates after the 1973 season when Ralph Houk moved on, Virdon had distant ties with the Yankees, who signed him out of high school in 1950. He was a center fielder, but the Yankees were pretty well set there with a kid from Commerce, Oklahoma, so after four years they traded him to the Cardinals. (Remember what I said about the depth of the Yankee farm system in the 1950s?) He was NL Rookie of the Year for the Cardinals in 1955, but early in the following season he was traded to the Pirates, where he spent the next nine years.

Really old-time Yankee fans will recall him as the slap-hitting Pirates center fielder whose hard grounder to short took a bad hop and hit Tony Kubek in the throat in game seven of the World Series, setting up the Bill Mazeroski home run that won it for Pittsburgh.

Virdon also had street cred—we didn't use that term back then, but it fits here—as a manager. His first year on the job with the Pirates, in 1972, they won the NL East.

But this was two years later, and he was new to the Yankees, and I was the team's highest profile player, and he'd just bumped me from my job, and I wanted to know why.

I just thought the change would be best for the team, Bill said.

Okay, I said, but don't you think I was owed a little advance notice?

I did it because I thought it was best for the team.

End of conversation.

The New York media, especially the daily tabloids, went a little nuts: "Murcer Out, Maddox In" and "Murcer Loses Job," that sort of thing. And they kept the story alive way past the time it ought to have been put to sleep. Over the next several weeks, I must have been asked a thousand questions, all variations of just one: "What do you think about the move, Bobby?"

My answer was always the same: "I don't like it, but I'll do whatever's best for the team."

Look, my relationship with the media has always been based on a bedrock principle: ask me a direct question, and I'll give you a direct answer. And both parts of my response to the Murcer-to-RF questions were honest: I *didn't* like it, not one bit, but I *did* want whatever was best for the team. Let's get on with the game.

Recently I asked my good friend Marty Appel, who was PR director of the Yankees at the time, to remind me just how much sound and fury was generated in the New York media by the move.

"A lot," Marty said, "and it's pretty easy to understand why. The Yankee center-field job was easily the most glamorous job in baseball. Earle Combs, Joe DiMaggio, and Mickey Mantle had all gone to the Hall of Fame from there—covering more than four decades. You had won a Gold Glove there. You were the team's glamour player. The story deserved the huge amount of attention it got because it represented a cultural change in something that defined the Yankees. The sacred area of real estate was being turned over to an unproven singles hitter who better fit Virdon's idea of what a center fielder should be. Someone like himself."

Mind you, I did okay in right. I threw out a dozen base runners in my first 50 games. But whether I could play the position was never the point.

What really annoyed me, then and even now when I think back on it, is that Virdon never sat me down and told me he was going to make the change. He was the manager; he decided who played where. I had no problem with that; there can be only one boss in the clubhouse. But you'd think he would have learned in Management 101 to tell your star player *beforehand* if you're going to do something like change his job title?

But as I said, let's get on with the game.

═══

To me, 1974 will always be memorable as the season I went off my rocker. Literally.

I've always been partial to rocking chairs, even when I was a little boy. There's a picture of me, I must have been four or five, rocking away in this little rocker. Later, when Kay and I started dating, I fell in love with this wonderful old Boston rocker in her house and with her, though not necessarily in that order. She used to tease me that I wouldn't ever have come over to her house if it weren't for that Boston rocker. I assured her that was nonsense, but it sure didn't hurt. I just flat-out love rocking chairs.

Ever since we got married in 1966, there's been a rocking chair in our household. That includes my time in the U.S. Army, when our home was this little tiny trailer. When we started living in New Jersey in 1969, I had one there.

But until 1974, there was one important place where I was rockerless: the Yankee clubhouse.

That spring I asked Pete Sheehy if I could bring one into the clubhouse and use it instead of the little stools that were there. He said sure, why not, and so I did.

From Opening Day, that plain, simple, sturdy wooden rocker became sort of my hallmark. I'd sit there rocking and relaxing before games. I'd sit there rocking and answering questions from reporters after games.

Murcer and his rocker, inseparable.

Make that *almost* inseparable. Once I was temporarily separated from my favorite means of clubhouse repose and relaxation in a most explosive way. Thank you, Sparky Lyle.

As I've mentioned, Sparky was the merry prankster of our clubhouse from the time he came to us from the Red Sox in 1972. His specialty was sitting buck-naked on birthday cakes, but once— during a long stretch without birthdays, I guess—he got another idea: saw the legs off my rocker, but fix it so that I wouldn't notice until I sat down.

And, in mid-June 1974, that's exactly what he did.

You've got to hand it to Sparky: he was a craftsman. Perfect cuts, perfect reassembly. I didn't notice a thing. But he'd alerted the other guys, so when I sat down and the rocker sort of exploded under me, I had a cheering, laughing audience.

At first I was a little ticked off, because I figured he'd ruined my rocker. But the grounds crew guys came to my rescue: they glued what was left of the base of the chair to the rockers themselves. Now the seat was only about six inches off the floor, but it still rocked, and so did I.

That little baby followed me to Candlestick, to Wrigley Field, and back to Yankee Stadium. But when I retired and became a broadcaster, it retired and went home to the Bobby Murcer Museum—my office in our home in Edmond—because there was no room in the broadcast booth.

Since then, I've made sure I've had a rocker everywhere I've lived, including hotels when I come up to New York to broadcast games. Today I'm into La-Z-Boys; at home I have one in the den and one in our bedroom. When I was going to be down in Houston for seven weeks of treatment, my brother-in-law Calvin Worth, who's the general manager of a big furniture emporium in Oklahoma City, sent one down to our hotel. Now the Marriott Medical Center keeps it in storage and ready for me when I go back for my monthly MRI and tests.

The only two people close to me who don't make any effort whatsoever to accommodate my rocking chair need are my two kids: neither Tori nor Todd has a single rocker, maybe because they think I'm off mine for making such a big deal out of a chair.

That's okay, I tell them, but it's your kids who're going to suffer when Bobby Pops stops coming around because he has no place to rock.

———

Except in one category, I had a solid season in 1974: I drove in 88 runs (about my usual number), and I hit .274 (pretty close to my career average), and I was named to the All-Star team again for the fourth season in a row.

But after averaging 26 home runs a season between 1969 and 1973, I hit just 10 in 1974. That's no typo: 10. I hit just 2 (yes, 2) homers in my "home" park. And they didn't come until late September.

Thank you, Shea Stadium.

But even though I hated every single at-bat I had in Shea, I loved the fact that we jumped from fourth place (80–82) in 1973 to second place (89–73) in 1974, to finish just two games behind the Orioles. (Bill Virdon was voted 1974 Manager of the Year in the American League. He deserved it.)

We were heading in the right direction.

Wait till next year!

LIFE IN EXILE

ello, Bobby? This is Gabe Paul. Did I wake you up?"

Hmmm . . .

"What time is it there? About 8, right? Sure I didn't wake you up?"

Hmmm . . .

"Look, Bobby, I'm just calling to tell you that we've decided to go in another direction, and we've traded you to the Giants for Bobby Bonds."

What?!

What?!

You've done what?!

I thought I was having a nightmare. Seriously. Many ballplayers in the off-season sleep late. At least *this* ballplayer slept late. For me, any time up until 10 A.M. is REM sleep time.

It's a pattern I carried over from the season. What with night games, and being on the road half the season, the chances of getting to bed before midnight between April and October fell somewhere between slim and none. And if you had a day game (Saturday) following a night game (Friday)? Makes me cranky just thinking about it. So I developed a habit of sleeping in *every* day, the year around.

That's why Gabe Paul's call at 8 A.M. on October 22, 1974, felt like the tail end of a bad dream.

Gabe had been part of Mr. Steinbrenner's Cleveland-based syndicate that bought the Yankees in January 1973. He'd taken over as president in April 1973 when Mike Burke was shown the door, and he became GM at the end of 1973 when Lee MacPhail was named president of the American League.

And now he was calling me to say that he had traded me?

No bloomin' way.

It was a nightmare.

———

Except it wasn't. It was true. I'd been traded away by the only team I'd ever played for. By the only team I'd ever *wanted* to play for. Traded across the continent, to a team in the other league. How could this be happening to me?

Gabe and I hadn't gotten along since day one. Oil and water. Fire and ice. We just didn't get along, and to this day I'm not sure why I rubbed him the wrong way.

Maybe it was because early on Mr. Steinbrenner and I had lunch a few times during which he sought out my views on where the club was going, what needed to be done, that sort of thing. The sort of thing that a certain president and general manager thought to be his exclusive concern.

Maybe it was because word leaked out that one of the things I thought might help the club was replacing Gabe Paul, who had the rep of being a bottom-line guy, not a baseball guy. I never expressed my reservations about him to anybody else, but whenever Mr. Steinbrenner asked me a straight question, I gave him a straight answer.

I certainly didn't go looking for those lunch meetings with Mr. Steinbrenner, and I know that I didn't feel it was my place to say to him, "Don't you think that Gabe ought to be here?" Mr. Steinbrenner was the Boss. If he said, "Let's just the two of us get together for lunch," my response was "What time?"

Maybe Gabe just didn't like the drop-off in my power output. (Can't blame him for that.) Just 10 home runs in 1974, from the guy who's supposed to be your principal power hitter? Not so good.

Maybe that was it with Gabe. The Yankees were going to be in Shea for one more season, and perhaps he feared another 10-homer season might be in the offing.

Maybe Gabe felt pressured to do something fast to shake up a team that hadn't won an American League pennant in 10 years, and maybe he figured that I would fetch enough in trade to turn the team around, provided he dealt me before I had a chance to put up another 10-HR season.

Or maybe he just didn't like my Oklahoma accent.

What I do know is that he took a lot of glee in making that wake-up call. I learned later that just before he called me, he waved Marty Appel, the Yankee director of media relations at the time, into his office and said, "Marty, Marty, come in, I want you to listen to this." And then, with a big smile on his face, Gabe put in the call to deliver the news that shattered my baseball life.

I have to tell you, I wasn't as shocked at learning about my brain tumor in that restaurant parking lot in Oklahoma City in 2006 as I had been at hearing Gabe's words in 1974: "We've traded you to the Giants."

I was no longer a New York Yankee.

———

"As long as I'm with the Yankees, you'll be with the Yankees, too."

That's what Mr. Steinbrenner had told me during one of those private lunch meetings after he took over the Yankees in 1973. Those were the most comforting words I had ever heard from a major league executive, since all I ever wanted to be was a New York Yankee.

So what happened? Did Gabe Paul make the decision to trade me without consulting Mr. Steinbrenner? Was Gabe acting on his own?

Of course not.

True, Mr. Steinbrenner had just come off a rough summer. He had pleaded guilty in August to obstruction of justice and to making illegal contributions to Richard Nixon's reelection campaign in 1972. And later that year, he would be suspended by the Commissioner of Baseball for two years. Mr. Steinbrenner had a lot on his plate that fall.

But the trade came on October 22 and the suspension didn't take effect until November 27. And since Gabe Paul wouldn't have a second cup of coffee in the morning without Mr. Steinbrenner's approval, I know in my heart that there is *no way* that Gabe would have traded me without Mr. Steinbrenner's approval of the deal.

No way.

———

I felt devastated, stunned, and betrayed.

All that first day after we got the news, Kay and I just stared at each other, shaking our heads, not believing that it could be true.

But what was I going to do, curl up in the fetal position and cry until spring training? As Kay would say much later, in a slightly different context (a week or so after my brain surgery in 2006): "We're glad we're not whiners, because whining is *so* bush league."

Hey, like it or not, I was a San Francisco Giant.

Gut-check time, Murcer.

That same day that Gabe Paul called me with the news, I got a very nice call from Mr. Horace Stoneham, the owner of the Giants, welcoming me to the club. Classy move by a very classy guy.

All fall and into the winter, I didn't complain or moan once in public about leaving the Yankees. Thanksgiving dinner might not have tasted as good as usual, and at Christmas I half expected to find a lump of coal with my name on it under the tree, and come midnight, December 31, "Happy New Year" sounded a little hollow, because the new year wasn't going to be spent in pinstripes. But I didn't take any potshots at the Yankees for trading me, and I sure wasn't going to be anything but upbeat publicly about moving to the Giants.

You know, new team, new league, new challenges, new city. After all, I knew the drill. I was a professional, and I was going to do my dead-level best to behave like one.

The Giants brought me out to San Francisco in January to meet the press. There's this picture of me and Kay that ran in the *San Francisco Chronicle*, the two of us holding a new Giants uniform top between us, both grinning from ear to ear. Let me tell you, that was your classic case of "laughing on the outside, crying on the inside." Even so, I tried to be as positive as I could be about the whole thing.

One question at that first press conference did make me smile: "Do you anticipate any problems trying to live up to Bobby Bonds's legacy?" Talk about your medium fastball down the middle: "No, I don't anticipate any more problems living up to Bobby's legacy here with the Giants than I anticipated living up to Mickey Mantle's when I succeeded him on the Yankees."

Then somebody asked me if I would be able to turn the Giants around and point them in the right direction: "I guess it all depends on how often the wind blows out to right field." (Little did I know at the time how prophetic that statement would turn out to be.)

Tell us, Bobby, do you see yourself as a team leader, a captain?

"There'll be only one captain on the Giants as far as I'm concerned," I said, "and that's our manager, Wes Westrum. Besides, the guys here are grown-up enough not to need a guy going around patting them on the fanny to motivate them."

I also pointed out that I was supposed to have been the leader on the Yankees, but that I obviously hadn't had much influence: we'd not been contenders for eight years.

As it would turn out, the Giants went from fifth in the NL West in 1974 all the way to third in 1975, while the Yankees dropped from second in the AL East all the way to third. The swapping of two $100,000 ballplayers—the first time that had ever happened—didn't do much for either club.

This was not a rebuilding move. "Murcer Dealt for Prospects" would have made sense, what with the Yankee farm system depleted, the team mired in the Great Depression of the post-Mantle years, and the free agent draft eliminating the ability of the Yankees to skim the cream off the top of the free agent pool.

But I will give Gabe credit for a trade he made after the 1975 season: Bobby Bonds to the Angels for Ed Figueroa and Mickey Rivers. Those two guys played key roles in helping the Yankees win the AL pennant in 1976 and the World Championship in 1977 and 1978.

<hr>

The Giants were nice people. I liked the guys on the team. But just about nothing in the whole situation felt right to me. It wasn't my team, it wasn't home, it wasn't the Yankees.

And then there was Candlestick Park.

To me, there's never been a worse baseball ballpark than Candlestick. Playing there for two full seasons, I developed a whole new level of respect for guys like Willie Mays and Willie McCovey and Juan Marichal, who had so many great years in that miserable place. My stocking cap and earmuffs are off to you gentlemen.

Let's start with cold and windy. *Really* cold. *Really* windy. There were days you just couldn't get warm in the outfield—and the dugouts were even worse. The cold started in your hands and then just penetrated your entire body. I used to put my bats in the clubhouse sauna and have the batboy grab one and hand it to me right before I went up to the plate. Anything to warm up my hands a little.

And because of the wind, every fly ball was an adventure. They'd enclosed the center-field section because they thought it would be some kind of windbreak for the gales coming in off San Francisco Bay. Before they built the enclosure, the wind blew straight from left field to right field, but when they enclosed the center-field section, it turned the straight left-to-right action into a whirlwind. I'd be standing in the outfield and watch a ball fouled off toward the third-base side be carried all the way across the infield and the first baseman would catch it.

They used to have to wire the batting cage down to keep the wind from blowing it away during BP. I'm not kidding. They staked it to the ground.

Pardon me, make that staked it to the artificial turf. Like every ballplayer from that era that I know, I hated playing on artificial turf. Especially that early stuff they had at Candlestick, which felt like a basketball court covered with a giant green nylon floor mat.

(I always liked what Dick Allen had to say about artificial turf: "If a horse won't eat it, I don't want to play on it.")

Kay

We loved San Francisco. Just loved it. A beautiful place, and plenty to do. The kids had a great time.

We loved the restaurants, the look and feel of the place, and the surroundings. When our folks came to visit, we loved playing tour guide and taking them to places like Alcatraz, Napa, Sausalito, Chinatown, and the Golden Gate Bridge.

We didn't love not being Yankees, of course, and nobody could love Candlestick Park. But we did love San Francisco.

The kids had a little adjustment period. Tori was seven, Todd was six, and they were just old enough to miss their pals back in New Jersey and at Yankee Stadium.

Sometimes, when you're adjusting to a new town, nothing breaks the ice quicker than calling on new neighbors for directions to the nearest ER.

That happened when we first arrived in San Francisco and Todd fell off his bike and split open his chin. He and a few boys from the neighborhood came to our house, and several hours and a few stitches later, we became friends with about three or four families.

As a way of saying thank you, I herded up a small gang of boys and hauled them and our two kids to a ball game. Everybody bundled up in coats and mufflers and caps and gloves, and we all went out to the 'Stick and loaded up on hot soup and hot chocolate and . . . everybody was so cold and miserable that we left in the seventh inning!

That was the first and last time we could persuade the neighborhood kids to go on a baseball outing.

Occasionally I would take Todd and Tori to a game, and we'd ask the ushers to let us go sit out along the right-field line. The team sometimes drew as few as 2,500 for a game, so the sections down the lines were blocked off. That worked fine for us because we could sit close to the foul line, and during a pitching change or before an inning started, Bobby could stroll over and talk to the kids, and we could discuss dinner or whatever.

After a few times, though, the club put a stop to that. I think they felt like it was embarrassing to have just us out there in this sea of empty seats.

One plus about my trade to San Francisco: I am pleased to report that in 1975, my first year as a Giant, I got my home run stroke back. I walloped 11 taters. Guess that proves that Candlestick was definitely a better power ballpark for me than Shea. A least 10 percent better. Life finally got back to normal in 1976, my second year in San Francisco—23 home runs.

Almost from the minute I set foot in Candlestick, I was on my hands and knees asking Mr. Stoneham to trade me—somewhere, anywhere. I knew I could not perform to my standards there, not in the cold.

Looking back, I guess I should be thankful that Major League Baseball didn't have a franchise in Alaska. Although I have to tell you, some days in Candlestick, they might as well have.

I actually considered quitting, although I had no idea what I would do. I was 29, a baseball player, in my prime years. Some days—more precisely, late afternoons before night games—Kay would practically have to shove me out the door to get me to go to the ballpark.

Remember the other great Dick Allen line? "I can play anywhere. First base, third base, left field—anywhere but Philadelphia."

That's the way I felt about Candlestick Park.

Evidently, most Bay Area baseball fans felt the same way. Half full was considered a great crowd. Many games, 5,000 people might be there in the first inning, fewer than half that by the seventh.

Over most of my two seasons as a Giant, Patty Hearst was on the lam from the FBI. I always thought a good place for her to go would be the center-field stands at the 'Stick. *Nobody* ever went there.

In fact, so few fans visited *any* part of Candlestick in the 1970s that Mr. Stoneham was negotiating to move the ball club to Toronto. He almost pulled it off in 1976. But at the very last minute, a local businessman named Bob Lurie stepped in and bought the club in a midnight deal with a pledge to keep the Giants in San Francisco. If he hadn't stepped up to the plate, we'd be talking today about the Toronto Giants.

My free agent year was coming up, so as soon as I could speak to Mr. Lurie, I told him he should try to work out a deal for me, because there was no way I was going to re-sign with the Giants. I liked and respected him, and I didn't want him to end up with nothing when I walked at the end of the 1977 season. He said he was sorry I felt that way. He tried to talk me out of it. He asked me, "If you were to change your mind, what would it take to come back?" I told him, "How about $1 million?"

Goodbye, Candlestick.

━━━━

Hello, Wrigley Field.

That fall, Mr. Lurie swapped me to the Chicago Cubs. The deal involved five players, but basically it was me for Bill Madlock. Two years earlier, I'd been part of the first-ever swap of two $100,000 players. This time, I'd been traded for the reigning NL batting champion. Guess I should have felt honored by that. All I really felt was disappointment that I was still half a continent away from home and still wearing a foreign uniform.

At least one had pinstripes. But they were the wrong color.

Once again, Kay and I liked our new summer place. Chicago's a fascinating town, filled with great restaurants. We bought a condo in Arlington Heights and settled in. The kids loved day baseball. And never having to wear their parkas and earmuffs.

For me, it was a kick to play in Wrigley Field. It's just a flat-out beautiful ballpark, a polar opposite to that other place I'd been incarcerated in for the previous two seasons. As Ernie Banks said, "Let's play two."

Naturally, I'd always heard about what a great place Wrigley was for power hitters—you know, the ball carries better in the warm days, the dimensions favor the batter, and the wind always blows out. Well, the first two things are true, but the third is more myth than reality. Fact is, most of the time at Wrigley you get a cross wind, left-field corner to right field.

But when the wind *does* blow out in the late summer, it's a great place to hit. That just doesn't happen often enough.

Couple of things about playing the outfield at Wrigley:

Whichever way the wind's blowing, it's pretty doggone tough on outfielders at all times, particularly right fielders and center fielders. Definitely not as tough as at Candlestick—no ballpark in the history of baseball has ever come close to that pit for bad wind—but some days Wrigley could be an adventure.

And then there are the ivy-covered walls. They're drop-dead gorgeous to look at, so green and soft and inviting. But the first time I ran into one, I learned a hard truth: brick walls don't have any give to them. My shoulder still hurts every time I think of hitting that ivy-covered baby trying to turn a long drive into an out.

As everybody knows, a ball that gets lodged in the ivy at Wrigley is a ground-rule double. What most people don't know is that an occasional possible triple can be turned into a ground-rule double by a little quick thinking on the part of the outfielder. More than once on a ball hit up the alley, I'd get there, reach down, kind of scoop the ball into the ivy, and stand up and hold both arms over my head. Ground-rule double.

Cheating? I prefer to think of it as gamesmanship. You know, taking sensible and appropriate advantage of an opportunity.

The fans at Wrigley were terrific. Must have been hard for them, given that the Cubs hadn't won a pennant since 1945, and had pretty much been in rebuilding mode ever since. But still they came out to support us.

My first year in Chicago was a typical Bobby Murcer season: 27 homers, 89 RBIs, .265 BA—plus I stole a career-high 16 bases. (Must have been on days the wind was blowing right to left.)

Even though I'd averaged just shy of 26 homers a year my first five full seasons (1969–1973), I never thought of myself as a pure power hitter. But I did think of myself as someone who could deliver consistently with men on base. Even when HR totals wobbled (10, 11, 23, 27 from 1974 through 1977), my RBI totals stayed steady: 88, 91, 90, 89.

And then there was 1978 . . .

Year two as a Cub wasn't so hot in the run production department: I hit .281, but I drove in only 64 runs and hit just nine home runs. What happened?

Well, numbers play a big part—and a legitimate one—in tracking performance in baseball. But sometimes numbers don't tell a complete story.

To understand the major reason (in my humble opinion) for my power outage in 1978, you need to know that Dave Kingman came to the Cubs that season. The year before, Kong had played for four clubs—the Mets, the Padres, the Angels, and the Yankees—in what has to be a record for Most Teams, One Season. But Big Dave was our left fielder now, and he was (of course) batting cleanup.

Great news for the number three hitter! You hit in front of Big Dave Kingman in Wrigley Field, you were guaranteed to see mostly good pitches, because a pitcher with any sense at all would turn cartwheels on the mound to keep from walking guys with him up next.

Guess who was hitting in the third slot? Yep, that would be Bobby Ray Murcer. And I have to tell you that I was looking forward to maybe having a career year. Hitting in front of Dave Kingman in Wrigley Field was a lefty power hitter's dream come true.

Only I didn't stay in the three-hole long. Early on, first baseman Bill Buckner went to manager Herman Franks and complained that he wasn't seeing anything to hit batting fifth, and could he flop with me. Herman said sure, if it's okay with Bobby. And Bobby, like an idiot, said sure, why not. Third, fifth, whatever helps the team.

Problem is, the bottom half of our lineup dropped off pretty sharply, as I soon found out. I never saw so many pitches just off the plate in my whole career. Didn't stop me from taking my hacks, but I have to believe it affected my power numbers.

Anyway, that's my story and I'm sticking to it . . . although I do hear Kay's voice in the other room, in a frequent refrain in our household: "Don't be a whiner—it's so bush league."

And Billy, how'd he do in the number three hole? All he did was hit .323, a hefty 39 points higher than the year before. Mr. Buckner and I later became good friends. Our daughter, Tori, who was 10 at the time, thought he was a real dreamboat. He even dated my sister-in-law, Cindy, once when she came for a visit. Even so, don't think I haven't reminded him now and then of how much he owes me for agreeing to that little switcheroo.

Billy and I both became health nuts at the same time, and for a while there we blended up power shakes using Shaklee's protein powders and bananas each day before heading out to the ballpark. I even toted a blender with me on road trips to whip up our power protein shakes.

We didn't know from PEDs—performance-enhancing drugs are a phenomenon of today's game—but we were hooked on our PPSs.

▬▬▬

Looking back on my Cubbie years, there's an inside-the-dugout story that still makes me smile. It involved Herman Franks and Peanuts Lowery, his de facto bench coach. (The term wouldn't come into common usage until years later.) Herman was very hard of hearing in his left ear; Peanuts was hard of hearing in his right ear. Neither, of course, would admit to any diminished function. But the "complementary" impairments manifested themselves so often that guys on the bench could barely hold back their laughter.

See, Herman would station himself at the extreme right end of our dugout, which was along the third-base side, at Wrigley, while Peanuts would usually stand a few feet away from him to the left. From time to time, Herman would issue an order to Peanuts ("Get Sutter up!") only Peanuts wouldn't hear him over the crowd noise. Next thing you know, Herman would turn to him and say, "I thought I told you to get Sutter up!" And there would be a little ruckus, both of them temporarily oblivious to the game.

Or it could go the other way. Peanuts would shout down to Herman, "Sutter's ready!" And a couple of minutes later, Herman would shout down to Peanuts, "Is Sutter ready?"

Their back-and-forths provided a constant source of diversion, especially in the dead of summer when the team wasn't going anywhere and the guys in the dugout were looking for laughs anywhere we could find 'em.

━━━

Except for the wrong color pinstripes, I found playing in Wrigley Field a sheer joy. Every ballplayer I've ever met would agree with that sentiment. (Pitchers, naturally, are excluded from the broad statement.) Part of it is the beauty of the place. Part of it is the history it represents. Wrigley's where Babe Ruth "called his shot" in game three of the 1932 World Series, where Ernie Banks swatted his 500th home run, and where Pete Rose tied Ty Cobb with career hit number 4,191.

Wrigley's nickname is the Friendly Confines, of course, but maybe a better term would be "Comfy Confines." Among the things about Wrigley that are so "friendly" are its small size (capacity: 37,741 when I was a Cub), the gorgeous ivy on the outfield walls, the absence of advertising billboards, and the close proximity of the fans to the action. (The foul area behind home plate and around to first and third is the smallest in baseball.)

Back in my playing days, most Cubs fans would have headed that list of friendly attributes with the fact that Wrigley was the only ballpark in baseball without lights. Cubs owners wanted night baseball at Wrigley, the better to sell more tickets. But

Wrigley remained lightless for one reason: local resistance. Because it's located smack-dab in the middle of a residential neighborhood, residents in the surrounding area—read: voters—didn't cotton to the after-dark commotion that night baseball would bring to the area. But finally, after threatening to quit the city altogether, the Cubs owners got their way, and the lights went on in 1988.

Now, the Good Lord might well have originally intended that baseball be played in the light of day. But the way I saw it, getting up early in the morning, going to the ballpark, and having to worry about rush hour traffic on the way home felt suspiciously like a day job.

Nowadays, of course, day baseball is virtually extinct. Personally, I call that progress.

———

Aside from the intimacy that its small size nurtures, the thing that makes the Friendly Confines so friendly—at least to hitters and fans—is that Wrigley breeds so many knock-down, drag-out slugfests. The two of those babies that I recall best I saw from radically different perspectives: the first from all over the field, the second mostly from the bench.

The first took place on July 28, 1977, against the Reds. We were leading the NL East at the time and feeling pretty good about things. The Reds were playing .500 ball in the NL West, but had several reasons (Pete Rose, Johnny Bench, Joe Morgan) for thinking things might pick up.

The 32,155 Wrigley faithful who showed up that day got a pretty good sense of where the game was going when the Reds scored seven runs in the top of the first and we came back with six in the bottom half.

That's right: a pitchers' duel.

We were tied at two touchdowns apiece—14–14—after nine innings. Both teams scored a run in the 12th, but we pushed one more across in the bottom of the 13th to crawl away with a 16–15 squeaker. (You spend 4 hours and 50 minutes battling it out on an

80-degrees-and-humid Chicago summer day, and you're lucky to be able to crawl.)

But what made the game special to me wasn't that we won (a darn sight better than the alternative) or that I hit a homer and a double in eight at-bats and drove in five runs (not a bad day's work). What made it memorable to me was the line in the box score the next day where they list a player's position.

Here was mine: RF—SS—2B—SS—2B—SS—2B—SS.

That's not an eye chart, or a rogue printing press asserting itself. What happened was that (1) we went through a lot of pinch hitters for the seven pitchers (including both Reuschels, Paul and Rick) who got abused that day; and (2) after outfielder José Cardenal pinch-hit for shortstop Iván DeJesus, we didn't have enough infielders to go around.

Follow me? I'm not sure I do. But what Herman Franks did, knowing that I'd had some experience in the infield, was bring me in from right and put me at SS. (He either hadn't heard about my arm or didn't care about the fans in the first-base boxes.) And then 2B. And then SS. And then . . .

Well, you get the picture. I flip-flopped with Dave Rosello, a legitimate infielder, depending on whether the batter was righty or lefty. Dave's line in the box score was even more impressive: *12* flips between SS and 2B. Señor Cardenal also got into the act (PH—2B—SS—2B—RF) because (I forgot to mention this) Herman also pinch-hit for our second baseman, Manny Trillo.

One of the times I was at 2B, Felipe Alou was at first after a hit. There was only one out. That could be trouble, because Felipe was notorious for knocking second basemen into left field trying to break up a double play. During a pitching change, I strolled over to first, all casual-like, and told my old teammate (Felipe had played for the Yankees in 1971–1973) that I'd appreciate his not barreling into second looking to hurt me, that I was a family man. I smiled. He didn't.

How did that middle infield platoon work out? Well, José made an error, Dave made an error, but Murcer was flawless in the field, with one force-out at second (of Felipe Alou, as a matter of fact; my plea for mercy obviously worked) and no other fielding chances. My fielding average: 1.000.

That was my first game in the infield in the majors since 1969—and my last.

Two summers later, I was present for another ringtailed-tooter of a Wrigley game. (That's what an old Texas pal of mine calls it, and it sounds right by me.) Only this time I spent most of the day spectating.

Phillies vs. Cubs, May 17, 1979.

Herman had given me the day off because the Phils started a lefty, Randy Lerch. Herm needn't have bothered with all that tactical thinking: Lerch faced just six batters, gave up a three-run homer to Dave Kingman (his first of three on the day), allowed five earned runs on five hits, and got exactly one batter out before heading for the showers in the first inning. We got another off Doug Bird.

Great, you younger Cubs fans may be thinking, the good guys are up by six after the first; this is going to be a laugher. Matter of fact, the Cubbies were *down* by a run because the Phillies had started the game with seven in the top half of the first. Mike Schmidt hit a three-run homer, his first of two round-trippers on the day, on his way to a typical (for him) Wrigley Field outing: 2-for-4 with two HRs and four RBIs.

The Phillies added an eight-spot in the third, another two in the fourth, another four in the fifth, and a singleton in the seventh after being blanked in the sixth, to bring them to 22. That's right: 22.

But we were a scrappy bunch, and we roared back with three in the fourth, seven in the fifth, three in the sixth, and three more in the eighth to go to 22. That's right: 22.

My contribution to this little donnybrook was modest: 1-for-2 after entering the game as a pinch hitter in the seventh and staying in to play right and center. But the day was young, I was just getting loose, and—yes—the wind was blowing out.

Neither team scored in the ninth, probably as a result of arm fatigue, and we went into extra innings knotted at 22.

Finishing the game the way he started it, Schmitty untied things in the 10th with his second homer of the game.

Phillies 23, Cubs 22.

All in all, a great day for the Wrigley concessionaires; a great day for the fans (at least until the 10th inning), who got two-plus games' worth of scoring for the price of one; and a great day for stats freaks. The 11 home runs by the two teams tied a National League record; it's been done four times, three of them involving the Cubs (all at Wrigley, of course), most recently in 1977 at the 16–15 game where I covered the infield.

And it was another great Wrigley Field day for Mike Schmidt. I swear, that man loved hitting in that park more than anybody I ever knew. It's pretty easy to understand why. In 1976 he hit four dingers in one game at Wrigley. Over his career, he hit 50 homers in 524 Wrigley at-bats. That's about one homer every 10.5 at-bats. His HR/AB ratio for his other 498 homers: 15.7. No doubt about it, Schmitty found Wrigley's confines *very* friendly.

Thing is, that 23–22 might well have been an even greater homer day for Schmitty. You got to wonder what he might have done if we hadn't walked him four times, twice intentionally and twice semi-intentionally.

———

Like most parents, Kay and I have often forged friendships among the parents of our kids' friends. That was the case with Ted Sizemore and his wife, Sam. Ted came over from the Phillies in a multiplayer trade in the winter of 1979 that was basically a swap of second basemen: Manny Trillo for Ted. During Ted's first spring training as a Cub in Mesa, Arizona, his and Sam's kids (Nickie and Tony) and ours bonded at the swimming pool, and generously allowed the parents into their group.

Over the years, the four of us have become close. Like us, they're "snowbirds" who spend the winter months in Southern California. Ted and I play golf. Kay and Sam do whatever women do when their husbands are playing golf.

For the last several years, Ted and I have done a lot of work with the Baseball Assistance Team, or BAT. He's the president and CEO; I'm the chairman of the board of directors. (So far, no

power struggles.) BAT, in case you don't already know, is an organization of ex–major leaguers devoted to helping other ex–major
leaguers in need. Here's our mission statement:

> *The primary objective of the Baseball Assistance Team is to aid those
> members of the "baseball family" most in need. B.A.T. strives to pro-
> vide a means of support to people who are unable to help themselves.
> Through charitable contributions from corporations, foundations and
> individuals, B.A.T. is there to assist those with financial, psychologi-
> cal or physical burdens.*

Ted has everybody in baseball on his cell phone, and the un-
canny ability to charm his way into the hearts and pockets of most
of them. He's been an enormous help to BAT, and to me.

Flash forward to June 1979. I was midway through a three-year
contract with the Cubs that had a no-trade-without-my-permission
clause. To me, that had been essential when I had negotiated my
deal. Kay and I liked Chicago. I liked Wrigley Field. If I was going
to be traded, and by now I knew that could happen at the drop of
a hat, I wanted to have control over where I went—and *if* I went
anywhere at all.

One morning before a game, GM Bob Kennedy came into the
clubhouse and asked me if I'd step outside for a minute. We went
up to the third-base boxes and sat down, and Bob got right to the
point: "There's been an inquiry from the Yankees about acquir-
ing you. You've got your no-trade clause, and I'm not saying we're
necessarily interested in doing anything. But I wanted to get your
feel on it—if we were able to make a deal with the Yankees, would
you accept it? It's a long shot, but before I start talking with them,
I need to find out if you'd accept a trade. So what do you think?
Would you waive your no-trade clause?"

I thought about it for maybe five seconds: "You bet."

The conversation between me and Bob took place at about

9:45 in the morning. The team was supposed to be dressed by 10. Bob obviously went straight upstairs and made a call, because the deal was done well before noon: Bobby Murcer for cash and a minor leaguer. No batting champion this time; the Cubs were just looking to shed my salary.

I gave all my Cubs teammates a big hug goodbye, hustled out to Midway, hopped on a plane, and flew to Toronto, where the Yankees were playing a night game against the Blue Jays.

That night, wearing a uniform that fit for the first time in four and a half seasons, I played right field, batted third ahead of Sweet Lou, and went 2-for-4.

Once again, I was what I had never stopped being in my heart: a New York Yankee.

HOMECOMING

My two full seasons in Chicago (1977–1978), we went 160–164. Meanwhile, *my* team—the Yankees, that is—went 200–125 and won two World Championships. Don't think I didn't notice.

Here's a little comparison chart that shows thumbnails of what happened during my first four full seasons in exile.

1975

You know how Tony Bennett sings "I Left My Heart in San Francisco"?

Well, I left *my* heart on the other side of the continent.

Score it Bennett I, Murcer 0.

1976

*F*orget the wind and the cold: what really hurt about playing my "home" games in San Francisco in 1976 is that the Giants dropped from 80–81 to 74–88, and from third to fourth.

Meanwhile, back at my real home in New York, the Yankees won the pennant, going 97–62 in the regular season and beating the Royals in the playoffs on Chris Chambliss's walk-off homer in the ninth inning of game five. Thurman was MVP and we—sorry, *they*—led the American League in attendance for the first time since 1964, the last season before the onset of the Great Depression.

Didn't matter that the Yankees were swept by the Reds in the World Series. Anybody who got in the way of the Big Red Machine that year got smashed.

What *did* matter was that the Yankees were back—and I wasn't.

1977

*T*he Cubs (81–81) led the NL East going into September, but then faded to fourth, an all-too-familiar ending to the Wrigley Field faithful.

Back home, Reggie Jackson, Thurman Munson, Graig Nettles, & Co. edged the Orioles and the Red Sox to win the AL East by 2.5 games.

Next they trimmed KC in the playoffs 3–2, with a come-from-behind win in the ninth inning of game five.

Then Reggie took over the World Series—and earned a new nickname, Mr. October, from the Boss. He hit three homers in game six to sew up championship rings for the Yankees.

And now a little footnote.

Before the season began, the Yankees had worked out a trade with the Blue Jays to acquire veteran starter Bill Singer; all they had to give up was a young lefty reliever who hadn't been used much the previous season, a kid named Ron Guidry. But Toronto's front office had to squelch the deal at the last minute when they realized that Singer was on the cover of their already printed media guide.

Bummed because they still needed a starter, the Yankees reluctantly converted Guidry. All Louisiana Lightning did was go 16–7 (with a 2.82 ERA) and pick up Ws over the Royals in the playoffs and the Dodgers in the Series.

Singer? He went 2–8 and retired at the end of the season.

What's the old saying about some of your best moves being the ones you don't make?

1978

The Cubs went 79–83 to finish third in the NL East, only 11 games behind the Phillies. Zzzzzzz . . .

And my Yankees? This is the one that hurt the most. This was the year of Cy Young Guidry (25–3, 1.74) and the Boston Massacre, of Bucky Dent and Brian (.161 lifetime) Doyle hitting .438 in the World Series, of Mr. October again. And another ring that I didn't get.

I was looking at another very long winter . . .

Looking back on my four-plus years in exile in the National League, I think that if the Giants and the Cubs had played all their games against the Dodgers, I might have opted to stay in the National League. In 63 games against L.A. during that period I hit .347 with 11 home runs. Project those numbers out over four and a half seasons and . . .

(C'mon, Bobby Ray, get a grip.)

Forget the numbers.

Of all the things ever said or written about me as a ballplayer, I'm proudest about something Sparky Anderson once said, and it had nothing to do with numbers: "Murcer's the kind of guy you do *not* want to see coming to the plate when the game's on the line."

That's what every ballplayer wants to hear.

The way I see it, I spent what would have been four-plus prime years wearing the wrong uniform. In the back of my mind, I'll always wonder whether my prime might have lasted a little longer if I'd stayed in New York, at Yankee Stadium, in pinstripes.

But you know what? Anytime you start playing woulda-coulda-shoulda mind games, you're just flat wasting your time. Leastways, that's what Kay tells me.

What hurt the most was that in the years I was with the Giants and the Cubs, the Yankees won three straight pennants and back-to-back World Championships.

It just ripped my heart out not to have been part of that.

＝＝＝

Now that I was back I found the same pinstripes, but a whole bunch of new faces in the clubhouse and a brand-new Yankee Stadium.

There's a famous American novel called *You Can't Go Home Again*. Well, I say you *can* go home again, so long as you don't expect it to look like the home you left.

In my forced absence, Yankee Stadium had been replaced. They called it a gut rehab, but it was really a new ballpark. Oh, they kept the famous façade so that from the outside the place looked the same. But inside, just about everything was different.

The locker in the clubhouse that I had inherited from Mickey? I could walk to the approximate area where it had been, but the locker wasn't there anymore.

The monuments to Yankee greats such as Ruth, Gehrig, & Co. that used to be in play in deep left center? Now behind a low outfield fence in "Monument Park."

The 296 feet down the right-field line? Now 310 feet. ("Only" 14 feet longer, you say? No big deal? Of course not, unless you happen to make your living hitting baseballs down the right-field line.)

New and more comfortable seats, better sightlines after the removal of some 100 steel girders, a new instant replay display (the first in baseball) on the new scoreboard, new and improved concession stands—new, new, new.

The term "Yankee Stadium II" never quite caught on, but it was *definitely* a new ballpark. And I was playing in it with a new number on my back, because when I returned to the team, my old number was taken.

Billy Martin, who played for the Yankees from 1950 through most of 1957, wore number 1. After his departure, Pete Sheehy assigned number 1 to Bobby Richardson. When Bobby retired after the 1966 season, he suggested to Pete that he hold number 1 for me until I returned from the army. So number 1 remained under Pete's lock and key until 1969, when it went on my back. Then Billy, who became manager in 1975, reclaimed his old number, and was wearing it when I rejoined the Yankees in 1979.

Enter Pete Sheehy again, bless his heart: he gave me number 2, formerly worn by Yankee great Frank Crosetti, who had retired after the 1978 season to cap a 37-year career as a Yankee player and coach.

I'd have preferred to have my old number, of course, but number 2 was doggone close, and anyway I'd have taken number 100 by then, provided it was on the back of the right uniform.

The Yankees I returned to were a lot stronger ball club than the team I said goodbye to four seasons earlier. These Yankees were coming off back-to-back World Championships and three straight American League pennants. We sent four players to the 1979 All-Star Game and six each in 1980 and 1981. (In 1974, we had just two representatives: Thurman and me; the year before, it had been me and Sparky.)

Among the new faces (new to me, that is) were Ron Guidry, Catfish Hunter, Tommy John, Luís Tiant, Bucky Dent, Willie Randolph, Oscar Gamble, and Mr. October himself, Reggie Jackson.

The most outsize personality, by far, was Reggie. He had an aura about him that made every at-bat an adventure. And he delivered. Thurman tagged him with the Mr. October moniker in a postgame interview with some reporters during the 1977 World Series against the Dodgers, the year he hit three homers in one game. Considering Reggie's postseason history—he reached the postseason in 11 of his 21 seasons, winning six pennants and five World Series—I'd say the nickname fit pretty well.

I enjoyed getting to know the new guys.

Catfish lived close by us in New Jersey, and he lived up to his rural North Carolina upbringing by transforming the big back-yard of his home into a vegetable garden. I swear, if the man hadn't already been making a pretty decent living pitching his way into the Hall of Fame, Catfish could have kept his family comfortable running a roadside market. He grew beautiful eggplant and corn and zucchini and tomatoes and lettuce. He kept the Murcers' re-frigerator filled with fresh produce all summer.

Tommy John was a talker. He talked about anything, every-thing, nothing—all the time. One of the sweetest guys you could ever want to meet, but you didn't want to find yourself sitting next to him in the dugout. In fact, the first assignment a new guy on the team—somebody who'd been called up or come over in a trade—received was to go down and sit next to Tommy.

I worked with him in the booth for a while, and I remember fighting to get a word in edgewise. But this special knack of his came in handy when there was a rain delay or when a game got out of hand.

I do believe that Tommy got as much out of his talent as any-body I ever played with. He didn't throw hard, and he had what I think even he would characterize as ordinary stuff. But he had pinpoint control and the heart of a lion. Plus he may have cut a ball or two in his day.

And then there was Oscar Gamble.

Good old Oscar had the biggest, most luxurious Afro in all of baseball, maybe in all the world. How big was it? So big that if a ball got stuck in there it would be a ground-rule double. That big.

He played a big role (17 homers in just 340 at-bats) on the Yankee pennant-winning team in 1976, then got traded to Chi-cago, then became a free agent and signed with the Padres in 1978. The story behind that signing became an instant legend inside baseball, among players and management alike.

It's only hearsay, mind you, but I heard it said so many times that I believe it really, truly happened this way:

Oscar and his agent were making the rounds during the off-season of his free agent year, looking for a multiyear deal. So far, they hadn't landed what they wanted, and next up was an appointment with Ray Kroc, who dabbled as owner of the Padres while turning out Big Macs by the million.

Oscar and the Padres weren't an obvious match. Oscar had spent the preceding five years in the AL, splitting time between DH and the outfield. He was no threat to win a Gold Glove, and in the National League, of course, he'd have to play in the field. Oscar had plenty of left-handed pop, but he'd always been a part-timer. (Only twice in his 17-season major league career did he record more than 400 at-bats.)

Even so, he and his agent had cooked up an aggressive plan to present to Kroc: three years, at $150K per. They were ushered into his office, hearsay says, but before they could open their mouths, Kroc said, "I'll give you $500,000 for one year. No long-term deal, take it or leave it."

Oscar and his agent looked at each other, asked Kroc if they could step outside to discuss it, and went out into the hall. There, once the door was firmly closed, they started dancing and high-fiving and hugging each other.

But wait—the story doesn't end there.

As soon as the ink was dry on the contract, Oscar closed another deal, this one on a brand-new Rolls-Royce. To celebrate, he and his wife, Juanita, went to pick up some lunch—at the nearest McDonald's drive-through.

Kay

Juanita was by far the flashiest dresser of all the players' wives. She often wore a hat to games. Not a Yankee cap, but a bona fide dress hat. And for playoff games, or maybe an important late-season series, she'd get decked out in a complete ensemble: hat, gloves, high heels, the whole deal. Very chic. That girl really enjoyed glamming out.

Oscar was born for the New York media circus. He positively thrived in it. Any time Reggie wasn't available for a comment about something, reporters knew they had an eager backup in the man with the hair. Oscar was only too happy to oblige.

We used to call him Ratio because he was always talking about his HR-to-AB ratio and how all he needed was some more cuts and he'd be up there among the league leaders in homers. He might have been on to something; the man delivered a lot of dingers for someone who was used mostly as a platoon DH.

One other distinctive characteristic about the man with the hair: his stance was so wide open that he would sometimes foul a ball off his *back* foot. Think about that one for a minute.

Oscar Gamble today is a successful sports agent—and bald as a billiard ball.

=====

But as much as I enjoyed meeting a bunch of new guys, the best thing about coming back to the Yankees was that it gave me a chance to reunite with two old pals, Lou and Thurman.

Lou and I didn't become teammates until 1974, when he came over to the Yankees from Kansas City, and then we split up while I was in exile those four and a half seasons in San Francisco and Chicago. We didn't get back together until I returned to the Yankees in mid-1979.

But Lou and I had already bonded on day one of that first season over a common passion: hitting. I couldn't begin to tell you how much time the two of us spent that first season together analyzing the most fundamental component of the game, namely:

> *How to strike a round object covered in horsehide (in the late 1980s it was replaced by cowhide) that is "9 to 9.25 inches in circumference" and weighs "between 5 and 5.25 ounces," which is propelled at you from a distance of 60 feet, 6 inches at speeds ranging between 86 and 100 mph, with a 36-inch length of seasoned ash.*

We sat next to each other in the dugout and talked hitting: *What did you see there? Shouldn't he square his shoulders more?* We sat next to each other on planes and talked hitting: *I think I need to drop my hands an inch or two—what do you think?* We stood in front of full-length mirrors in the clubhouse and analyzed each other's stances. We gave running commentaries on each other's swings during BP. We talked about adjustments to different situations, different counts, different ballparks, different pitchers. We were full-time batting instructors for each other. We would wear each other out talking about hitting. (Correction: Lou would wear *me* out.) We probably would have discussed hitting all through double dates if Kay and Anita would have permitted it.

Lou was a guess hitter; I was not.

He'd go to the plate with a theory, deciding that the pitcher was going to throw him such-and-such, and looking for it there. If he was right, *bingo!* If he was wrong, adjust his theory for the next pitch.

I'd go to the plate looking dead red—fastball—all the way, every pitch, and try to adjust to the breaking pitch when it came. Now, everybody's looking dead red at 3–1, 2–0, but I'm expecting a fastball every time. I never trusted myself to be a guess hitter.

As you can imagine, these conflicting approaches came up now and then in our endless conversation about hitting.

When we both wore pinstripes, Lou was my adjoining room-mate on the road, my soul mate in the dugout, and my dinner date as often as we could manage it. If Kay and Anita had not been in the picture, we would have become the *real* Odd Couple. Guess who would have been Oscar and who would have been Felix?

I am utterly and absolutely punctual. Tell me you're going to call me at 9 A.M. CST and I'm tapping my toe at 9:02.

Lou? If he gets the day right you're lucky.

I am something of a neat freak. (In the other room, Kay is saying, "What do you mean 'something'?") I like things orderly.

Lou? Have you ever seen a hotel room after a whirlwind's whipped through?

I am a cleanliness-is-next-to-godliness maniac. The first thing I do when I get to a restaurant is go to the men's room and wash (and thoroughly dry) my hands. I exit by shoving the door open with my shoulder, the way they do in TV hospital shows. (You never, ever want to touch the door handle of a public restroom.)

On the way back to my table, I've solved the problem of people wanting to high-five me (I don't even want to imagine where their hands have been) by either four-knuckling them or, if they stand up, by pumping forearms. (Howie Mandel taught me that one.) At my table, I carefully wipe down my utensils with my napkin. Let's eat!

Lou? Clean enough, by normal people's standards, I guess.

My dear friend exhibited one especially quirky trait on long road trips: he'd typically start off with nothing but his shaving kit in his suitcase. At the first stop, he'd buy enough clothes to last him until he got home. Said he couldn't be bothered to pack. Occasionally he'd stay over with us in New Jersey, if Anita was away or something. A few times, after a road trip, Kay would commandeer his suitcase and launder his (new) clothes. (Not a task I would undertake, as much as I liked the guy.) She was always perplexed to discover that amid the jumble of wadded-up garments, Lou's socks were always mated—and tied into tight knots.

One year before spring training, Lou bought a new 50-foot Hatteras. He loves to fish, and he figured he'd have the boat hauled down from New Jersey to Fort Lauderdale, where we'd live on the boat, fish—and talk hitting. Sounded good to me.

Somehow, though, the boat got damaged on the way down and had to go into dry dock in Miami for repairs. Three days before we were to break camp and head north for the season opener, Captain Lou got a call that his flagship was ready. Want to go with me to pick her up? Sure, I said, and off we went.

But a little something happened on the way to Fort Lauderdale from Miami: Captain Lou ran his precious rig into a drawbridge on the intercoastals. We were jammed against this big pylon, which was lucky, because another foot or two to the right and the top of the boat would have been peeled off. I crawled out of the boat and onto the bridge, and got the drawbridge operator to call the coast guard. The coast guard came and pulled us off the bridge, but the front of the boat was all torn up.

This was Captain Lou's shortest voyage.

The bottom line? I love Sweet Lou for his quirks, his neuroses, his tics, and his insatiable, mad, unquenchable love for the game. But not for his seamanship.

Thurman came up for a cup of coffee in 1969, but 1970 was his rookie season, and he made the most of it, hitting .302 and winning Rookie of the Year honors. He'd been a first-round pick in the 1968 draft, and I have to say that initially he came across as cocky. Soon I'd amend that to confident, but another C word also springs immediately to mind: combative. Thurman was as combative and intense as anybody I ever played with or against.

That combative streak came across in his dealings with the New York media. He was wary of them, and they sensed that, and pressed him that much harder. Thurm didn't like to be pressed, and he let them know that. The long, droopy mustache he wore made him look meaner than he actually was, and I think he used his readily available scowl to keep people—especially reporters—at bay.

He was a great defensive catcher, with a quicker release to second base than any catcher I've ever seen. He often threw from his knees, firing a bullet that never got more than four feet off the ground. He won three Gold Gloves, but I think he deserved more. He was that good.

Shoot, in 1971 he made just one error all season, and that came when he was knocked unconscious by a runner on a play at the plate that dislodged the ball. (That must have been some kind of tough official scorer is all I can say.)

Thurman and his wife, Diana, were real homebodies, and they had three little kids who were a bit younger than ours, so Kay and I didn't see them as a family that much when the Yankees were at home. It was when we were on the road that Tugboat—my nickname for him—and I got close, and it cost me big-time.

Tugboat, Gene "Stick" Michael, Mel Stottlemyre, Yanks broadcaster Frank Messer, and I had a semipermanent floating poker game on the road. We called ourselves The Web, because we were always looking for some new talent to lure in and trap. Later on, that would often be Lou, although more times than I care to remember, I would be the one trapped, even though I was supposed to be part of The Web, not one of its victims.

We played for meal-money stakes (that was $75 a day back then), which meant a big winner (Munson) might walk away with $300–350, while a big loser (Murcer) could drop that amount. We played mostly high-low, because—looking back, I'm sure of this—one of the double-secret bylaws of The Web required that Murcer be trapped in the middle.

You have a lot of time on your hands when you're on the road. Golf was a rarity, because you don't have that many off days on the road. (Plus I never cottoned to the idea of playing with rented clubs.) An occasional movie filled up a couple of hours, but it was as hard to find anything good to see then as it is now.

So poker it was, or going out for a good meal—or, when we were in Detroit, combining the two. There was a hot dog stand close to our hotel in Detroit, near Tiger Stadium, and after a game we'd pick up a couple of bags of coneys and convene a meeting of The Web in somebody's room. I know there's a tendency to see the past through rose-colored glasses, but I still remember those Detroit coneys as the best I ever had. Or maybe they just got rid of the bad taste of losing at poker.

As I said, one of the beautiful things about coming home in 1979 was that I would be reunited with Lou and Thurman as they argued back and forth, back and forth, about hitting and every other aspect of baseball.

It was worth me getting caught in The Web to be part of that again.

The three of us would finish our careers together and then ride off into the sunset together, three Yankees for life.

═══════

My best game in pinstripes came on the worst day of my baseball career: Monday, August 6, 1979.

The morning of that terrible day, the Yankees flew as a team to Canton, Ohio, to bury our captain, Thurman Munson. That night, with a hole in our collective heart, we stepped out onto the field at Yankee Stadium to play a baseball game that none of us wanted to play. And the only reason we did play it was that we all knew our captain would have insisted.

Five days earlier, on Wednesday afternoon, the Yankees had completed a three-game sweep of the White Sox in Chicago to cap a short road trip. (We lost three straight to the Brewers at the front end.) Lou and I had come out with the team; Thurman had flown out from Teterboro Airport in New Jersey on a six-seat Cessna Citation I/SP jet that he'd recently purchased.

We still had our condo in Arlington Heights, so Tugboat and Lou bunked with us. Tuesday night, after a postgame dinner, Kay and I went to bed, leaving the two of them arguing over who was going to be the better pinch hitter when they were no longer regulars. Some things never change.

Thursday was an off day, so Tugboat planned to fly home to Canton after Wednesday's game to be with Diana and their three children and to practice with his new toy. Lou would fly back to New York with the team; I was staying in Chicago to spend the off day with Kay and the kids.

Wednesday night, after we thumped the White Sox 9–1, Kay and I drove Thurman out to the airport. The kids came along with us. He took us into his new plane and sat us down. With Neil Diamond serenading us from his state-of-the-art audio system, Thurman pointed out the plane's special features like the proud papa he was.

Tugboat asked to borrow a little cash money for fuel, so I loaned him $200, and after he filled up, he asked us to go to the end of the runway and watch him take off.

We stood by our car and waved him goodbye as he roared off into the dark night. That's the last time we ever saw him.

The following afternoon—Thursday, August 2, 1979—Thurman went out to the Akron-Canton Regional Airport to practice takeoffs and landings. On the third touch-and-go, he let the plane sink too low before revving up engine power, and he clipped a tree about a thousand feet from the end of the runway. The skidding plane then hit a tree stump and burst into flames. Two passengers, one of them his instructor, were injured. Thurman was trapped in the cockpit. He died of asphyxiation in the burning plane.

He was 32.

A longtime dear friend, Jimmy Lindstrom, whom we'd gotten to know back in New Jersey in my early years as a Yankee, called to tell us as soon it hit the news in New York. I couldn't believe it. Kay couldn't believe it. We were devastated, in shock. Less than 24 hours earlier, we had been sitting in his plane with him. And now . . .

We got a flight down to Canton late that afternoon, and arrived at Diana's house around 8 in the evening. We stayed there that night. There was nothing we could do, nothing anybody could do, but hug Diana and Tracy and Kelly and Michael. Hug them and tell them how much we loved their father, and how much we loved them, and cry together.

The next morning we returned to Chicago, picked up our kids from neighbors who had taken them in, and flew out that afternoon for New York. The Yankees were playing the Orioles that night in the opener of a four-game series. I don't recall ever asking out of a game before in my entire career, but I called Billy before we left Chicago and told him I just didn't think I could go that night, even if we got back in time. He understood.

There was a brief memorial service before the game. The Yankees in the starting lineup took the field but left the catcher's position vacant. Robert Merrill sang "America the Beautiful." Bob Sheppard asked for a moment of silence. And then the 51,151 people at the Stadium that night stood and gave our captain a nine-minute ovation.

We sleepwalked through the next two days. The clubhouse was subdued, absent the usual raucous banter. We had suffered a death in the family, and we were still groping for ways to cope with it.

As soon as the funeral arrangements were finalized—Monday, August 6, at 9:30 A.M.—Mr. Steinbrenner chartered a plane and announced that the New York Yankees would be attending as a team. But we were scheduled to play a nationally televised game (ABC's *Monday Night Baseball*) that night against the Orioles. What if we were delayed by weather or something, didn't get back in time, and had to forfeit? Didn't matter, said Mr. Steinbrenner. We were going to bury our captain.

The funeral was conducted in the Canton Civic Center on a bright, sunny morning. About 700 packed the auditorium. Another 1,000 or so were outside to say goodbye to one of their own.

Lou gave the first eulogy and captured our dear friend perfectly:

> *He played hard. He played tough. He played fierce. He played to win . . .*
>
> *We don't know why God took Thurman away. We'll remember him as long as we live. Diana and the children, I hope God gives you the strength and conviction to carry on . . . the way Thurman would have wanted you to.*

And then it was my turn.

The night before the funeral, I had talked about what I might say—what I could *possibly* say—with Kay and our dear friend Jimmy Lindstrom. How do you sum up a star that shone so brightly, that illuminated the lives of his friends and loved ones, only to be snuffed out so suddenly and prematurely?

When I stepped up to the podium and looked out over the sea of faces, many so familiar, many others new, all showing the strain and pain of the moment, I practically broke down. It wouldn't be the last time.

As I began to read my remarks, I discovered immediately that I couldn't look at my teammates. Each triggered a memory of something Tugboat and I had done together, joked about together, experienced together. And so I focused on Diana and the kids, the ones who suffered the greatest loss. I broke up several times and had to stop to collect myself. But somehow I got through the words that came from my heart.

> *He lived. He led. He loved.*
>
> *Whatever he was to each one of us—catcher, captain, competitor, husband, father, friend—he should be remembered as a man who valued and followed the basic principles of life.*
>
> *He lived blessed with his beautiful wife, Diana; his daughters,*

Tracy and Kelly; and his son, Michael . . .

He led his team of Yankees to three divisional titles and two world championships . . .

He loved the game, his fans, his friends, and, most of all, his family . . .

He is lost, but not gone. He will be missed, but never forgotten.

As Lou Gehrig led the Yankees as the captain of the 1930s, our Thurman Munson captained the Yankees of the 1970s. Someone, someday, will earn the right to lead this team again, for that is how Thurm—Tugboat, as I called him—would want it.

No greater honor could be bestowed upon one man than to be the successor to this man, Thurman Munson, who wore the pinstripes with number 15 on the field.

But history will record Thurman as number 1.

We got back to Yankee Stadium just in time to suit up and get ready for the game. Nobody felt like playing baseball, but we knew we had to, because Thurman Lee Munson would have insisted on it.

The game was broadcast on ABC's *Monday Night Baseball*, so there was a national audience. Howard Cosell, Keith Jackson, and Don Drysdale were in the booth. I recently screened a video of that game, the first time I'd ever seen it. I found Cosell, as one would expect, both dramatic and poignant as he praised Thurman at the top of the show in the slow, measured cadence he often employed: "He was . . . the best there ever was . . . at what he did."

The Orioles, with Dennis Martinez on the mound, scored one in the second, another in the fifth, and two more in the sixth to take a 4–0 lead. In the seventh, I hit a three-run homer to make it 4–3. Then, in the bottom of the ninth, I hit a two-run single. Yankees win, 5–4.

I never used that bat again; eventually I gave it to Diana. The rest of the year, we wore black armbands. To this day, Tugboat's locker in the clubhouse remains empty. The number 15 has been retired. Thurman Munson has a plaque in Monument Park.

These are the things people do as part of the healing process.

But some things never heal.

THE LONG GOODBYE

orget the holiday season: August and September are the best months of the year when you're in a pennant race. You're more alert. Sights and sounds and smells are sharper. Food tastes better. You notice more things. Sleep may sometimes be slower to come, but it's sweeter when it does. And waking up . . . hey, is it time to go to the ballpark?

But if you're 12 games out on August 1, and you've been around the horn long enough to know that you don't have a snowball's chance of seeing any October baseball except on TV, those last two months of the regular season can be tough going. And the older you get, the tougher the going gets.

The clubhouse is less fun to be in—fewer jokes, fewer laughs, and a whole lot less energy. The loud music throbbing from a dozen tape decks that used to lift the room is now simply irritating.

After a game, you shower and dress and leave a whole lot quicker than you did when your team still had a chance. If you're lucky, you have a family waiting for you outside the clubhouse to lift your spirits and refocus your attention.

On the field, you find your mind wandering every time you're down by four runs in the sixth—and that seems to happen every other day.

Little aches and pains that come with the turf of being a ball-player and that you used to ignore all of a sudden become the reasons why you went 0-for-4 against a pitcher you should own and why you failed to hit a cutoff man and cost your team a run and why you played a single in the gap into a double.

There are more empty seats in the ballpark at the start of games, and there's a large exodus in the seventh if you're behind by three. Fans, even loyal, diehard fans, know the score.

Believe me, I do, too. Most of my career, I've spent August and September that way. It's one thing in the early part of your career; then it's "Wait till next year!" It's another thing altogether when you've been around long enough to read a box score. Then it's "Been there, done that."

Even so, you try to stay focused, you try to stay positive—after all, baseball history is chock-full of big September comebacks. Besides, you're a professional, and you play hard, because that's what you're paid to do.

But you're also human, and a realist to boot. If your team simply doesn't have the horses, and you know it, then August and September stink.

All that's what made 1980 and 1981 so special, in entirely different ways.

———

We had a terrific season in 1980. Won the AL East with a record of 103–59. Got great seasons from Reggie (41, 111, .300), Rudy May (his 2.46 ERA was the AL's best), Tommy John (won 22 games, with 16 of them complete—at age 37!), Goose (tied for the league lead in saves with 33), and Rick Cerone. Rick had an impossible job, of course, taking over behind the plate from the captain. But he came through strong: 14, 85, .277.

Oscar Gamble and I had a solid power year: 27 homers, 107 ribbies. Problem is—and I'm sure Oscar would agree—we did it together, splitting the lefty DH job and time in the outfield. Between us, we had 491 at-bats, just about 50 shy of what a full-time player would.

Didn't matter, I told myself. We're going into the playoffs. My first time. What I'd been playing for my entire career. October baseball!

But then we ran into Kansas City in the playoffs—or, more precisely, we ran into George Brett.

Brett had 24 homers and 118 RBIs in 1980. Good, you say, but 17 fewer dingers than Reggie and only 7 more ribbies than Jax. Right, but Brett got those 118 ribbies in *117* games. The man missed 45 games because of injuries and still drove in a run a game. Oh, and did I mention that he was hitting over .400 in late September and tailed off to "only" .390? Needless to say, he was named American League MVP.

You'd think maybe he might have been worn out by the time we faced off against the Royals in the ALCS. I wish. He hit two homers and drove in four runs as they swept us in three games.

My contribution in my maiden appearance in postseason play? Not something to write home about: 0-for-4 in one start. But my feeling was that I'd made it into October, I'd gotten a taste, and maybe this was just the beginning.

———

A lot of ballplayers try, in the off-season, to make a few extra bucks. In the old days, that would mean barnstorming. Guys would put together a couple of all-star teams and tour the country, playing each other in non–major league venues. In those days, back in the 1940s and early 1950s, when there were only 16 major league teams and no TV, most of the country had never seen big league baseball players, only read about them in *The Sporting News* or heard about them on radio. A troop of barnstormers coming through town was a big deal.

Later on, before there was an established card show and memorabilia circuit, there was a kind of catch-as-catch-can effort by players to turn an off-season buck.

My first endeavor on that front came when on an off day in 1972 I did a photo-signing appearance at the Woodbridge Center in Woodbridge, New Jersey, a gigantic three-story mall that contained every top store in retailing. This was organized by Jimmy Lindstrom, my dear friend from Wayne, New Jersey. I had met him in Fort Lauderdale during spring training my rookie year. Over the years, he became an honorary member of my family.

The idea behind my first adventure in trading on my celebrity was that I would go to the Woodbridge Center and autograph photos of me for two hours. The photos would be free; the idea was to draw crowds to the mall. I would get $500 from the management of Woodbridge Center, not an insignificant amount at a time when my salary was still south of $100K per year. Two hours of signing, and then I'd be on to another gig at a sports store in another mall for another $500.

Good money, no heavy lifting.

But we turned out to be victims of our success. Jimmy and the mall management figured 500 people, tops, would show up. Wrong. More than 2,000 came out. In the rain. More than Santa Claus usually pulled, the mall manager said. Good for the ego, but not only did we run out of photos for me to sign, I had to quit after two hours and get over to my next signing. So I slipped out the back way, the mall manager announced that Elvis had left the building, and more than a thousand now ex–Bobby Murcer fans were left crying in the rain.

Nearly 34 years later, a month or so after my brain surgery, I received a letter from a woman who wished me well and told me that she had been in that crowd at Woodbridge, and that she had been shut out before she could get a photo. She said she'd been a true-blue Yankee fan and still was. I thanked her for her loyalty to the Yankees all the years, and promptly sent her an 8x10 with my autograph and a note. It was the least I could do; she'd been waiting more than three decades.

Jimmy and I kicked around a few other schemes, but then in 1980 he and another good friend, Richie Levinson, hit on a really big idea: a baseball school run by real, live New York Yankees for young teenage boys who loved baseball the way we did when we were their age. To be held in Florida, during Christmas–New Year's break.

Sounds like a grand slam homer, don't you think?

The Bobby Murcer Professional Baseball School

FROM THE MISSION STATEMENT: "My sole intention is to offer the finest instruction, equipment, and facilities so that I may help a future professional baseball star develop more rapidly and with great insight into the world of professional baseball."

WHEN: From December 27, 1980, through January 1, 1981.

WHERE: At the Yankee Spring Training Complex in Fort Lauderdale, Florida. You couldn't ask for a better campus for a baseball school, right?

THE STUDENT BODY: Teenage boys, 12–18. (Sorry, we weren't evolved enough to think coed at the time.)

THE DISTINGUISHED FACULTY: Mike Ferraro (Dean of Administration); Rick Cerone (Professor of Catching); Sammy Ellis (Professor of Pitching); Lou Piniella (Professor of Outfield and Hitting); Charley Lau (Distinguished Professor of Hitting and Special Instructor to Superstar George Brett); and your humble servant (President, Provost, and Dean of Faculty).

GOAL NUMBER ONE: Provide a bunch of eager, hardworking, talented young boys a chance to hone their baseball skills and stoke their dreams under the tutelage and guidance of bona fide major leaguers.

GOAL NUMBER TWO: Provide the founder, the faculty, and their families with a free midwinter vacation in sunny Florida, along with the chance to pick up a few extra bucks during the off-season.

Tuition and Fees

PLAN A: $450 Instructional School only (plus lunch)

PLAN B: $600 Instructional School, lodging at Holiday Inn (three meals daily)

PLAN C: $930 Instructional School, lodging at Holiday Inn (three meals daily), round-trip air transportation via Eastern Airlines from Newark/NYC to Fort Lauderdale.

And how did it work out? Depends on whom you ask.

When it was the faculty and the student body out on the field, it was great. They looked up to us and followed our every word as if it were gospel. (Professors love that.) I've never been around more enthusiastic, high-energy young boys in my life. It was positively thrilling to watch a bunch of kids pouring their hearts into learning more about the very game that *you* love enough to have devoted your entire life to.

Off the field, it was a whole different deal.

Forget all the headaches involved with setting up the structure, making decisions on the housing and dining and travel arrangements, and working out the details of the curriculum with my Distinguished Faculty.

Jimmy did most of it, to be sure, but I got way more involved than I'd counted on. As much attention as I pay to every tiny detail of everyday life, I guess I should have expected that. But frankly I didn't count on getting sucked in as far as I did.

The real burden was being responsible for a hundred teenage boys (some away from home by themselves for the first time in their lives) every hour of the day for six days. (It felt more like six years.) Making sure they didn't sneak off to buy beer or go joyriding in some older kids' cars or spend all their spare time chasing girls on the beach—you know, all the things teenage boys do. Wondering what I would do if something awful happened. Filling my mind with all the awful things that could happen.

We got through it. Nobody strayed from the reservation. Nobody got hurt. Everybody had fun. Everybody learned something, including the faculty members with children of their own.

We had one full-ride scholarship student: Todd Murcer. And one of our alumni—Mike Stanley—went on to a solid major league career as a catcher that spanned 15 seasons, including 4-plus with the Yankees. (I take full credit.)

The school lost about $20,000 for its investors. Fortunately for me, I was not one of them. I had told Jimmy and Richie at the outset that they could use my good name but not my good money: my capital investment was exactly zero. So was my profit.

So maybe you're thinking things got even better and a lot easier in year two? Think again. There was no year two. There will *never* be a year two.

From time to time over the next decade, Professor Piniella would occasionally suggest that the Bobby Murcer Professional Baseball School reopen. And every time he did, I would—acting in my capacity as President, Provost, and Dean of Faculty—smack him upside his head.

═══

If ever a baseball season deserved an asterisk, it's got to be *1981. Consider this:

- The Yankees finished first in the AL East—and they finished fifth in the AL East.

- I was paid $100K less than my contract called for.

- Major league attendance dropped from 43 million in 1980 to 26.5 million.

- The home run leaders of the American League were Tony Armas, Dwight Evans, and Bobby Grich with 22. The year before, Reggie Jackson and Ben Ogilvie had tied with 41.

- There were eight division champions in the four major league divisions.

- Four pitchers (Dennis Martinez, Steve McCatty, Jack Morris, Pete Vukovich) tied for the American League lead in wins with 14. The year before, *18* AL pitchers had more than 14 wins.

- And so on. A game known for its continuity and tradition was turned upside-down in *1981.

How? Why? What happened?

A strike happened.

A strike called by the Major League Baseball Players Association began on June 12. We walked out because MLB's owners were unilaterally trying to steal back something they had already lost in the courts and at the bargaining table: our right to sell our services in the free market to the highest bidder.

You know, free agency.

The owners wanted to push through a rule whereby a team would be compensated for losing a free agent player to another team that signed him. The compensation in question would be a player selected from the signing team's roster (excluding 12 "protected" players).

The players maintained that any form of compensation would undermine the value of free agency. It's simple, really: if I sign you after your contract expires with another team for $1 million because I think you're worth it, the new rule the owners were trying to shove down the players' throats would compensate your old team for not valuing you as high as I did by allowing them to take a player from my roster. All of a sudden you're costing me $1 million *plus* another player. My incentive to pay you what I think you're worth? It drops. Who loses? You do.

The whole principle of free agency—the right of a player to participate in a free market for his services—was at stake, and so we went on strike. Most sportswriters placed most of the blame where it belonged: on the owners. *Sports Illustrated* ran a cover headline that read, "Strike! The Walkout the Owners Provoked."

The owners provoked our strike because the free market system, applied to baseball, was costing them a lot of money. Between 1978 and 1981, they had—of their own free will in a free market—shelled out 43 contracts for $1 million per year or more to players they wanted to keep or to acquire from another team. Shoot, it wasn't so much earlier that $100,000 a year had been considered a huge salary for a baseball player. (At least it sure seemed huge to me in 1973.)

We were the clear winners in the July 31 settlement that ended the strike after two months. In the compromise agreement, teams that lost a "premium" free agent could be compensated by drawing from a pool of players left unprotected from all the clubs rather than just the signing club. Some compensation, yes, but not enough to inhibit a player's right to take advantage of the free market system.

But the nearly two-month strike was painful and costly. Players lost $4 million a month in salary. The owners lost upward of $75 million in revenues.

The fans were the big losers, of course, to the tune of more than 713 games that got canceled.

(Oddly enough, the Murcers *as a family* were big winners. For the first time, we got to spend a big chunk of a summer together. We went water-skiing with friends and their kids, we went fishing on the Jersey Shore, we went on picnics with other players and their families in the middle of the week. For us, it was like a real family vacation. The only downside was that it was an *unpaid* vacation.)

So what was MLB going to do? Simply pick up the season where it left off was, of course, one option. In retrospect, that seems like it might have been the smart thing to do. But the owners, fearful that the fans wouldn't come back, decided instead to split the *1981 season into two halves, with the first-place teams from each half in each division meeting in a best-of-five divisional playoff series. The four survivors would then move on to the two best-of-five League Championship Series.

We came back to work on August 9 with the All-Star Game (NL 5, AL 4)!

A whole new season!

Everybody's got a (second) chance to go all the way!

Let's play ball!

That's when it got a little weird. The split-season idea would generate more playoff games, which was the point, because they would generate additional revenues. (The owners had lost a ton because of the strike—deservedly so, because they drove us to it.) But there was a huge flaw: the winner of the first half, already guaranteed a place in the playoffs, had no incentive to play hard in the second half.

Consider the Yankees. We finished the first half in first place with a 34–22 record, two games up over the Orioles. We were in the playoffs. We finished the second half in fifth place with a 25–26 record. Didn't matter; we were in the playoffs.

Did we quit like dogs in the second half? Did we just go through the motions even though fans were still paying the same ticket prices to watch us? No, not exactly. But we certainly didn't play with the edge that we had during the first half.

More weirdness in the *1981 season. Neither the Reds, who had the best full-season record in the NL West, nor the Cardinals, best in the NL East, made the playoffs. Meanwhile, the Royals had the fourth-best full-season record in the AL West—and did make the playoffs. The Orioles, who had a better full-season record in the AL East than we did (59–46 vs. 59–48), didn't make the play-offs.

But we did. We beat Milwaukee in the division series in five games, and we swept the A's, and—bingo! Unfurl the bunting, because Bobby Murcer was finally going to get to play in his first World Series!

Somehow, it didn't feel the way I had expected it to, the way I *know* it would have felt 10 years earlier. That's because I wasn't really part of it. Against the Brewers in the division series, I pinch-hit twice and went 0-for-1 with a walk. Against the A's in the League Championship Series, I started one game and went 1-for-3 with a walk. Against the Dodgers in the World Series, I started in one game and went 0-for-3.

Far, far worse, we lost to the Dodgers in six games.

It was my first World Series after 12 seasons in the majors, and I sensed it might well be my last.

All the waiting, all the hoping, all the dreaming for all those years came down to this. Not exactly how I imagined things would turn out when I signed a contract to play baseball for the New York Yankees in 1964.

Truth of the matter, I was happy to have the *1981 season behind me, even though I wasn't too thrilled by what I thought was coming next.

———

Every veteran ballplayer is all too familiar with the one key stat that tells him where he fits in his team's plans for the future: at-bats. For 10 seasons, from 1969 through 1978, I averaged 559 at-bats—about par for a regular who steers clear of the DL. But then, over the next 3 seasons, my at-bat totals were as follows: 454, 297, 117. True, the last number was so low in part because of the mid-season work stoppage in *1981 that wiped out 38 percent of the season, but I still averaged only one at-bat per game. And in 1982, that dropped to less than one at-bat a game.

My other stats—HR, RBI, BA—suffered accordingly, of course, for the simple reason that I wasn't getting enough plate appearances to stay sharp. I don't care who you are, if you go a week or so without cracking a lineup, except maybe for a pinch-hitting appearance every so often, you aren't going to be able to hit major league pitching the way you did when you were in the lineup every day. You don't play, your performance plummets.

Teams, of course, see a chicken-and-egg factor here. They'll conclude that Old So-and-So isn't producing so they use him less. Meanwhile, Old So-and-So takes the position that they're not using him enough to keep him sharp so he can't possibly produce.

A handful of exceptions prove the rule. Somebody once said of Smokey Burgess, the old Cubs–Phillies–Red Sox–Pirates–White Sox catcher and pinch hitter extraordinaire in the 1950s and 1960s, that he could fall out of bed on a cold winter morning and hit a line drive. The player most like that today would be, I suppose, Manny Ramirez.

But those guys are the exceptions.

On top of that, I was getting old, borderline ancient by baseball standards of the time: 33 in 1979, 34 in 1980, 35 in . . . You see where this is going, don't you?

And what was I supposed to do? Go to Billy Martin, Dick Howser, Stick Michael, Bob Lemon, Stick again, Clyde King, Billy again—the seven managers I played under in the three-plus seasons that I was a born-again Yankee—and beg for more playing time? Not my style. Anyway, as you can probably guess from the turnover in the manager's office during that time, they had bigger problems to deal with than a frustrated outfielder from Oklahoma who thought—*knew*—that he had plenty left, and that all he needed was a chance to show it.

In 1981, the final year of the three-year contract I had signed with the Cubs, I hit only six home runs and drove in just 24 runs in my 117 at-bats. Project that over 500 at-bats, and it would be a typical Bobby Murcer year. But my days of getting 500 at-bats were behind me, and I knew it.

Kay and I talked it over, and we decided that I wasn't going to go out there and test the free agent waters if I didn't re-sign with the Yankees. I'd begun my career in pinstripes; I'd end it in pinstripes. And I would consider myself one of the luckiest men alive . . . even if I did think I had a couple of good swings left in me.

So in late September 1981, before the season ended, I called Mr. Steinbrenner, and I asked him point-blank: "Am I going to be asked back?"

He said, "I don't know, Bobby. Let me talk to my baseball people."

A couple of days later he got back to me and said what I thought he would: "Sorry, Bobby, it doesn't look good."

Kay and I had prepared for this eventuality, and frankly we weren't too surprised. So we began to make preparations, knowing that our biggest immediate problem was to sell our house in Franklin Lakes, New Jersey. All those years before when I was with the Yankees, we rented. But the winter after coming back to the Yankees in 1979, we bought a nice two-story home on an acre of land in a good community. Only now, with interest rates at 18–21 percent, we faced the prospect of being stuck with three houses: our home in Oklahoma, our condo in Chicago, and our New Jersey home. Fortunately, the neighbor across the street heard we were leaving and made an offer. We sold the house without even having to put it on the market.

So now it was time to move on.

We headed back to Oklahoma after the World Series.

Time to begin the next stage of our life.

Three weeks later, Mr. Steinbrenner called and offered me a three-year contract.

Where do I sign?

Fact is, I didn't sign right away. It was a handshake deal. Teams juggle their rosters all winter. I officially became a free agent on November 13, 1981. I went to spring training in 1982 as a non-roster invitee. I signed a three-year contract for $1.25 million on April 5, 1982, six days before Opening Day.

But much as I appreciated the new contract, I never deluded myself into thinking that the Yankees had suddenly decided that I was going to play a central role in the team's future.

By now I was strictly a DH against right-handers. I hadn't played in the field at all in 1981, and wouldn't for the rest of my career. Problem was, Oscar Gamble was also a lefty DH and occasional outfielder, and there wasn't enough work to go around.

On Opening Day in 1983, a cold, misty, miserable day, I walked into the clubhouse and, as ballplayers routinely do, checked the starting lineup posted on the wall outside the manager's office. I did a double take: Billy Martin had penciled me in to start in left field. What? I hadn't even so much as taken a fly ball in the outfield in spring training. In fact, Billy had told me down in Fort Lauderdale that "you won't even need a glove this year," so I was just a tad rusty.

I walked into Billy's office and politely reminded him I'd do anything to help the team, but that playing left field without a glove would be tough. He looked at me like he didn't know what I was talking about, so I explained. Billy, who in those days was drinking pretty heavily, finally got it. He realized that he had confused Oscar and me. (At least in our roles on the ball club; we didn't look that much alike.) He switched me to DH and Oscar to left.

I've always wondered why Mr. Steinbrenner re-signed me to that three-year-deal, and I think I have the answer. I believe he was trying to make up for what he'd done seven seasons before—trading me to the Giants a year after telling me that as long as he was with the Yankees, I would be a Yankee as well. I'm not sure that was his motive for re-signing me, mind you, but if it factored into his thinking, it shows a side of the man that might come as a surprise to people who have seen him in only one dimension.

We went from the penthouse to the outhouse in 1982, from the World Series the season before (albeit in that wacky split-season format) to fifth place in the AL East, 16 games behind the Brewers. Three managers—Bob Lemon, Gene Michael, and Clyde King (the last two interim appointments)—failed to stop the team-wide collapse. It wasn't pretty. And it wasn't fun.

What nobody could have predicted, though, was that the *1981 season marked the beginning of the Second Great Depression; the Yankees wouldn't come within sniffing distance of the postseason again until 1995, when they won the AL East but were knocked out in the first round of the playoffs.

The Second Great Depression ended for sure the following season, 1996, the first of an unprecedented 12 straight seasons of making it to the postseason under the leadership of Joe Torre.

When you play on a winning team, baseball's fun.

When you play on a losing team, it's a job.

And when you don't even play . . .

11

HOW DO I GET UP TO THE BOOTH?

*T*he first time I set foot in a broadcast booth to do color commentary for the Yankees was in Baltimore's Memorial Stadium on June 20, 1983. At that time, I knew as much about TV-radio broadcasting as I did about brain surgery. Over the years, I've learned a few things about both, but on that night in Baltimore I was the greenest of rookies: no spring training, no rookie league ball, just straight to Opening Day.

What do I do?

"You don't have to 'do' anything," answered WPIX producer Don Carney before that first game. "Just watch the game and talk baseball."

Whew! What a relief! At least that was a topic I knew a little something about. And that's what I've been doing every summer for the last quarter of a century: talking baseball.

Only on that warm June night in Baltimore, I had expected to be *playing* baseball—it was the first game of a three-game series against the Orioles in Baltimore, and I had to be ready to DH or pinch-hit or whatever. I hadn't been used much lately, but I still had to be ready to go.

Then, early in the afternoon, I got a telephone call in my hotel room.

"Bobby, we're in a pennant race, and we have a problem . . ."

No "Hello, Bobby. This is George. How ya doin'? How's the weather down there?" Introductions weren't necessary—I recognized the caller's voice at once; it's not one you ever forget.

Small talk and pleasantries? Never the caller's strong suit.

The business about us being in a pennant race? In *June*?

You have to understand this about George Michael Steinbrenner III: to him, the Yankees were *always* in a pennant race, and *every* game mattered, from Opening Day on.

Proof? Back in 1980, when I was in Oklahoma City to bury my father, the Red Sox were coming into Yankee Stadium for a "key series." All Yankees–Red Sox series are, by definition, "key," and Mr. Steinbrenner didn't want us to be a man down. So he called me in Oklahoma City and asked if it would be okay with me if he sent a plane to fly me directly to New York after the funeral so that I wouldn't miss a game.

Why, uh, sure, Mr. Steinbrenner. I'll go get packed.

Now, back to that phone call in June 1983:

"Griffey's hurt, and he can't play. But we don't want to put him on the DL, because we'd lose him for two weeks, and he'll be ready to go before then."

Yeah, that's a problem, I thought, but what's it got to do with me? And then I found out.

"Now, we've got this kid first baseman in the minors who could stabilize us at first until Ken gets healthy. He's supposed to be a great fielder but not much of a hitter. Young kid by the name of Don Mattingly . . ."

Well, he certainly got the fielding part right.

". . . only we don't have a roster spot for him. So here's what I'm thinking: I've always thought you'd be great in the broadcast booth. Would you consider retiring and moving up there? No pressure. I'm not pushing you. You think about it. I'll call back in 30 minutes."

Me?

The *broadcast* booth?

Now?

Retire and move up to the *broadcast* booth?

I was bowled over. I didn't know what to think. But I did know that I'd better think fast, because I'd need to have my answer ready in *exactly* 30 minutes.

So I quickly took stock. (Make that *very* quickly.)

I was 37 years old, positively ancient by the standards of the day. I was in the second year of a three-year contract. As sparingly as I had been used for the last season or two, it had been even worse so far this year—two-plus months of the 1983 season, I'd had only 22 at-bats in nine games. At that rate, I had zero chance of building the kind of numbers that would make me an attractive free agent in 1985. I believed I had plenty of game left in me, but I had to get a lot more at-bats than I'd been getting to prove it.

Heck, my last base hit had come 19 days earlier, in Anaheim against the Angels. It was a home run, off Dave Goltz, but still . . . A player can't be an effective designated hitter unless he gets to hit on a regular basis.

Frankly, sitting on the bench had become a drag, even if I was wearing a Yankee uniform.

On the positive side, the broadcast booth would be a new adventure, a complete departure from anything I'd ever done. I'd still be in baseball. And I'd still be a Yankee.

The idea that had seemed so shocking 17 minutes earlier was now looking like it made good career sense and good personal sense as well. Just 13 minutes to go, though, so I called my chief adviser in all things, Kay. I laid it all out for her, with all the pluses and minuses, and she gave me exactly the response I had expected: "Do what you think is best, dear."

So I was ready with my answer when, exactly 30 minutes after my first call of the afternoon from New York, I received a second one. And my answer:

Yes.

"Bobby, I think you've made the right decision. I think you'll be just great. We'll hold a press conference this afternoon and make the announcement. You'll start tonight.

"You'll be great."

========

It was over. Time to hang 'em up. Time to move on.

My first hit in baseball was a home run.

My last hit in baseball was a home run.

In the nearly 18 years in between, I had built up a million great memories, forged dozens of friendships for life, had way more fun than any one person deserves, and lived out a dream that I first started dreaming 30 years before.

I came into the majors in pinstripes, and I left in pinstripes.

All I had to do now was take off one uniform and put on another, to trade playing baseball for talking baseball, to move to the next stage of my life.

How do you get up to the broadcast booth?

========

My three partners that first season of broadcasting—Scooter, Bill White, and Frank Messer—couldn't have made it easier on a raw rookie. They were great teachers, mostly by example. I did a lot of careful listening, and between innings I pounded them with questions. They answered each one, no matter how naïve, patiently and directly. And there was no rookie hazing.

I got to work with everybody, and on both TV and radio, from the start. Two of us would do TV and the other two radio for six innings, then we'd flip. The following game, we'd reverse it. Then in the next series, we'd switch the pairs. Technically, I was the color guy, at least at first. And when I was paired with Scooter, I got some early training in play-by-play when he'd go out for coffee after the seventh inning and make a beeline for the George Washington Bridge.

During our years together in the booth, Scooter caught me off guard more times than you've had hot dinners, and he gave me a taste of what was to come that very first weekend in Baltimore.

Scooter was scheduled to interview a very special guest—the distinguished author, noted Washington personality, and huge baseball fan, George Will. Great, I remember thinking: I'll pick up a few tips on how to do a one-on-one interview with a big-name guest. Except that when our guest entered the booth, Scooter had conveniently "left the building." Now pinch-hitting for Phil Rizzuto . . . me.

Poor George. I don't remember a word of what I said or asked, but I'm pretty darn sure it wasn't very profound or probing.

Early on, I mangled a bunch of syntax, misused more than my share of words, and trotted out a few baseball clichés. When Howard Cosell described my broadcast voice as "guttural," I had to look up the meaning.

One critic sniffed that my Oklahoma accent sounded a bit incongruous—looked that one up too: "out of keeping or place; inappropriate; unbecoming"—emanating from the broadcast booth in Yankee Stadium, a hallowed place formerly inhabited by the likes of Mel Allen and Red Barber. Never mind that the former grew up in Alabama, the latter in Mississippi and Florida.

Too bad: I'd spent almost four decades perfecting that accent, and I sure wasn't going to change now.

I did do some homework, though. I took a crash course in broadcasting, including a few sessions with the great sportscaster Marty Glickman. (Now there's a guy who most certainly did *not* have an Oklahoma accent.) After a couple of embarrassing interruptions, I learned certain basics such as holding up my hand to signal to my broadcast partner that I wanted to say something. And I internalized the cardinal rule that sportscasters going back and forth between TV and radio must, *must* follow: talk more on radio, talk less on TV.

That last thing sound a little obvious? Sure it does, but it doesn't sink in until you find yourself saying, "Smalley goes to his left in deep short, scoops up a two-hopper, flips it underhand to Randolph, who fires it on to Balboni to complete the bang-bang double play"—and saying it to all the fans who are watching it for themselves on TV!

Uh, Bobby Ray, the people you're talking to just *saw* that.

═══════

About six weeks after I went up to the booth, I was back on the field for a big party that Mr. Steinbrenner and the Yankees threw at Yankee Stadium. Twenty-five years later, it still gives me chills to think about it. I'm talking about Sunday, August 7, 1983—Bobby Murcer Day.

From the minute Kay and I, Tori and Todd, my mother, my brother DeWayne, and Diana Munson and her three wonderful kids (Tracy, Kelly, and Michael) walked out onto that historic field together before a game against Detroit, I was overwhelmed with emotion.

We lined up along the first-base line in front of the Yankee dugout and stepped forward as Bob Sheppard introduced each of us.

My old colleague and friend Frank Messer presided over the festivities as emcee. Upstairs, Mr. Steinbrenner and his family cheered us from their box. In one of the luxury suites a contingent of Oklahoma pals mingled with a gaggle of New York friends. Dave Winfield, Ron Guidry, Goose, and Lou stepped out of the Yankee dugout to take the mike and present me and Kay with a staggering array of gifts: a luxury cruise to Rio de Janeiro, a set of Louis Vuitton luggage to pack our travel gear in, a Cartier watch to make sure we wouldn't miss our boat, a bright red Chrysler LeBaron convertible, a set of golf clubs (boy, did Todd's eyes light up), and enough other wonderful things to stock a Fifth Avenue department store.

The best gift of all, though, was the incredible ovation from the capacity crowd that may have registered on the Richter scale.

The only blemish on the day was delivered by the spoilsport Tigers: they beat us 8–5.

Following the game, our whole posse—about 45 strong—boarded a bus chartered by the Yankees and headed off on a familiar trail across the GW Bridge for part two of the biggest party of my life. Our destination: the Livingston, New Jersey, home of old and dear friends Sharon and Barry Halper.

A minority owner of the Yankees, Barry was one of the most famous collectors of baseball memorabilia of all time. You name it, he had it—or would soon get it. His collection included what is very likely the first baseball (yes, the *first baseball*), a handmade ball dating from Alexander Cartwight's New York Knickerbockers, who played the first "baseball" game in 1846; Babe Ruth's bathrobe, along with that camel coat the Bambino was often photographed in; Christy Mathewson's checkerboard and Ty Cobb's dentures; a baseball card collection that dated from the 19th century and numbered more than 500,000 cards; more than 1,000 game-worn uniforms, including at least one from nearly every member of the Hall of Fame; enough signed baseballs to supply the major leagues for a season. . . . And, well, let me just say it was always a great treat to visit Sharon and Barry and inspect his latest acquisitions.

(A huge fan of Mickey Mantle, Barry snapped up just about every bit of Mickey memorabilia that came on the market. When Mickey had his liver replaced in 1995, two months before his death, he told reporters that he figured Barry had probably bought it.)

Barry, who died in 2005, sold his collection at auction through Sotheby's in 1999 after stipulating that the Baseball Hall of Fame had first crack at anything they wanted. The Hall took about $5 million worth of stuff. The remainder fetched another $17 million.

The party that wonderful day in 1983 featured a fantastic home-cooked meal by Sharon and a tour of Barry's museum. During the party Sharon let on that this was the first time a bus had ever been parked in their driveway, so Kay later needlepointed her a pillow that said, "The Bus Stops Here."

Over the years, I worked for seven different broadcast entities: WPIX and WABC Radio (1983–1984); SportsChannel (1986–1989); WPIX (1991–1997); WPIX and MSG (1998); Fox 5 (1999–2001); and YES Network, along with Fox 5 and WWOR-TV (2002–present).

Close readers will have noticed two gaps in that résumé. I spent 1985 as assistant GM, establishing to my complete satisfaction that I wasn't front office material; and I left the booth in 1990 to create a telecom startup in Oklahoma City, where I proved in short order that I could steer a new business into bankruptcy.

Initially I preferred radio, because it let me talk more, but that required a 162-game commitment. TV was a little easier on my personal life, at least in those first years. When I started with WPIX, we carried only about 100 games; another 40 or so were on SportsChannel. Nowadays, of course, all 162 Yankee games are on TV, about 120 on YES and the remainder on ABC, Fox, and MY9.

In 2008, I'm planning to work 50 regular-season games.

My routine on a day I'm working—make that *night* I'm working, because most games these days are played at night—hasn't changed much over the years:

- Wake up around 7 A.M.

- Watch SportsCenter on ESPN.

- Read the local papers. When we're in New York, that means the *Times*, the *Daily News*, the *Post*, and *Newsday*—plus *USA Today*.

- Hit the gym for a workout.

- Eat lunch (usually with Kay, because she's been traveling with me since our kids grew up) at about 1:30.

- Head for the ballpark so as to arrive about three hours before game time.

- Stop off at the booth for a look at the stats of starting pitchers and the briefings from production.

- Go down onto the field and into the dugout to talk to Yankee players. Not an interview—just a chat to stay in touch.

- Sign a few autographs for early arriving fans—always.

- Back in booth an hour or so before game time: exchange ideas with broadcast partners, review stats again, greet occasional visitors to booth.

- Stay until the last out. (Unlike Phil.)

My three goals:

1. Help fans learn more about the team.

2. Help fans learn more about baseball.

3. Help fans enjoy the game more.

Like just about everything else, broadcasting has changed over the years—a *lot*. The biggest change, of course, is in the sheer number of games in all sports that are on air.

But there's also been a big change in how we broadcasters approach our craft. When I started, the distinction between the play-by-play guy and the color guy was pretty clear. That distinction has long since been blurred.

There's also more talking today, at least on TV. I can't prove it, but I can feel it. It just seems like broadcasters now feel a need to fill every moment with something besides crowd noise.

Finally, the whole business has gone a little stat crazy. Every booth has a computer (or 10) with instant access to just about everything you'd want to know—and a lot that you don't really *need* to know, like how such-and-such a batter hits against left-handed pitchers when there's a full moon.

I believe statistics can tell you a lot about the game. I think they can also get in the way sometimes.

My weakness behind the mike in the beginning was that I talked a bit too much sometimes. See, I *love* talking about baseball, and people were paying me money to do that, and . . . well, sometimes I may have gotten a little carried away. (But I promise you: we weren't being paid by the word.)

As to my main strength today, I think it's that I'm not afraid to say something is a bad play, even if it's made by a Yankee. Fans know baseball, too. You try to gloss over a bonehead move by a player, even if he's wearing your old uniform, and they're going to nail you. As they should.

The way I see it, I'm going on 25 years in the booth—already 8 more than I spent on the field—and I'm still learning.

———

Every broadcaster has his nightmare game, and usually it's one that goes on and on and on for so long that you start thinking about breakfast.

Length's not necessarily so bad if the lead changes hands a lot, and there are some exciting plays—and your team wins. But I sure wouldn't have wanted to be the announcer for the Orioles when they hooked up with the Rangers in a pitchers' duel in Baltimore on August 17, 2007.

The final score was 30–3.

I'm not kidding: 30–3, Rangers over Orioles.

The O's got off to an early lead, scoring 1 run in the first inning and 2 in the third, and carried that 3–0 lead into the top of the fifth. Even after the Rangers posted a 5-spot, it was still a ball game, with neither team scoring in the fifth, but in the seventh the sky fell in on Baltimore, as Texas scored 9 runs. I'm guessing that with the hometown heroes down 14–3, the seventh inning stretch was more of a seventh inning sprint to the parking lot by Orioles fans. Neither team scored in the seventh—the Rangers were probably exhausted from running the bases—but Texas ended all suspense with 16 runs in the eighth and ninth.

My dream game, on the other hand, is a seesaw deal with a fair amount of scoring—say, 7–6—with the lead changing hands three or four times, and the game-winning hit coming in the bottom of the 10th after the other guys went up 6–5 in the top half.

A game like that, you're likely to see some decent, if not great, pitching. And naturally you'll see a lot of hitting. No home runs are necessary, thank you, but a lot of doubles and at least one triple with a close play at third. Couple of key stolen bases. Couple of circus catches in the outfield to save runs. No walks, no errors. And the whole deal would be wrapped up in 3:21, *tops*.

Oh, and I guess it goes without saying that the dream game I just described takes place on a perfect, warm summer night with a sky full of stars—in Yankee Stadium.

===

As I said way back in the Introduction, I've had 31 different broadcast partners over the years. And I stand behind the pledge I made then to give a free bottle of my brother Randy's grand-slam barbecue sauce to anyone who can name all of them. Meanwhile, I'll give you a head start by spotting you a baker's dozen, in alphabetical order, just to give you a sense of the quality of folks I've had the good fortune to work with.

Mel Allen

How about that!

A person doesn't often get a chance to work alongside a legend, and I got to work with two: Mel and Scooter.

When a young guy from Birmingham, Alabama, with a law degree (and a serious addiction to baseball) named Mel Israel went to work for CBS in 1937, the network "suggested" that he change his last name. He picked Allen, his father's middle name, and legally changed it in 1943.

Mel was the voice of both the Yankees and the Giants until 1943, when he went into the service. After the war, Allen was the Yankees' exclusive voice for the next 18 years. Over the years, he called 18 World Series in a row from 1946 to 1963. The Yankees appeared in "only" 14 of those, but Mel was the go-to guy for World Series play-by-play.

The Yankees fired him after the 1964 season—sponsor pressure, make room for new blood, yackety-yak. Maybe it was just a coincidence, but that was the last time the Yankees went to the World Series until 1976, when Mel rejoined the Yankees' broadcasting family, where he remained until his retirement in 1985. All that time away, Mel's heart stayed loyal to the Yankees. (Hey, I know the feeling.) During Mel's last nine years with the Yankees, they went to four World Series and won two.

Mel died in 1996. Two years later, the Yankees dedicated a plaque in his memory in Monument Park at Yankee Stadium. The plaque calls him "a Yankee institution, a national treasure" and includes his signature line:

"How about that?"

Hawk Harrelson

The first player I knew to wear custom-made Nehru suits. Years later, Cecil Fielder tried to bring back that style when he was with the Yankees. At 6-foot-2 and 190 pounds, Hawk could pull off the look. An inch taller and some 50 pounds heavier, Cecil couldn't.

A nicotine fiend when we were broadcast partners, Hawk practically smoked me out of the booth. I'm happy to report that he has since given up the habit.

But I bet he's still making his famous "duck snort" calls!

(Don't know what a duck snort is? Well, let's say a batter hits a lazy little pop fly that lands for a single just beyond an infielder running out and just in front of an outfielder racing in. To 99.5 percent of us folks up in the booth, that's a "dying quail." To Hawk, it's a "duck snort." Where he came up with the term, I do not know.)

Jim Kaat

One of the best. Easy, effortless style. I always envied Kitty's virtually photographic memory. I swear he had instant recall of every play in every game he'd covered since sitting down in front of a microphone.

Over his 25-year pitching career, Kitty won an astonishing 16 *consecutive* Gold Gloves. The Veterans Committee of the Hall of Fame next meets in 2009 to consider candidates for the Hall.

C'mon, guys—let's put Kitty in Cooperstown!

Michael Kay

A former newspaper beat writer for the *New York Post* and the *New York Daily News,* Michael went into the booth with plenty of expertise about the game. What's astonishing to me is that he can gobble peanuts and do play-by-play without skipping a beat. Me? I can't even take a sip of water while we're on the air—it throws off my concentration.

Mickey Mantle

Mick's brutally honest personality sometimes brought a little too much color to his color commentary: "Hell, [player to be named] should have caught the damned ball!" The production crew back in the truck had to be on their toes when Mickey was on air; even then, they sometimes couldn't hit the two-second bleeper button fast enough.

Much as I loved the guy, I have to admit that broadcasting wasn't his strongest suit. But man, did we have some fun together over the years. (More to come in chapter 13.)

Tim McCarver

Very, very smart, and always—I mean, *always*—prepared. Loves good restaurants and knows the best places to eat in every town—not only the hot new places, but also the offbeat, "locals-only" joints. T-Mac's something of a wine connoisseur, so we always ate *and* drank well.

Once, when we were in Seattle for a series with the Mariners, Kay and I took Tim to one of *our* favorite spots just outside the city near the Chittenden Locks, a fish restaurant called Ray's Boathouse. We were set to order our usual—bucket of steamers and catch of the day—when Tim, after consultation with our waiter, told us with considerable excitement that "halibut cheeks are in season."

(Old joke: Guy suggests a restaurant to a friend. Friend says, "You really like the place?" First guy says, "Not particularly. I go there just for the halibut.")

But halibut *cheeks*? I didn't even know halibuts had cheeks. Now I do, thanks to Tim, and let me tell you, they're some mighty fine eating.

Frank Messer

A pro's pro. Frank helped me greatly there at first, when I didn't even know how to shut off my mike if I had to sneeze. He was the first traditional play-by-play announcer to work Yankee games since Mike Burke fired Red Barber after the 1966 season. A man of great poise—and a member of our regular poker game on road trips.

Lou Piniella

My dear friend Lou and I had the same broadcast employer in 1998: I did play-by-play and color for WPIX and MSG, while Sweet Lou did pregame and postgame shows with Greg Gumbel for MSG. We never actually worked in the booth together. Too bad. Can you imagine it, Felix and Oscar working a Yankees–Red Sox game side by side? What's even harder to imagine is a broadcast booth large enough to hold Lou's XXL baseball personality for nine innings, but the fact is that Lou's one heckuva broadcaster. Talk about having a fire in your belly for the game!

Tom Seaver

Tom was quite a prankster. Once, just before a game, he told me, "If Scooter asks you a question, say, 'I don't know, ask Seaver.'" Well, I went along with him, and when Scooter asked me something, I said, "I don't know, ask Seaver." Scooter did, and Seaver's response was "I don't know, ask Murcer." I thought we were going to dance around that floor all day.

I like to check out hands, whether of a hitter or a pitcher (or even a brain surgeon). So much is in the wrists, and in the length and strength of the fingers. I was studying Tom's left hand as he gripped the mike one day and I noticed that it was all scratched up, like he'd been in a catfight. Then I noticed his right hand when he made a note on his scorecard; same thing. I asked him what was up, how did his hands get so scratched up.

"Oh, that's from working with my roses," he said.

Next thing I know, he's flashing pictures of his flower beds the way a new grandfather would show off pics of his twin grandbabies. (By the way, have you seen mine . . . ?)

Turns out that Tom and Nancy Seaver were avid and accomplished gardeners at their place up in Greenwich, Connecticut, where they lived for 30 years. I use the past tense because the Seavers now live near Calistoga in the northern Napa Valley, where Tom's refocused his attention on becoming a winemaker. The first vintage of a cabernet sauvignon named Seaver was released this year.

And you know what? I bet Tom Terrific could still throw that hard slider on the outside corner.

Ken Singleton

Singy is probably my best friend from the booth. A tough opponent, too: he played for the Orioles in the Munson tribute game in 1979 after we returned from Thurman's funeral. We first got to know each other later that year when we traveled together for three weeks in Japan as members of a U.S. all-star team.

Speaking of that three-week tour to promote baseball in Japan, a stunt in one game gets my dander up to this day: Earl Weaver, our manager, called time and sent me in to run for Rod Carew, who was on third.

Say what? In the first place, why pinch-run for anybody at third unless the guy there was limping with an injury? Second, me running for Rod Carew made no sense whatsoever because—as Weaver knew perfectly well—Rod could spot me 5 yards and beat me in a 30-yard dash.

The only reason that Weaver, who hated the Yankees like the plague, made that move was to show me up. I was the only Yankee on the American team, and the little twerp wanted to embarrass me by using me in a meaningless way.

Fortunately, that little banty rooster's strutting didn't get in the way of me and Singy getting to be tight. Our personalities meshed too well, on the field and in the booth.

Suzyn Waldman

Only the second woman in history to be a play-by-play announcer for a major league team. A fellow cancer survivor (breast cancer, 1996) and a good friend. Used to be a Broadway singer, with her biggest role as the female lead in *Man of La Mancha*. Has performed the National Anthem at many Yankee home games.

Suzyn caught a lot of flak when she cried on air while describing the somber mood in the Yankee clubhouse on the postgame show for WCBS 880 AM after the Yankees were eliminated in the 2007 playoffs. The players were down, and some of the Yankee coaches were crying, because they feared—with good reason—that Joe Torre's days with the Yankees were numbered.

Suzyn, being Suzyn, didn't exactly take the criticism lying down. In a *Newsday* interview, she had this to say:

This one's getting me angry, because I don't play this card a lot, but this is as sexist as it gets. What's the big damn deal? That I cried for four seconds of a 10-minute post-game? The idea that I can't choke up because a man I went through cancer with 11 years ago is going to lose his job and I was describing his coaches crying? It's absolutely ludicrous.

Kay's reaction? "You go, girl!"
Mine, too. Suzyn is as quality as they come.

Bill White

A perfect straight man for Scooter, of course, but much, much more. Soft-spoken, perceptive, a master of the less-is-more school of broadcasting. Bill was the first black play-by-play broadcaster in baseball.

Like me, Bill's first hit in the majors was a homer. But unlike me, he got it in his first *at-bat*. Terrific first baseman (seven Gold Gloves) and deadly clutch hitter for the Giants, Cardinals, and Phillies. Got a pretty good promotion when he was named president of the National League in 1989.

A joy to have as a partner.

And, of course, Scooter . . .

I have so many Scooter memories that I decided to put them in their own chapter. (See chapter 12.)

═══════

One of the many reasons that I enjoyed working alongside Scooter so much is that he and I saw things eye-to-eye when we were in the booth together. I'm not talking about agreeing on most things, even though we did, but literally seeing eye-to-eye.

See, since Scooter retired in 1996, I've almost always been the runt of the booth. During the first broadcast of the 2006 season, I was squished between Jim Kaat and Michael Kay, both of whom are at least 6-foot-4. (Although from my perspective, they sure seemed taller.) In the pregame show on TV, I looked like I was standing with my two bodyguards. The next day, it was Singy and Kitty on either side of me. (*Hey, who's that guy with the Southern accent standing in the hole?*)

That was it. I told the production team that they had to get me a block of wood or something to stand on, or they had make those other guys sit on the desk while I stood, so we would at least look like we evolved from the same species.

So now, whenever I work with giants (not Giants: been there, done that), I've got my very own concrete slab that says, "Bobby's Block."

If you can't beat 'em, step up so you can join 'em!

———

At the end of the 1984 season, just a year and a half after I went up into the broadcast booth, Mr. Steinbrenner "asked" me to turn in my blazer and move into his front office as assistant general manager. His idea was that I would serve a one-year apprenticeship under GM Clyde King and then take over the following year as general manager, with Lou Piniella taking over as manager. He put it to me as an offer, but that was really two letters away from what it really was—an order.

And the result?

What an honor! What an opportunity! What a mistake!

Naturally, I did as I was asked by the man who owned the ball club, but it didn't take long sitting behind a desk for me to realize that I was as out of place wearing a tie and sitting behind a desk as I had been playing shortstop back in 1966.

Square peg, meet round hole.

Can pigs fly?

Am I making myself perfectly clear?

Much as I loved baseball, I couldn't love it from the perspective of a front office man. If I couldn't play—and that was no longer in the cards—I still needed to be following the flow of the game, reacting to what I saw on the field, anticipating what I might see next, trying to make it clear to fans who were watching and listening with me.

Being on the field was best.

Being above the field, taking in the action and interpreting it, was second best.

For me, there was no third best.

There was, though, one brief respite in that white-shirt-and-tie year that I quite enjoyed. Early in the season, Mr. Steinbrenner asked me to work a little with my successor on the 25-man roster back in 1983, Don Mattingly, who was going through a little rough stretch. I guess the Boss figured that since I had been a successful left-handed hitter in Yankee Stadium, I might impart some special insights to Don. Yes sir, right away—but first I had to request permission to speak with Don from our current hitting coach, Mr. Lou Piniella.

That permission was forthcoming (along with a few smart remarks), and I did in fact work with Donnie a few times. I suggested a little adjustment of his hands here, a little shifting of his feet there, nothing major, because after watching the man swing a bat up close, I knew nothing major was wrong. Not surprisingly, Don pulled out of his little slump soon thereafter, as he would have done if I'd stayed behind my desk back in my tiny little windowless office.

Mr. Piniella took this brief intervention with ostentatious grace and mock gratitude. Fact is, Lou was as good a hitting coach as he was a hitter and as he later was a manager and occasional announcer. That didn't prevent me from claiming full credit for the season that Don went on to have: 35, 145, .324.

Mr. Steinbrenner was not pleased when, at the end of the season, I asked that I be permitted to return to the broadcast booth: "You're making a really big mistake, Bobby. You have the potential to be one of the top young executives in baseball."

Mind you, I was mighty flattered that Mr. Steinbrenner thought I had the stuff to make a good GM. But I respectfully disagreed with him.

In 1986 I was back where I believed I belonged—up in the booth, trying to get a handle on what Scooter had just said and figure out what he might say next.

My favorite press box, it will come as no surprise to you to learn, is the one at that big ballpark at the corner of 161st Street and River Avenue in the Bronx, New York.

But my second favorite press box over the years was on the other side of the country at the Big A in Anaheim. The ballpark was originally called Anaheim Stadium; then it became Edison International Field of Anaheim; and today its official name is Angel Stadium of Anaheim.

As I said, the Big A.

We could always count on two things when we worked games at the Big A: really good food in the press box, and really good weather. (Games *always* started on time.)

One other thing that made visits to the Big A special to me was my special relationship with the Cowboy, Gene Autry. I had first met him many years before, when I was just a teenager, through my uncle, the country singer Johnny Bond. They were both from Marietta, Oklahoma. and Uncle Johnny toured with the Cowboy over the years.

Every time we went out to California to do a game, I had fun visiting with the Cowboy talking about old times. When he died, his wife, Jackie Autry, was always very gracious to us. She had a box right next to the press box, and she would bring over chocolate cake or cookies to welcome us.

My favorite *town* on the road was Seattle, hands down. Kay and I both liked the town so much that she would often fly out to be with me when we had a series, especially when an off day allowed us to squeeze in a little more time there.

*H*ere I am at the ripe old age of eight in February 1954. What's missing in this picture? *(Courtesy of the author)*

*W*hy am I smiling *(front row, center)*? Because I know the Fillmore Falcons are just the first stop on my way to Yankee Stadium. *(Courtesy of the author)*

*S*enior prom, 1964 . . . and we lived happily ever after. *(Courtesy of the author)*

With that other center fielder from Oklahoma, spring training, 1965.
(Jim Lindstrom)

My first hit in the majors was a home run. September 14, 1965.
(Associated Press)

Me with my super-proud Dad, 1966.
(United Press International)

*T*wo Yankees for life: me and a raw rookie named Thurman Munson in 1970. *(Mike Grosbardt)*

*P*laying center in Yankee Stadium: a job with a lot of history behind it. *(Mike Grosbardt)*

*J*ust another day at work, 1971. *(Mike Grosbardt)*

With Kay, Tori, and Todd at Family Day at Yankee Stadium, 1972. *(Mike Grosbardt)*

Signing a new contract next to general manager Lee MacPhail to join the "100K Club." Funny, a hundred grand seemed like a lot of money in 1973. *(Mike Grosbardt)*

Four for four: On June 24, 1973, I hit four consecutive dingers. Now, if only I'd kept up that pace for the rest of the season . . . *(Mike Grosbardt)*

Murderers Row: Ron Bloomberg, Jim Ray Hart, Thurman Munson, Graig Nettles, Roy White, and me in 1973. *(Mike Grosbardt)*

What time do we tee off? The Oklahoma kid and sweet Lou Piniella, spring training, 1973. *(Jim Vervack)*

$\mathcal{N}$ot lookin' so bad for a guy in exile. *(Jim Lindstrom)*

$\mathcal{M}$y final bow, 1983. Off the field . . . *(Major League Baseball)*

. . . and into the broadcasting booth. Fox Sports broadcaster Curt Menefee and me interviewing Derek Jeter after the Yanks' 2000 World Series win. *(Steve Crandall)*

$\mathcal{M}$y "ringing out" ceremony after my completion of radiation therapy in 2007. *(Courtesy of the author)*

$\mathcal{H}$ome sweet home: with Yogi at the Yankees' Welcome Home Dinner following Opening Day, 2007. *(Courtesy of the author)*

$\mathcal{W}$ith my new teammate Aaron Gaberman in the broadcast booth at Yankee Stadium, Old-Timers' Day, 2007. *(Teri Gaberman)*

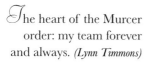

$\mathcal{T}$he heart of the Murcer order: my team forever and always. *(Lynn Timmons)*

A Yankee for life. *(Mike Grosbardt)*

Kay

*S*eattle's a gorgeous place, with a nice, cool climate in the summer. Downtown's good for walking around and people watching. Great stores, great parks. You have the mountains to the east, and the ocean to the west. And you can take various day and half-day excursions to interesting, close-by places. We liked to take the ferryboat ride out to Bainbridge Island. We loved to visit Chittenden Locks, a chain of devices that raise and lower water levels to permit boat traffic between Puget Sound and two nearby freshwater lakes.

There's also a beautiful botanical garden nearby, and a glassed-in area at this fish ladder where you can see these huge salmon swimming upstream during spawning season.

The locals call them the Ballard Locks, for reasons that no local's ever explained to us. And I don't pretend to know how all that raising and lowering gear works. But I do know I could sit there all day and watch all those yachts and barges, sailboats and motorboats and tugs, just about everything but rafts coming and going. Especially if we're sitting outside eating steamers and grilled fish at Ray's Boathouse, where Timmy McCarver introduced us to halibut cheeks.

Not surprisingly, a Murcer description of good places and good times has turned to food.

Seattle now also has a ballpark that's worthy of the town. The Kingdome was a dump, at least for baseball. But Safeco Field is one of the top ballparks in the game, an absolutely first-class 21st-century sporting facility.

So it's not New York, and it's not Oklahoma, but Seattle is a great place to visit.

There's one key member of the Yankee family who sits up in the broadcast booth level but who never speaks directly into a microphone on radio or TV, someone everybody who's been to the Stadium has heard and just about nobody has seen, a man as linked with Yankee tradition as anybody I can think of.

Saying that Bob Sheppard is the PA announcer at Yankee Stadium is sort of like saying the Mississippi is a stream. I can close my eyes and hear that rich, melodious voice—Reggie Jackson once called it the "Voice of God"—rolling out over Yankee Stadium. The first time I would come to the plate in a game, it was always the same: "Batting third for the Yankees, number 1, Bobby Murcer. Center field. Number 1."

Shep has been a Yankee more than 50 years; I've known him 40 years and counting. No question about it, Bob Sheppard is *the* voice of the Yankees.

Let me say one other thing about Bob Sheppard that goes beyond him being legend at Yankee Stadium, with his unique voice and his special way of announcing names and numbers and pitching changes and the like. What a lot of people, including many Yankee fans, may not know is that he was also a longtime professor of English literature at St. John's University in New York. I mean, the man's a scholar!

Every once in a while, Bob would hear a broadcast that I'd done and come to me and tell me, "Bobby, I just want to bring to your attention that you used a word the other day on the telecast, and it's not exactly proper in that context." And then Shep would proceed to give me a little English lesson. (Goodness knows, I could use some educating back then. Still can.) I took it as a mark of his generosity, and I loved it when he would bother to point out any miscues that happened in the broadcast. I'm proud to say that there have been fewer and fewer encounters of that sort as years have gone by.

For a couple of decades, Bob has called me Governor, as in "Governor, you'd be great in the political world." We've talked about issues that I'm interested in, like raising funds for cancer research and my anti-tobacco campaign. (See chapter 17.) And so one day he said, pretty much out of the blue, "You run for governor of Oklahoma, and I'll be your campaign manager. You've got a winning message."

If I ever did run for anything, I would definitely want to have Bob Sheppard on my side, but I've seen too many politicians up close and personal ever to want to be one of them.

———

Another member of the Yankee Stadium institution best known for his work behind a mike was the great Metropolitan Opera baritone Mr. Robert Merrill.

In 1969, my first full season, Mr. Merrill sang the National Anthem on Opening Day at Yankee Stadium for the first time. There would be many encores over the years. Despite my solid roots in country music, I thought his voice was flat-out gorgeous, and I came to look forward to hearing it year after year, first as a player, then as an announcer.

Merrill never lacked for singing gigs at the Met; he took on the Yankee Stadium job for the simple reason that he was a huge Yankee fan. He hadn't always been, though. As a kid growing up in Brooklyn in the 1920s, he was naturally a Dodgers fan. A colleague of mine explained years later how and exactly when Robert Merrill saw the light.

One day the father of his best friend in Brooklyn took a few of the neighborhood boys over to enemy turf, the Bronx, to see a Yankee game. They sat in the right-field bleachers, where the boys silently rooted against the Yankees. Then something truly transformative happened: young Robert Merrill caught a home run ball hit by . . . Babe Ruth.

And that turned him into a Yankee for life.

The pinstripes came in the 1970s, when Mr. Steinbrenner instructed his people to suit up Mr. Merrill with an official uniform top with the number 1½. From then on, he always wore that jersey at Old-Timers' Days when he sang the anthem.

Since I had worn number 1 and number 2 as a Yankee, it was practically inevitable that I got to know number 1½.

Bob was a sweet man. Not surprisingly, he and I talked mostly about baseball, and how the Yankees were doing, and what kind of moves we needed to make. The man knew his baseball; he'd pitched some semipro ball in the late 1930s to earn money to pay for singing lessons.

But he also tried his best to introduce me to his world.

"Bobby, you and Kay need to go see an opera."

Bob, I don't think that's for me.

"C'mon, Bobby. I'll pick one out for you."

Bob, I dunno . . . so how about those Red Sox?

I don't know why I resisted. By the time I got to know Bob, when I was working out of the broadcast booth, Kay and I were dedicated New Yorkers. We'd been to the New York City Ballet, we'd seen a fair amount of theater, and under our daughter Tori's prodding, we had even spent some quality time in museums. But opera? It just didn't seem like a good fit.

Score it E-Murcer for not taking up Robert Merrill's offer to pick out an opera for us.

A baseball fan to the very end, Mr. Merrill died in 2004 while watching game one of the 2004 World Series. I looked up his epitaph on the Internet:

> *Like a bursting celestial star, he showered his family and the world with love, joy, and beauty. Encore please.*

The Yankees haven't yet officially retired number 1½. But they will.

———

As I mentioned in the top of the first, back in the Introduction, about my years behind a microphone, I've been thrilled by many great individual performances (David Cone's perfect game), startled by others (George Brett and the Pine Tar Incident), and continually amazed at the way the game has evolved while retaining its essential, eternal beauty.

But the best part of it all is that I have been able to keep in close touch with the fans, with the game itself, and with my team, the Yankees.

And I owe it all to having the good sense to accept an offer I couldn't refuse nearly 25 years ago.

Oh, and Mattingly, that kid who replaced me on the 25-man roster when I took a hike up to the booth in 1983?

He worked out all right, too.

"MURCER, YOU HUCKLEBERRY!"

*E*very time I think about the Scooter—in case you picked this book up by mistake and need to be told, that would be Philip Francis Rizzuto, Hall of Fame New York Yankee shortstop and longtime broadcaster—I smile. And then I get a little teary because he's no longer with us. But then I smile again when I think how thankful I am for what he gave us, and especially for the time I spent with him in the broadcast booth.

I first met Phil Rizzuto in September 1965 when he introduced himself to me in Washington, D.C. The Yankees were there to play a three-game series with the Senators. As I recall, the broadcast team at the time was Red Barber, Joe Garagiola, and the Scooter. I thought it was pretty classy, this Yankee legend going out of his way to make a raw 19-year-old September call-up feel comfortable. He didn't have to do it; I hadn't even won a place on the 25-man roster yet. But that's the kind of guy Phil always was: generous, unpretentious, down-to-earth.

As most of you surely know, Scooter was a local boy, born and raised in Brooklyn, and Yankee fans embraced him as one of their own, even if he did grow up in that other borough. He played on some of the greatest Yankee teams of all time, and played his way into the hearts of Yankee fans. Later, when he retired and went up to the booth, it was like, one of their own makes good again. He talked their language. He was a *true* Yankee for life.

For a ballplayer, I think one of the greatest things in the world is to play in the same area where you were born and raised, play for your local major league team, and be there for your entire career. Phil did just that.

Scooter and I started working together in the summer of 1983, the day I announced my retirement in a pregame ceremony before a game against the Orioles and then went straight up to join the Scooter, Frank Messer, and Bill White in the broadcast booth for the first pitch. Talk about your quick career transitions—it was the very first time I had ever been in a broadcast booth anywhere. I know I'd have felt a lot more comfortable if I'd still been in my uniform instead of civvies, but Scooter, Frank, and Bill made the transition very easy.

But my first actual taste of what it would one day be like to broadcast baseball games with Phil Rizzuto had come much earlier, way back in the early 1970s, when I was still a player. And it came—literally—out of the blue.

The Yankees were in Kansas City for a night game against the Royals, and Scooter had just asked me a question in a pregame interview. The drill back in those days was for a member of the WPIX broadcast team to do a live interview with a player right before each game. You know, a little pregame teaser with somebody who was on a hot streak, or somebody who has just joined the club, or whatever. This was one of those deals.

Now, as everybody knows, you can get some pretty violent storms out in the Midwest in the summertime, and they often hit without warning, especially in the late afternoon and early evening. In Kansas City that day, it had been hot and hazy, but the forecast hadn't called for any bad weather.

So there we were, the Scooter and me, standing next to the Yankee dugout, live and on the air. Scooter had just asked me his first question, and as he stuck the microphone under my chin for me to answer—*zap!*—this big lightning bolt and clap of thunder hit really close by. Without so much as even a "Holy cow, Murcer!" he flipped the microphone up in the air and bolted for the dugout. (I learned later that Phil was absolutely terrified of thunder and lightning, especially when he had a microphone in his hand.)

Suddenly I'm standing there, the mike's on the grass, the camera's red light is on, we're live, and Scooter's long gone. I thought, Well, what in thunder am I going to do? So I just picked the microphone up off the grass, looked into the camera, answered the question Scooter had put to me, and said "Okay, folks, we'll be back right after this."

Scooter thanked me later for—literally—picking up where he left off. Looking back, I see the incident as my September call-up in broadcasting, and I have Scooter to thank for it.

———

Note: I sat alongside Scooter in the broadcast booth for nearly 10 seasons, during which time we called upward of 1,000 games together, and I accumulated maybe 1 million Scooter memories. ("Oh, these Yankees can get the clutch hits, Murcer. I might have to go home early, I just got a cramp in my leg."—and 999,999 more.) So I've got the goods to bend your ear all season about my dear, departed colleague. But I have to warn you: it's pointless to try to tell Scooter Stories in any kind of logical order, any kind of orderly sequence, because he didn't broadcast that way. He just said whatever came into his mind. That's the way I remember all my Scooter Stories, so let me honor my old and dear friend by recalling a few that way.

———

We were in Detroit one summer night in 1991, Scooter and I were doing radio, and Cecil Fielder was at the plate for the Tigers. Cecil was a big, strong guy who could hit the ball over the moon. Was 6-foot-3, 240—at least that's what the program said. Now, in old Tiger Stadium there in Detroit, you could hardly see a high fly ball in the air from up in the broadcast booth. You had to bend down and look up, really strain your neck to follow the flight of the ball. As you can imagine, it was especially tough during night games.

So this night Fielder hit a ball a mile high in the air. Scooter was doing the play-by-play, and then and there, almost at the crack of the bat, he called it the longest home run in Tiger Stadium history. "Way back . . . out of the ballpark . . . totally over the roof . . . a towering drive"—I mean, I was getting goose bumps.

Next thing you know, Alvaro Espinoza caught the ball. At short.

That's right, the Yankee *shortstop* caught what Scooter had just called the longest home run in Tiger Stadium history.

Scooter goes, "Holy cow, I can't believe . . . That huckleberry! . . . I can't believe this! The shortstop! Murcer! How can the shortstop catch . . . oh, Murcer, I can't talk any more! I can't believe it. Holy cow! You've got to take over."

And he just stopped talking.

Can't blame him, really. He'd just called what may well have been the highest *pop fly* in Tiger history the longest *home run* Detroit had ever seen. No doubt about it, that ball had more hang time than any I'd ever seen before or since. Enough for Phil to dig himself a deep hole and fill it in with words.

It wasn't the first time, and it wouldn't be the last.

═══

One day at Yankee Stadium we were doing a game, and I noticed what I thought was a pipe tobacco can on the table in front of us. We did three innings, and I kept looking at it, and I kept thinking, Well, I don't believe I've ever seen Scooter smoke a pipe, so what could he be doing with pipe tobacco?

Finally, during a commercial break, I asked him, "Scooter, what's with that pipe tobacco can?"

And Scooter said matter-of-factly, "Oh, that's Harry."

And I said, "Harry?"

And he says, "Yeah, my friend Harry." (Scooter told me his last name, but I forget it.) "Harry and I made a pact that if he went before me, I'd bring his ashes here to Yankee Stadium and sprinkle him out in center field. He was a big Yankee fan, and he asked me to do that for him, and so that was what I was going to do."

(Okay, I'm thinking. That's a touching, very Scooter-like thing to do for a friend.)

"But when I showed up earlier today," Scooter went on, "and I started walking out toward center field, the grounds crew chief stopped me and said, 'Scooter, where are you going? What are you doing?'"

(As you can imagine, I didn't know where Scooter was going, either.)

In fact, he was just getting started: "'Look, I promised my friend Harry that I'd sprinkle his ashes out here in center field.' And the crew chief said, 'Well, I can't let you do that.' And I said, 'But I made a pact with Harry, I promised him I'd do this.' But the chief said, 'Scooter, we just can't allow you to do it. If we let everybody who wanted to have his ashes sprinkled here at Yankee Stadium, can you imagine how high it would be?'"

And Scooter said to me, "I couldn't sprinkle his ashes on center field, so that's Harry."

So we broadcast the whole game together: Scooter, me—and Harry.

But every good story, even a Scooter story, has to have an ending. So the next day, I asked my dear friend and mentor, "Say, Scooter, what'd you finally do with Harry?"

"Well, Murcer," he said, "as I was driving home over the GW last night"—that is, the George Washington Bridge, which spans the Hudson River and joins New York and New Jersey—"I was remembering that Harry always liked to fish. So I just pitched him out of the car window into the river. Today Harry's out there on the Hudson, or floating out to sea, depending on the tide."

Yep, that was Scooter.

There was only one downside to working next to Phil in the broadcast booth: I gained weight faster than ever before in my life. And I still blame the Scooter.

My first Opening Day as a Yankee, in 1966, I weighed 160 pounds, soaking wet. That's not much meat to spread over a 5-foot-11 frame. My second Opening Day as a Yankee, in 1969, after two years in the army, I weighed 175–180. That's the weight I played at until I retired and moved up to the broadcast booth in 1983.

Now, I'm a pretty self-disciplined guy, and pretty conscientious about working out, and pretty careful about watching what I eat, and while I knew that when I stopped playing I'd have to be even more careful, I didn't really expect any problems maintaining my *new* playing weight up there in the booth.

I hadn't counted on the Cannoli Factor.

That first couple of seasons I shared the booth with Scooter, he introduced me to all this wonderful Italian food, including all kinds of cheeses and sausages and lasagnas, and always cannolis. Sometimes he'd bring something from home that his lovely wife, Cora, had made. Sometimes it would be a big antipasto platter that a friend of his would send over. It was always good stuff, way better than anything we could get there at the Stadium. But the cannolis, they almost did me in.

We ate before the game. We ate during the game. Sometimes it was like a three-hour, five-course dinner, and always with cannolis, sometimes as dessert, sometimes as a first course, whenever. Boy, I can taste them now.

And before I knew it, I'd put on a good 10 pounds. From 180 to 190—now that's quite a bit *too much* meat for a 5-foot-11 frame, especially since my new job didn't require chasing down balls in the outfield or running the bases.

In my prime, I could have served as a judge in any cannoli contest in town. Because of Scooter, I'd sampled every variety known to man. Multiply 1,000 games by 2.5, a conservative estimate of the number of cannolis I ate per game. Imagine, a kid from the South Side of Oklahoma City becoming a connoisseur of Italian pastry!

If only Scooter had published a *Phil Rizzuto's Cannoli Diet Book*, it would have sold millions—to people looking to bulk up a little.

━━━

Ever hear about Scooter's WW?

If you have, skip on over to the next section. But if you haven't, this Scooter Story starts with the fact that he didn't work with a scorebook up there in the booth. The rest of us did. So far as I know, every other baseball broadcaster in the business does. But not Phil.

Scooter would show up at a game—with not too much time to spare before the first pitch, I might add—and write down a lineup on whatever he had, just a piece of paper, or a napkin, or whatever was handy. That's how he kept score.

Today, of course, broadcasters have laptop computers with access to every stat in the world, and they use a scorebook, complete down to pitch count and ball/strike ratio and pitch location.

That wasn't Scooter's way. I don't know what he did with all those napkins and all those pieces of paper; he probably threw them away as he was on his way out to the parking lot during the seventh inning. But that's how he kept score, and it worked for him. He could always tell you what happened, remind fans in the eighth inning that so-and-so had grounded out to second back in the sixth, everything essential to keep fans abreast of the game.

Scooter would use some of the standard symbols, like K for a strikeout and 4–3 for a grounder to second, that sort of basic stuff. And a little curve over F–7 to remind him that in the batter's previous at-bat he lofted a lazy fly ball to left. Nothing elaborate, but enough for Scooter to track the game and keep fans informed and involved.

Once, though, after longtime sidekick Bill White returned to the booth after a bathroom break or something, he asked Scooter, "Did I miss anything?" Bill had missed a couple of batters, so Phil said, "Oh, yeah, White. Go ahead. Look over my scorecard." It was on a napkin or something, and it was pretty clear, except that

Bill didn't recognize one symbol that Scooter had written down there: "WW."

So Bill asked Scooter, "I haven't seen that before, what does WW mean?"

And the Scooter told him: "Wasn't Watching."

══════

Very early in my broadcasting career, maybe a week or 10 days after I retired as a player and went up to the booth, Scooter and I were paired up. We were supposed to be doing the seventh, eighth, and ninth innings on TV. So just before we took over, Scooter asked me if I wanted a cup of coffee and I said, "Well, yeah, thanks," and he said, "I'll be right back." So he got up just before the beginning of the eighth inning and took off to get us some coffee.

That's the last I saw of him that night.

I'd never done play-by-play before, but that was okay, I could watch the ball game and explain what viewers had just seen take place on the TV screens. The problem was that I'd never done any of the other necessary components of a telecast—announcements and lead-ins to ads and promo stuff and the schedule for the rest of the week—that a broadcast team normally would do. And, of course, I'd never worked solo.

By the middle of the eighth, it dawned on me that Scooter was probably on the GW Bridge heading home, which in fact he was. So I did the rest of the game, got through it somehow.

The next day, I got up to the booth, and a few minutes later here came Scooter with a cup in his hand: "Here's your coffee, Murcer."

I learned quickly enough that Scooter often left the ballpark early, but when he didn't, he'd sometimes sort of just disappear anyway. He'd mess up a play or something and go, "Oh, Murcer, Murcer. I can't talk anymore. You're going to have to take it from here."

Talk about your initiation into broadcasting!

Phil made his major league debut in 1941 and took his last at-bat in 1956. That made him a relic, a piece of ancient history to today's ballplayers, most of whom seem to think that the game of baseball was invented about a week before they tied on their first pair of spikes.

They'll stand on the dugout steps on Old-Timers' Day and go, "Who *are* those old dudes?" Rizzuto? The announcer guy? Didn't he used to play for the Yankees?

That's understandable. They don't mean any disrespect. It's just that we live in a fast-moving age, lightning fast compared to when I was breaking in, much less the era when Scooter was building his collection of championship rings.

"Old" to some guys today is last night's highlight tapes.

One huge exception to that generalization is Derek Jeter. Almost alone among his contemporaries, Derek demonstrates his respect for the players who came before him by taking the trouble to learn about their accomplishments. The Scooter retired from the booth after Jeter's 1996 rookie season, but I know he loved to watch Jeter play. In turn, Derek knew all about Scooter, about what a great Yankee he'd been.

Sometimes you'd see them standing side by side—Jeter at 6-foot-3, Scooter maybe 5-foot-6 when he stretched—and you'd wonder if they came from the same planet, much less whether they played the same position in the same game. Jeter was always ribbing Scooter about that, but deep down Derek knows that Scooter had to have been pretty doggone good to have played as well and as long as he did, despite being somewhat vertically challenged.

Scooter Rizzuto and Derek Jeter, two Yankee shortstops for the ages.

Who knows what critics would do today with the Scooter style of broadcasting, but it wasn't a "style," really. All the birthdays and the hellos and leaving early to beat the traffic, and the "special" way he called certain plays—that was certainly no act, no "style." It was just Scooter being Scooter.

The man knew the game. He knew it inside and out. And he gave his listeners plenty of baseball. But he also gave them plenty of entertainment along the way, because he believed, instinctively, that you're supposed to have fun watching (or listening to) a game.

Why would they call it a "game" in the first place if you weren't supposed to enjoy it?

Fans loved listening to Phil. They loved him for doing his best to bring them a good time. And at the end of the day, isn't that all that matters, having a good time at the ol' ball game?

———

Funny thing, I sat next to Phil Rizzuto in the broadcast booth for more than a decade, and he and I played a ton of golf at charity events over the years. But in all that time, I never, ever suspected that Scooter lived a whole secret life—as a poet.

That's right, a poet.

Back in 1993, Ecco Press published a slim paperback book titled *O Holy Cow!* The subtitle: *The Selected Verse of Phil Rizzuto.*

The selected *what*?

Holy cow!

Editors Tom Peyer and Hart Seely created *O Holy Cow!* by taking transcripts of actual WPIX telecasts, selecting passages of comments Scooter said on air, and recasting them—word for word—as 94 poems.

Roy Blount, Jr., only one of the funniest writers on the face of the planet, contributed an introduction.

(Note: A new edition of *O Holy Cow!* was published by Ecco Press in March 2008 with a new introduction by some huckleberry named Bobby Murcer.)

It finally made sense. All those times that Scooter would come out with something out of left field and then turn to me and say, "So what do you think, Murcer?" That was just him road-testing a new sonnet. And those many occasions when he'd leave the booth after the seventh inning to "grab a cup of coffee" or "stretch his legs"? Must've been because he felt he did some of his best poetizing in his car heading back to his New Jersey home and his beloved Cora.

At least one poem in *O Holy Cow!*, called "Asylum," I remember as clearly as if it were yesterday. (It was actually June 17, 1992, Yankees–Red Sox in Boston, Roger Clemens pitching to Mel Hall in the sixth. Two outs, bases empty, Sox up 2–1.)

> *Got some chocolate-chip cookies here*
> *Murcer.*
> *So don't ask me any questions*
> *For a batter or so.*
> *All right?*

Many of the selections will make you scratch your head—as, for instance, "Colorado," presented here in its entirety:

> *They're having more snow*
> *Out in Colorado.*
> *Which is not in Montana.*
> *But it is not far from Montana.*

But my favorite—it still makes me cry—Scooter "wrote" on August 6, 1979. That was the terrible day the Yankees flew out to Canton, Ohio, in the morning to bury our captain and my best friend, Thurman Munson, and then flew back to play the Orioles in Yankee Stadium.

Scooter's poem that night is called "The Man in the Moon." Here are the last two stanzas:

> *You know, it might,*
> *It might sound a little corny,*
> *But we have the most beautiful full moon tonight.*
> *And the crowd,*
> *Enjoying whatever is going on right now.*

They say it might sound corny,
But to me it's some kind of a
Like an omen.

Both the moon and Thurman Munson,
Both ascending up into heaven.
I just can't get it out of my mind.
I just saw that full moon,
And it just reminded me of Thurman.
And that's it.

If there's a Hall of Fame for poets, Scooter belongs in that one, too.

ME AND MICK

$\mathcal{M}$ickey Mantle was going out when I was coming in. I shared clubhouse space with him for a month when I was called up in September 1965, went through one spring training with him in 1966, and started the 1966 season as his teammate. But that year I was up with the Yankees only briefly before being sent down to Toledo, and the following two years I was in the U.S. Army. By the time I got back, Mick had retired, so I didn't get to know him that well when we were both players.

Mick and I only became friends after I retired in 1983, but in that all-too-short period before his death in 1995 at the age of 63, we became very close. We played a lot of golf together, talked a lot of baseball, and compared Oklahoma accents. I miss him.

He stayed with the Yankees as a part-time coach after he retired. He would be with us in spring training as a special adviser. And later, he and I were in the broadcast booth together briefly for SportsChannel.

The year (1986) that we partnered up in the booth was one strange trip. Mickey was a no-holds-barred guy. He was liable to say anything. By comparison with the Mick, Scooter was Mr. Smooth.

The best example of Mick's tell-it-like-it-is approach came a couple of years later, shortly after he opened a restaurant in Manhattan called Mickey Mantle's Restaurant and Sports Bar. When I say "opened," I really mean that he lent his name to the joint. Anyway, it was a fairly upscale restaurant in a definitely upscale neighborhood—on Central Park South, between the Ritz-Carlton and Park Lane hotels. Still there, as a matter of fact. Draws a lot of tourists.

Anyway, Mickey Mantle's had just opened, and I told Mick before a game we were doing together that he ought to plug the place on air. "Sure," he said, "why not?"

And so, during the game, I said something like, "Mickey, I know you've got your new restaurant open now. How are things going?" Mick said, yeah, he did, and it was great, and they were doing really well down there, and he enjoyed going and greeting the guests.

But then he got a little specific: "As a matter of fact, Whitey and I were there for lunch this afternoon. We both ordered steaks, and Whitey's steak was as tough as shoe leather. It was the worst thing you've ever . . ."

This caught me way off guard, and I start gesturing to him and running my finger across my throat, trying to stop him from saying all this negative stuff about his own restaurant on the air. But Mick, he just kept going, saying how Whitey couldn't chew his steak, it was so tough, and how he couldn't even cut his, and on and on.

Finally there was a third out, and during the commercial break I said to him, "Mick, you shouldn't be saying that about your own restaurant, even if it was bad." And he said, "Aw, well, that's just the way it was."

The next day when he came in I asked him, "Did you get any feedback from your partners about what you said on the air last night?" And he said, "Boy, did I. I got myself in a heap of trouble. They got all over me for talking about the steak being tough. You better not be asking me any more questions about the place."

But that was Mick. He was going to tell you exactly how he felt, answer any question you asked him as straight as he could. Didn't matter one whit if it cast him in a bad light.

What you saw was what you got with Mickey. Sometimes he got himself in hot water being so blunt, but I think his willingness to tell it how he saw it was his strongest quality.

By the way, I can tell you from personal experience—and Kay agrees—that the food at Mickey Mantle's has improved tenfold since Mick cut loose on air. The restaurant is now 20 years old and going strong.

═══════

As I mentioned back in chapter 3, there were many superficial similarities between our early careers. Both of us were young kids from Oklahoma. Both of us had been signed by the same scout, Tom Greenwade. Both of us were 19 when we first made the 25-man roster. Both of us came up as shortstops. Both of us got moved to center field. And both of us were power hitters, the only difference being that Mickey's power took the ball *over* the fence a lot more often than mine did.

Then there was the fact that I was a lefty all the way while Mick was a switch-hitter. And as Yogi once observed, "Mickey can hit just as good right-handed as he can left-handed. He's just naturally amphibious."

Early on, reporters used to ask me, "Well, what's it like, being compared to Mickey Mantle?" And I said, "Well, I'm not worried about being compared to Mickey Mantle; I'm worried about what *Mickey* thinks about me being compared to him."

Later in my career, and even after I retired, I still got asked if I had felt a lot of pressure in the early days from all those expectations that I was going to be the "next Mickey Mantle."

My answer was always the same: "Are you nuts?"

Okay, maybe I said it more politely, but that's the way I felt. Sure, it was flattering to be considered in the same ballpark as him, but there was only one Mickey Mantle—the guy with seven championship rings (1951, 1952, 1953, 1956, 1958, 1961, 1962), three MVP awards (1956, 1957, 1962), and one Triple Crown (1956).

Oh, and speaking of numbers, consider this one: Mickey hit 536 homers in 18 seasons, while I hit 252 in 17.

Ralph Houk hit the nail on the head: "You don't replace people like Mickey Mantle."

But if I never did become the next Mickey Mantle, I did become the next occupant of the one and only Mickey Mantle's locker in the Yankee clubhouse.

That was thanks to the oldest Yankee of them all.

———

Mickey retired in 1968, and I came back from the army in 1969. When we got back up to Yankee Stadium after spring training, I discovered to my delight that my new locker in the Yankee clubhouse was . . . Mickey's old locker!

Legendary clubhouse manager Pete Sheehy, who was in charge of such critical matters as locker assignments and uniform numbers, explained how it had happened: "Mickey came to me at the end of the season and said, 'Pete, how about you just give my locker to Bobby.'" As simple as that. Talk about being blown away—I couldn't have dreamed of a better kickoff to my first full season as a Yankee.

Every Old-Timers' Day until Yankee Stadium was shut down after the 1973 season for renovations, Mickey would always come to his old locker—*our* locker—and dress there or hang his coat or whatever he needed to do. Talk about making me feel proud to be a Yankee!

When Yankee Stadium reopened in 1976, the lockers in the clubhouse had been completely remodeled. I could have shown you where Mickey's locker—our locker—had been, but it wasn't the same. Now it was just floor space, not a special place.

(As an aside, the locker I had when I came back to the Yankees in 1979 in the new, remodeled stadium is where Derek Jeter now lockers. It's right next to where Thurman Munson lockered. And those, too, will be gone after the current Yankee Stadium gives way to the new one in 2009.)

I certainly never put myself on the same pedestal that Mickey Mantle so richly deserved, but I've got to tell you: it felt pretty good to lace up my cleats while sitting at his locker.

———

Mickey Charles Mantle was a bona fide, genuine, truly good guy. He was also an incredibly generous man. In his speech at the dedication of the Mickey Mantle Memorial statue in 1998 at the Bricktown Ballpark in Oklahoma City, Tony Kubek said that Mickey would have been the richest man ever to come out of Oklahoma—including all those oil barons—if he hadn't picked up so many restaurant checks and bar tabs over the years. So true. As Tony also said, Mickey was generous with his praise of his teammates and his treatment of rookies. I can speak to that last attribute from firsthand experience.

How generous? Nobody rooted harder for Roger Maris than the Mick did in 1961 when they were both chasing Babe Ruth's home run record. I'm guessing that Mickey was every bit as happy that Roger got to 61 as he would have been if he himself had.

Even though he owns a piece of the Diamondbacks, Billy Crystal is one of the biggest Yankee fans in the world, and in 2001 he directed a made-for-TV movie called *61*. The subject, of course, was the home run race in 1961 between Mickey and Roger Maris.

I loved the movie from first pitch to last out, and I also learned something that I hadn't known before: Mickey and Roger lived together that summer in an apartment in Queens. Talk about taking the home run race home from work!

After Mickey retired, you can just imagine how in demand he was for appearances and signings and memorabilia shows. He had one stipulation: old Yankee buddies Hank Bauer and Bill "Moose" Skowron had to be included as well. He wanted them to get a payday along with him.

(And yet Mickey was always a little embarrassed by his own celebrity. He never could understand why so many people sought him out for autographs.)

Being a good teammate—to Mickey, that was the highest honor he could aspire to. Not long before his death on August 13, 1995, Mick videotaped a message to be played on Old-Timers' Day, which he was unable to attend because he was too ill. In it, he said his number one goal had always been to be a "great teammate."

From the unanimous testimony of guys he played with a lot longer than I did, he more than lived up to that goal. The way he treated people explains why guys like Clete Boyer and Tom Tresh named sons after Mickey.

Yes, Mick, you were a great teammate.

If he hadn't been a pretty fair country ballplayer, Mickey would have made a great scout. During spring training in 1966, after watching me take some grounders at shortstop, he told Kubek that "This kid's going to make a great outfielder some day." Tony pressed him on that assessment a little, and Mickey was happy to explain: "The Yankees will lose money if they play this young man at shortstop. I've watched him field a dozen ground balls and throw to first. They're not going to be able to sell out the first-base boxes at Yankee Stadium with him out there. With that arm he'll pick off five or six paying customers a game."

Mick might also have made a great hitting instructor if he'd put his mind to it. The year he coached first base for the Yankees (1971), he got on my case in spring training about bunting more—or at least faking a bunt: "You'll get the infielders cheating in a couple of steps." He said I was robbing myself of 20–25 hits a year by not using the bunt as a weapon. I knew that he'd been a great bunter himself early in his career when he still had two good legs, so I took his advice. The result: I hit .331 that year, my career best, and 54 points higher than my career average.

In that fine speech in 1998, in which he praised Mickey's generosity, Tony said a lot of things that every Yankee present that day felt in his heart:

> *Mickey never put himself on an unreachable pedestal. He was a humble man. He didn't have a phony bone in his body. He always put winning before personal achievement. He was selfless in his approach to the game. He had an abiding love and respect for baseball, its players, and all for which it once stood.*

Mick was also one of the best golf buddies you could ever have in your foursome. We played many, many times over the years—often to raise money for various charities—but the one round I'll always treasure the most is the day I got a hole-in-one at Barton Creek in Austin. Mickey Jr. was part of our group that day, too, and I have some great pictures of us celebrating the historic event.

Let me tell you, the man could hit a golf ball just about as far as anybody this side of John Daly. It didn't always go where he wanted it to, but until he became ill toward the end, Mick could definitely go deep.

The part of golf that gave Mick the most trouble, I'm sad to say, was the 19th hole. It was really hard to watch the liquor take hold of him, as it did increasingly over the years.

You've undoubtedly heard what Mickey once said about his condition, referring indirectly to his struggles with alcohol, but I'm going to repeat it here because it captures Mickey's self-mocking sense of humor: "If I'd known I was going to live so long, I'd have taken better care of myself."

(One of Mickey's golf buddies, former University of Texas and Detroit Lions great Bobby Layne, who also died in part as a result of alcohol abuse, is supposed to have said it first. Doesn't matter. Mickey always had an ear for a great line.)

According to Yankees who played ball with Mick, booze spurred an interest in meteorology. He would call the weather bureau after a game to get the next day's forecast. If there was a 30 percent or higher chance of rain predicted for the next day, he knew he could "toss back a few extra ones" that night since the next day's game might be called. More often than not, of course, the weatherman got it wrong. Didn't matter. Mick would go ahead and play his heart out even though he wasn't quite, ah, 100 percent.

———

Back in the 1980s, Kay and I attended several of the Mickey Mantle Charity Golf Classic events held at Shangri-La Resort near Grand Lake in northeastern Oklahoma. Mickey had partnered up with the Make-A-Wish Foundation, which helped bring in many big-name athletes from all areas of sports. You couldn't swing a five-iron without clipping a hall of famer in one sport or another. The local people from that part of the state loved playing golf and rubbing elbows with Mickey and his all-star cast. To-gether, they raised a ton of money over the years.

I remember that throughout the two days of those events Mickey was always very accessible, very affable—and by the end of each evening, always very "over-served." At those moments, when his alcoholism was so painfully evident to his adoring public and close friends, I wished for Mickey some privacy, but—who knows?—being by himself might have only made it worse for him.

I'm sad to say that one terrifically upsetting moment will always stand out in my memory. On the first night of each of those events, a big talent show and dinner took place. Well, this one time, Mickey spoke briefly, and then an assortment of performers put on a show. One highlight was when Stan Musial popped up on stage and played a tune or two on his harmonica.

Then, at Mickey's request, Roy Clark sang "Yesterday When I Was Young," and Mick pulled a chair to the center of the dance floor and sat there alone, looking very sad, very lonely. I just hated seeing Mickey look so vulnerable. I knew another side to him, the funny, self-mocking, shy country boy, and I wished *that* Mickey could be the only one the public would see.

Mickey loved that song so much that he asked Roy to sing at his funeral. Roy honored that request in 1995, when Mickey died at the age of 63.

I'm sad Mickey's life ended so soon, before he could reap the benefits of his newfound sobriety and his work as a spokesperson for the Mickey Mantle Donor Awareness Foundation. Boy, we just never know what kind of curveball is headed our way, do we? But he will always remain a sports hero, a mentor, and a special friend to me.

As I said after his funeral, if Mickey Mantle was your friend, it was for life.

A FAMILY AFFAIR

*A*nybody who's ever had a Little Leaguer or two around the house knows that baseball can take over a family's life for part of the summer. Driving kids to practice and picking them up, taking them to games and picking them up, serving as everything from equipment manager to groundskeeper to third-base coach—all that eats into your day.

Multiply that by 100, and you get a sense of how professional baseball can dominate a family's schedule.

"Normal" hours for a baseball family might look a little crazy to a nonbaseball family. For instance, if I had a night game at Yankee Stadium, Kay and the kids would arrive at the ballpark at 8 or 8:30. (I'd have come out at about 3 with some of the other players who lived in North Jersey.) Then, assuming the game didn't go into extra innings, we'd all leave together at 10:30 or so and head on out . . . to dinner.

If we hadn't followed this wacky schedule, with dinner at 11 or 11:30, we'd never have been able to sit down for a family meal together for six months of the year.

Kay

*T*he kids and I didn't go to watch the game, really. For us, it was mainly a social thing. Oh, we'd pay attention when Bobby came to bat, but we didn't follow the action pitch by pitch.

When Tori and Todd were little, they weren't sure what was going on, except that it was loud and they got to run around.

Later, when they were older, going to a game meant they got to hang out with friends they'd made among the other players' kids. Sometimes I wouldn't even see them for innings at a time, only when they dropped by for money for the concession stand.

Sometimes, during our second time around with the Yankees when Tori and Todd went from children to teenagers, we'd drive into Manhattan to the Carnegie Deli after a game for one of their giant hot pastrami sandwiches on rye. Most times, though, we'd stop off at one of our favorite all-night diners in New Jersey. Either way, we wouldn't get to bed until 1:30 or 2, and then we'd all sleep in till 10:30 or so.

When I was on the road, the kids got to bed somewhat earlier, but they'd often stay up to watch the Yankee game on TV—or so they assured me.

The trade to San Francisco changed a bunch of things, of course, but one really big change was that it cut back on the number of games that Kay would bring the kids to. It was just too cold for them, especially in the early part of the season. And so if we were playing a night game, there wouldn't be any of those late-night Murcer family dinners.

Kay

*F*ollowing a night game, when Bobby was sleeping in, my job was to keep the kids quiet. Once they got to be four or five, they understood. Sort of. But there was a lot of shushing and tiptoeing in our household, let me tell you.

One Saturday morning when Todd was four, I heard a little hum coming from the other side of the house, where our bedroom was. We lived in Fort Lee, New Jersey, upstairs in a two-family house, and the owners, an older couple who lived down below, were always complaining about the kids running around and making noise. So we had to try to keep a four-year-old and a five-year-old really quiet all the time— Mission Impossible!

Anyway, I went to investigate, and just as I was rounding the corner of the hallway, I heard Todd give out a loud whisper: "There he is!" Our bedroom door was ajar, and outside it Todd and four or five neighborhood boys were huddled down and peering in.

Seems that Todd was conducting his own little private tour: "See, that's the Yankees' center fielder!"

The funny thing was that back then Bobby slept in the buff. I told Todd, after I'd hustled everybody to the other side of the house, "No more show-and-tell!"

Thank goodness, Bobby didn't wake up. If he had, Todd might have tried to get his dad to sign autographs!

Through age five, the kids were always with me and Kay, from spring training through the last out in September. After they started going to school, Kay would stay with them back in Oklahoma the duration of the school year, from September 1 through the end of May, when the three of them would come up and join me.

Once the season ended, of course, we'd all head back to Oklahoma, where we'd go back to an early-to-bed, early-to-rise-routine. The only one of us to resist that flip-flop, who to this day remains a dedicated night owl, was Tori. She fine-tuned that up-at-all-hours routine in the 14 years or so she lived in New York and after graduating from the Fashion Institute of Technology.

Between 1969 and 1983, we lived in nine different houses, seven of them rentals. We did buy a condo in Chicago (1978) and a house in New Jersey (1979) the second time around with the

Yankees, and we did stay in a couple of New Jersey places twice.

Confusing? Yeah, I suppose, but that comes with the turf when you're a ballplayer and you have a family and your home base is in a different time zone from your home clubhouse.

———

Family Day at Yankee Stadium was a big hit every year. The kids wore little uniforms with their dad's number on the back. Each family was introduced on the field, and a quick three-inning game allowed the kids to hit and run the bases. Clowns cavorted around to keep the smaller kids happy.

Kay captured a lot of those fun and games on a trusty old camcorder, and has since transferred everything to DVDs. (It will come as no surprise to learn that she heads the Information Technology division of the Murcer household.) Of course, our grandkids will probably grow up playing soccer, and may never know what a DH is, but at least they'll be able to see their parents having fun when they were little.

Back in 1972, when Todd was just shy of three years old, a photographer from the *New York Daily News* took a shot of him crouched down at third base, holding a glove almost as big as he was, looking as intent and serious as Graig Nettles ever did. The photo made the front page of the paper the following day. Today, it has a position of honor in the Murcer Family Album.

One of Todd's uniform tops from those years made a comeback on Old-Timers' Day in July 2007. Once again, number 1 was proudly worn by a Murcer in Yankee Stadium—this time by Todd's son, Jack (age four), our oldest grandson.

———

I played for Billy Martin for only parts of two seasons, 1979 and 1983, and I know he had a lot of personal troubles, but I always respected him for his attitude toward the kids of players. Most major league teams permit male members of players' families to come into the clubhouse only after games. Billy's policy was far more generous. He allowed the sons of players to come into the clubhouse before games, play around in the bullpen and even on the field if they got there early enough, and hang out in the passageway behind the dugouts during games.

Mr. Steinbrenner continued that policy even after he fired Billy following the 1979 season. He recognized that it helped build a strong family attachment to the team, and Mr. Steinbrenner had the vision to know that building team spirit would contribute to turning the Yankees into winners again.

Billy's open-door policy was a big reason that, after I returned to the Yankees in 1979, Todd came to almost every home game the rest of my career. I'm pretty sure that if he'd been required to sit up in the family section, Todd would have stayed home in New Jersey the way Tori often did when she became a teenager. As a consequence, Todd and I got to spend a lot more time together, driving to and from games, and seeing each other in the clubhouse.

Yankee players with young sons had Billy to thank for initiating that policy, and Mr. Steinbrenner for recognizing its positive impact on the team.

Kay

*L*ate in the 1973 season, just after Todd turned four, I took him and Vinny, one of his little friends from our neighborhood, and Vinny's mother to a Saturday afternoon game at the Stadium. After the game was over, I walked the boys down to the clubhouse entrance, the attendant there called Bobby, and Bobby led the boys on into the clubhouse. That was the standard drill.

I rejoined the group of players' wives and family members up by a Stadium exit at the top of the ramp leading down to the clubhouse. That's where we always waited and chatted while our men showered and dressed.

After 20 minutes or so, players started up the ramp in ones and twos. Pretty soon I spotted Bobby—he was always dressed and out pretty quick unless reporters cornered him to talk about the game—and by his side were Todd and Vinny. Then all of a sudden, Vinny saw us and started racing up the ramp as fast as his little legs could carry him. I'll never forget what happened next.

"Ma! Ma!" Vinny screamed at the top of his lungs as he reached us. "Mama, [Player X] has a giant wiener, a giant wiener! It's this big!" And the little dear held his hands up about two feet apart.

Needless to say, everybody burst into gales of laughter.

Vinny was a little older than Todd, but too young to adhere to the Yankee policy posted on the inside of the main door in big, bold letters so that it was the last thing a player saw every time he left:

WHAT YOU SEE HERE, SAY HERE, DO HERE, STAYS HERE.

The family section at Yankee Stadium was in the lower grandstand, behind home plate toward the first-base side up behind the box seats, and extending just beyond the edge of the backstop. Wives would come with the kids, even babies, knowing they could depend on a built-in network of support from other players' wives. There was also a small corps of teenage girls—mostly from the Bronx, I guess—who came over from other sections and congregated around the family section and served as de facto babysitters once we got to know them.

On a warm summer evening, particularly if we'd just returned from a long road trip, there'd be 30 or 40 family members and kids up there. You'd come to the on-deck circle for your first at-bat, look up and spot your family, and give a little nod. It was great just to see them.

The kids had a ball. They weren't about to sit still for nine innings, of course, but between the ushers watching over them, the "babysitters" always around, and more than one set of mothers' eyes on them, they could move around and make friends and, best of all, pay frequent visits to the concession area behind the seats.

By the third inning, Kay assured me, a whole gang of fun would have broken out back of the stands.

Kay

*T*hat feeling of being together, of taking care of each other, was super-important. We were out in a big public place, and unless you made your kids sit right next to you the entire ball game, you couldn't keep your eyes on them the whole time.

Because we were all together as one really big family, that didn't bother me, but it sure bothered my mother back in Oklahoma.

In the summer of 1973 there had been a spate of kidnappings of little kids from upper-middle-class neighborhoods in New Jersey, and as soon as it made the national news, my mother was on the horn to me: "You be sure to tell Tori and Todd they must never, never tell their names to strangers at the ballpark. You don't want somebody taking them for ransom."

I'd already thought of that, of course, but being a dutiful daughter, I reminded them never to tell their last names to any strangers at the ballpark who asked them.

Next thing you know, Todd is coming back from the concession stand with one of his babysitters with this big smile on his face. He runs up to me and says, proud as a peacock, "Mom, I did just like you told me. A man buying popcorn asked me if one of the Yankees was my dad, and I said yes, and he said which one, and I said Graig Nettles!"

At one game Todd, about four years old at the time, was sitting on the lap of our good friend Bob Halloran, in a seat on the aisle in the family section. "Can you get me a foul ball, Uncle Bob?" Todd started saying even before the first pitch of the game. "Catch me a foul ball, *please!*"

Bob said he'd do what he could, and they settled in to watch the game.

Bottom of the first, an ice cream vendor with a big white box strapped to his shoulders came by. Todd wanted an ice cream sandwich, naturally, and Uncle Bob was happy to get one for him. The ice cream vendor flipped open the lid of his box at the same instant that—*crack!*—a foul pop sailed up into the stands and landed . . . smack-dab in the middle of the ice cream box.

Bob, who was getting his change from the ice cream sandwich, grabbed the ball just before a scrum of fans descended on the spot fighting to get a souvenir. Nobody was hurt in the melee, but the poor vendor's box got knocked six ways to Sunday, with ice cream sandwiches flying everywhere.

The batter who sliced that weak pop up?

Number 1 for the New York Yankees, Bobby Murcer.

Kay

Todd held on to that ball for dear life all through the first four or five innings. Then, sometime in the middle of the game, he and I went back to the concession area. As I was paying for our popcorn, I heard Todd say, "Hey, you want a baseball?" And he handed the ball to another kid in line behind us.

"Why did you do that, Todd?" I asked him when we got back to our seats.

"I could tell he wanted it," Todd said, "and Daddy can hit me another one."

As Kay and I were thinking about this chapter and the role baseball played in our family life, she suggested that I ask Tori and Todd what memories they had of growing up as baseball brats. So we asked them both, tell us off the top of your head what you remember from those days. Not big games or special moments necessarily, but just whatever comes to mind.

Here's what they had to say.

Tori

I remember Mom doing needlepoint in the stands all the time and not really paying attention to the game . . . fans coming up to us and asking for autographs . . . cruising the Stadium for cute boys . . . hanging out after the game with other families in the family room . . .

counting the number of multiple back handsprings Kenny Griffey (he was just a little kid!) would do outside the locker room . . . playing Truth or Dare and Spin the Bottle while waiting for our dads to come out of the locker room . . . staying up REALLY late and eating at the Carnegie Deli at midnight.

I remember Dad sleeping in until noon . . . eating fried bologna sandwiches, his favorite . . . the boy who sent me a letter after seeing me on Bobby Murcer Day in 1983 after Dad retired (Flash: That boy is now a man who works for MLB.) . . . getting ice cream at that little place in Franklin Lakes we loved and seeing Brooke Shields there once, shopping at the malls . . . seeing Dad walking through the stands to our seats and being cheered by people at the last game of the World Series; this was the first time he'd ever sat in the stands to watch a game . . . being away from the ballpark, at a mall or something, and having fans freak out when they noticed Dad like he was some big celebrity.

Todd, being a boy, of course had the advantage of getting to hang out in the clubhouse and in the runway behind the dugouts during games.

Todd

I remember playing bumper pool with Billy Martin after he got thrown out of a game . . . fighting with the other kids over the chocolate-chip cookies he'd bring into the clubhouse for us . . . listening with a bunch of kids to Pete Sheehy talking about Babe Ruth and DiMaggio and Mickey Mantle and all the Yankee greats—and finding a coat hanger hooked on the back loop of my pants after I walked away (that was one of Pete's favorite tricks) . . . seeing Luís Tíant roller skate up and down the passageway behind the dugouts in nothing but his jockstrap and a big cigar in his mouth, with a Speak & Spell in his hand so he could study English . . . eating all the junk they had laid out for the players . . . sitting around and listening to Ron Guidry play drums. (He was cool.)

I remember playing in the batting cages before games . . . driving back with Dad late at night through the Bronx after a game and kids coming up with rags to clean the car windows at street corners (one threw a hubcap at the car once after Dad didn't roll down his window to give them money) . . . rubbing down game balls with mud in the umpires' room after they showed us how . . . taking tape and sanitary socks from the trainer's room to make a ball so that we could play scrub with it underneath the stadium during the game . . . stopping when a loud noise erupted and running down to the grounds crew's dugout to see what was going on . . . scoring a brand-new set of golf clubs that Dad gave me after Bobby Murcer Day in 1983 . . . being awed by Kenny as he'd go back-flipping up and down the passageway under the grandstand . . . telling Dad on the way home one night that Kenny was "the greatest athlete I'd ever seen."

Even though baseball enriched our lives in many, many ways, we all paid a big price for being away from home six months of the year, and having to build a new home in a different place every summer. I missed a whole lot of Tori's and Todd's growing up. I missed way more dance recitals and Little League games than I ever saw, and I don't think spring vacations every year in Florida made up for that. They sure didn't for me.

But it worked out pretty good all around, I think.

After a semester at the University of Oklahoma, Tori went to the Parsons School of Design and the Fashion Institute of Technology in New York. She worked in New York for 14 years doing PR for the likes of Calvin Klein and Anne Klein before getting married and starting her own family. (She also did unpaid volunteer work as our own personal guide to the Big Apple. Without her, all we'd know is that the Bronx is up and the Battery's down, and that people ride in a hole in the ground.)

Todd went to the University of Oklahoma on a golf scholarship and earned his BA with a major in economics. Later, he got his MBA from Boston University. He played a couple of years on the mini-tour circuit before deciding to go get a real job and restrict his golf to taking money off his old man. He's now a director of a small firm in the telecom business.

They're both happily married to wonderful people, and between them Tori and Todd have given Kay and me five wonderful grandchildren. Not even Mr. Steinbrenner could ask for a better starting nine than that.

PINSTRIPE ALL-STARS,
1969–TODAY

M y New York Yankee All-Star Team (1969–today) is
almost certainly going to cause a little buzz among
Yankee fans, each of whom most likely has a favorite
or two I'm going to have to pass over. (Let's hear it, Steve Balboni
fans.)

So have a look. And while you're doing that, I'm going to go
unlist my telephone number.

Starting Lineup

C   **THURMAN MUNSON**. A no-brainer, at least in my heart.
Thurman's my captain, and always will be. Can't leave
your captain off your All-Yankee team. The AL Rookie
of the Year in 1970, when Thurm and I first really got to
know each other, and the AL MVP in 1976, when he led

the Yankees to the AL pennant while I was trying to figure out the wind in Wrigley Field. I miss him to this day.

C   JORGE POSADA. Head and shoulders, the best all-around catcher in baseball today. He and Yogi are the only Yankee catchers in history to hit 30 home runs in a season. He's a switch-hitter with a lifetime .277 BA. Since 2000, he's driven in more runs—603—than any catcher in the game. He's a terrific defensive catcher and a leader. He turns 37 in August 2008, and that's a little long in the tooth for a guy who dons the tools of ignorance every day, but the Yankees would be nuts to let him walk.

Q: Hey, Murcer, you got two catchers in your starting lineup? What's going on?

A: It's my team. Get used to it.

1B   DON MATTINGLY. Remember this about the Hit Man: he owns *nine* Gold Gloves. He may well be the greatest fielder at his position that baseball has ever seen. Anybody with that kind of talent around the bag *and* Yankee Stadium power *and* a .307 lifetime BA can play first base for me any day of the week, and twice on Sundays (in the unlikely event that baseball ever returns to Sunday doubleheaders).

2B   WILLIE RANDOLPH. Look up the definition of "solid" in the dictionary and you'll find a picture of Willie. Turned the DP better than any second baseman I've ever seen.

Think baseball's not a contact sport? Try being the second baseman trying to turn a 6–4–3 on a medium hard grounder to short with a fast base runner on first. You've got your back turned to a guy barreling up behind you trying to knock you into left field, and you can't waver for a nanosecond, even if that guy's Kirk Gibson. Willie was utterly fearless in such situations.

SS   DEREK JETER. My pick at shortstop for the Pinstripe All-Stars, 1969–today, is also my pick as the best shortstop in all of baseball in that time frame. He can hit, he can run, he can field, and, most important, he can lead. Of all the Yankees today, he's the most knowledgeable—and most respectful—of the great Yankees of history.

Got a legacy you want guarded and honored? Derek's your man.

3B   ALEX RODRIGUEZ. In my opinion, A-Rod made a *great* move when he listened to Warren Buffett's wise counsel, benched agent Scott Boras, and cut his own deal with the Yankees. My prediction is that it will turn out to be a great deal for the Yankees *and* for Yankee fans *and* for Barry Bonds haters as well. A-Rod entered the 2008 season with 518 dingers. At the same age, Bonds had 274. Barring a major injury, and figuring a conservative 30 homers a year, A-Rod will pass Bonds in nine seasons or so, rendering moot any question of an asterisk.

LF   RICKEY HENDERSON. As exciting a player to watch as anyone who ever pulled on a jockstrap. I used to love the way Rickey would talk to himself, twisting his shoulders and neck, as he dug in at the plate. And I also used to love how opposing pitchers got rattled whenever he got on base.

CF   BERNIE WILLIAMS. One of the classiest players ever to wear pinstripes. Clutch hitter. Plays a mean classical guitar. He and Paul O'Neill (drums) used to serenade the clubhouse. Joined the Boss—that would be Bruce Springsteen, not George Steinbrenner—for a great rendition of "Glory Days" at the big Joe Torre Safe at Home Foundation Benefit in November 2007.

Talk about your high expectations. When Bernie came up in 1991, he was pegged as a 50–50 guy, as in 50 home runs and 50 steals a year. How high were those expectations?

Consider this benchmark: Mickey never came *close* to a 50–50 season.

People in the front office were licking their chops. So was Mr. Steinbrenner, an avid reader of scouting reports. But I remember vividly that in Bernie's rookie year he looked—and played—like a deer caught in the headlights. He knew what the expectations were. And the harder he tried to deliver on them, the more frustrated he—and the brass—became.

Take the 50 SB. Bernie was fast, plenty fast enough to turn long drives up the alleys into outs. But it took him one and a half steps, maybe two, to get up to full speed, which meant he was only an average base stealer. (His best: 17 in 1996.)

(Rickey Henderson, in contrast, took only half a step to get up to top speed. Rickey would have killed Bernie in a 30-yard dash; Bernie might have held his own at 100. (Guess how far it is from first to second.)

And the power? Bernie topped out at 30 homers in 2000.

Bernie was a terrific center fielder and an outstanding hitter. He had eight .300 seasons and finished with a lifetime .297 in 16 years. But he never made it within shouting distance of 50–50.

It's a measure of Bernie's character that he persevered and had a wonderful career in pinstripes despite all the pressure to deliver beyond his means.

RF DAVE WINFIELD. "Wait a minute!"—I can see the switchboard lighting up as those words hop off the page—"What about Reggie Jackson? How can you possibly leave Mr. October off your Yankee All-Star Team? Murcer, Scooter was right—you *are* a huckleberry!" Calm down, calm down— don't get your jock in a twist. For one thing, Big Dave was a better all-around ballplayer, but it doesn't matter, because the Yankees are still in the American League, right? So . . .

DH REGGIE JACKSON. I would never even dream of leaving Mr. October off my Yankee All-Star Team.

Pitching Staff

SP DAVID CONE. I was in the booth when he pitched his perfect game in 1999, and I have to tell you that I saw him pitch a bunch that were almost as good. One of the top strikeout pitchers in major league history, a five-time All-Star, and one of the grittiest competitors I've ever seen on the mound.

SP RON GUIDRY. As a lefty hitter, I can only thank my lucky stars that I didn't have to stand in against Gator and his nasty slider with the game on the line in 1978, when he had the best season by a pitcher in the modern era: 25–3, 1.74 ERA, 9 shutouts. He held opposing batters to a *.193* BA, and he was even tougher in the ninth inning, when they hit just *.119*.

What I want to know is how he ever lost those three games that kept him from going 28–0.

(Special note for trivia freaks: the winning pitchers in Gator's three losses were all named Mike—Mike Caldwell of the Brewers, Mike Flanagan of the Orioles, and Mike Willis of the Blue Jays. And one other thing: they were all lefties.)

SP   CATFISH HUNTER. He never overpowered anybody with his stuff; he won by being one of the savviest pitchers ever to take the mound. He died in 1999 at the age of 53 from amyotrophic lateral sclerosis, or ALS, also known as Lou Gehrig's Disease. A terrible loss for baseball, but somehow fitting, considering that Catfish and the Iron Horse were both such great, bighearted Yankees.

SP: ANDY PETTITTE. In an era when hitters have pretty much dominated the game, Andy has been a rock of consistency. One of the toughest lefties I've ever watched work. Like the Gator, Andy's a guy I wouldn't like to be standing in against with the game on the line.

As every Yankee fan knows, Andy was named in the Mitchell Report in December 2007 as one of the major league baseball players who allegedly used steroids and/or human growth hormone.

Later, Andy stepped forward and admitted in a deposition under oath that he had used human growth hormone on two occasions (in 2002 and 2004) without a prescription. He explained in a press conference on February 18, 2008, that he had used HGH in an attempt to speed his recovery from injuries, not to gain a competitive edge.

Andy expressed his profound regret for doing so:

> *I am sorry. I know in my heart why I did things. I know that God knows that. I know that I'm going to have to stand before Him one day. The truth hurts sometimes and you don't want to share it. But the truth will set you free.*

Naturally, I was saddened to learn all this, but I was sincerely proud of Andy for standing up like a man, telling the truth, and accepting responsibility for his actions.

Admitting an error, telling the truth, and accepting responsibility for your actions—three traits that make Andy Pettitte an outstanding role model, and a deserving member of my Pinstripe All-Stars.

SP MEL STOTTLEMYRE. A great pitcher on a series of so-so (at best) Yankee teams during the Great Depression. Number six on the all-time Yankee career wins list. Plus he had maybe the greatest single day any pitcher has ever had. On September 29, 1964, against the Senators in Washington, Mel threw a two-hit shutout—I know, I know: what's so special about that?—*and* went 5-for-5 at the plate with 2 RBIs. Is that special enough for you?

But What About the Rocket?

*T*here is, of course, a glaring omission from the starting rotation of my Pinstripe All-Stars, 1969–today.

Roger Clemens.

True, he spent only six of his 24 big-league seasons as a Yankee—and most of his best work was done in Boston, where he pitched 13 seasons and won three Cy Young awards (1986–1987, 1991) and one MVP award (1986); and in Toronto, where he picked up back-to-back Cy Youngs (1997–1998).

But in those six seasons in pinstripes, Roger compiled a record of 83–41 and won his sixth Cy Young. (He won his seventh Cy Young at age 41 in 2004, when he was with the Astros.)

So why am I not putting him in my Pinstripe All-Stars rotation?

Because of my belief that Roger used performance-enhancing drugs, or PEDS.

On February 4, 2008, Andy Pettitte gave a two-and-a-half-hour, 101-page deposition under oath. In it Andy spoke of two conversations that he had had with Roger in late 1999 or early 2000, in which Roger told him that he had used human growth hormone.

On February 13, 2008, Roger vehemently denied under oath before the House Committee on Oversight and Government Reform that he had ever used steroids or human growth hormone. He also denied that he had ever told Andy that he had used human growth hormone. He stated on the record that Andy had "misheard" or "misremembered."

If I believe Andy—and I do—then I cannot also believe Roger.

Baseball—the commissioner, the owners, the players' union, and the players themselves—must take a stand to preserve the integrity of America's game.

My small, symbolic stand is to leave Roger Clemens off my Pinstripe All-Stars.

RP GOOSE GOSSAGE. Talk about your split personalities! With his uniform on, Goose was fierce, focused, driven, and downright mean. (And did I mention the 100-mph fastball?) Off the field, Goose is a gentle, sweet, caring, lovable, big teddy bear of a man. If you have a bat in your hands and a different logo on your cap, you never wanted to encounter the first Goose, because it meant the game was on the line and he believed with all his heart that it belonged to him.

Goose had just one pitch: a fastball. Oh, he'd throw a changeup or a curve once in a blue moon, but batters knew that when Goose was on the mound they could sit on dead red. Problem is, when the guy out there's throwing the fastball at 100–102 mph with pinpoint control, there's not much you can do with it.

Back in Goose's heyday, when "closer" as a job title was relatively new, he often worked two, sometimes three innings. That would never happen today, when your closer is strictly a one-inning guy. In 2004, when Mariano Rivera notched 53 saves, his most as a Yankee (so far), he pitched $77\frac{2}{3}$ innings—spread over 74 games, only slightly more than an inning an outing.

Goose is the latest Yankee to be elected to the Hall of Fame. He'll be formally inducted on July 27, 2008.

Way to go, Goose!

RP SPARKY LYLE. The first AL reliever to win a Cy Young (1977). I've long since forgiven him for sawing through the legs on my rocker. So I can't think of any reason to keep one of the grittiest lefty short men I've ever seen out of my bullpen.

(Now, if Sparky had sat down butt-naked on one of my birthday cakes the way he "christened" several other cakes over the years, I might have second thoughts.) .

Lyle's trade to the Rangers in 1978 after the Yankees got Goose Gossage prompted one of the all-time great lines from Graig Nettles: "Sparky went from Cy Young to Sayonara."

RP DAVE RIGHETTI. You've been a solid starter for three years. You've thrown a no-hitter against the Red Sox—on the Fourth of July, for goodness' sake. (The first by a Yankee lefty since 1917, which was also the first in Yankee history, when a southpaw named George Anthony Morgridge blanked the . . . Red Sox.)

And your reward? You get sent to the bullpen the following year. Don't feel sorry for Rags, though. Coming out of the pen, he averaged 32 saves a season for seven more years (1984–1990).

His best year in pinstripes was 1986, when Rags saved 46 games to break the ML record shared at the time by Dan Quisenberry and Bruce Sutter.

Oh, I almost forgot—in October of that year, Rags saved both games of a doubleheader against . . . the Red Sox. A Yankee for life always likes to remember things like that.

Hard fastball, hard slider, hard attitude when the game was on the line, which it always was when he stepped onto the mound.

RP MARIANO RIVERA. The greatest relief pitcher in baseball history. Period. Okay, okay—that may sound a little excessive, so let me amend it slightly: Mariano's the greatest relief pitcher *I've ever seen or expect to see. Period.*

What's amazing to me is that Mariano does it with one pitch. *One.* Ninety-nine percent of the time, he throws a cutter. The hitter knows what's coming, but it doesn't help.

The cutter, as best this old shortstop-outfielder-DH understands it, is a hard fastball with a nervous tic. It moves—in on lefty batters like a buzz saw, away from righties just enough to miss the bat—and it gets home quick: Mariano brings it at 90–92 mph.

As I said, the batter knows it's coming, but that knowledge is of little use. His WHIP—you rotisserie and fantasy players know what I'm talking about; for everybody else, that's Walks + Hits per Inning Pitched, the purest statistical assessment of a pitcher's command—is a shade under 1.00 in the 12 years he's been a Yankee reliever.

One top of all that—and I bet you're thinking, isn't that enough?—Mo is the best all-around athlete on the Yankees. I seriously believe he could play any position. He's quick as a cat, and a great fielder, so don't even think about bunting on him.

Now, if he could just leap tall buildings in a single bound . . .

Bench

With a starting lineup like the one listed above, you hardly need a bench. Those guys are all gamers, and they could probably beat most teams playing just six guys in the field.

But let's fill out the 25-man roster anyway:

3B   GRAIG NETTLES. A two-time Gold Glover, an eight-time All-Star (once with the Padres), and a hall-of-fame wisecracker. Next to his Cy Young–to–Sayonara line about Sparky, my favorite Nettles-ism has to do with fulfilling his boyhood dream: "When I was a little boy, I wanted to be a baseball fan and join the circus. With the Yankees, I've accomplished both." Every team needs somebody to keep the clubhouse and dugout loose: Graig's that guy for me.

1B   TINO MARTINEZ. Patented lefty Yankee Stadium swing. Clutch hitter. Great team player. I've always been puzzled that he never won a Gold Glove. Tino dug *everything* out of the dirt, and he was automatic at turning the 3–6–3 DP. (That's a much harder play for a righty like Tino than for a lefty. Righties have to swing around to their right to make the throw to the shortstop covering second. But I never saw Tino blow a 3–6–3 chance with a bad throw.)

Tino was under huge pressure when he came over from Seattle in 1996 to replace one of the most popular Yankees of all time, Don Mattingly. He managed to do it, and helped the Yankees win four World Championships.

UTIL LUÍS SOJO. You could feel perfectly at ease sending him in to play any of the four infield positions. Now *that's* what I call a utility player. On second thought, I never did see Luís go behind the plate . . .

OF   PAUL O'NEILL. A classic warrior, and he even looks like one. Now that he's been my colleague in the broadcast booth, I can assure you that he talks as good a game as he played.

Only one problem: Paul's 6-foot-4, so we may have to haul out the Bobby Block again.

OF   LOU PINIELLA. My very dear friend since 1974, Sweet Lou was simply one of the greatest hitters in the clutch that I've ever seen. And I don't need to tell anyone who's ever watched Lou *discuss* a call with an umpire how fiery and passionate a ballplayer he was.

Manager

Of all the managers I played under, RALPH HOUK stands head and shoulders above the rest.

First and foremost, Ralph was a players' manager. He believed in positive reinforcement, though I doubt he ever used the term in his life. He believed in building guys up, accentuating their strengths, as a means of getting them to deal with their weaknesses.

And Ralph never, ever reamed out a guy in front of the other guys in the clubhouse, no matter how much the guy might have deserved it. If a player did need a little talking to, Ralph would have him come into his office and close the door. It was between the two of them, end of story.

Ralph was especially good with young players, giving them encouragement and boosting their confidence, never ripping them. If you have the tools to reach the major leagues in the first place, then the rest is a matter of hard work and confidence. A kid with a bunch of talent can get spooked, get down on himself, and wash out in the blink of an eye.

Ralph understood that instinctively. Ralph saw it as his number one job to build up the confidence of young kids so they could go as far as their talent could take them. If he saw something that needed fixing, he'd say something—but usually in a way that made the young player feel like he'd come up with the idea himself.

Finally, Ralph always stood up for his players to the media.

Some managers, if things are going sour, will let on to the press that so-and-so was letting down the team and was in fact the cause of the slump. Maybe not directly, but clearly enough—say, by not countering a reporter's assertion (often in the form of a question) that so-and-so was letting the team down and was the real cause of our 10-game losing streak.

Not Ralph. To him, the 25 guys in the clubhouse were a team. We played as a team. We won as a team. We lost as a team.

At first, Ralph didn't know anything about losing. He was named manager of the Yankees in 1961, when he was 41: World Championship. The next year: World Championship. And in 1963, "only" an American League pennant.

Ralph may have thought, What the heck, no challenge here, and moved into the front office as GM. Three years later, after most of the great stars of the World Championship teams of the late 1950s and early 1960s had retired or come to the end of their careers, he decided to return to the dugout as manager.

That was 1966, the year the Yankees finished dead last for the first time since 1912, and the beginning of the Great Depression.

The next seven seasons that Ralph managed the Yankees the

results were better, but during that time we didn't come close to a pennant. Plain and simple, as I discussed in chapter 6, we just didn't have the horses.

As Ralph always said, we win as a team, and we lose as a team.

Postscript

An obvious question—and a fair one—is why not Joe Torre?

Well, there's no doubt that Joe was far and away the most successful Yankee manager in the period 1969–today: 10 AL East titles, 6 AL pennants, 4 World Championships.

But see, I never *played* under Joe. I think you can judge a *player* by watching him play: fans do it all the time. But only the players can truly understand what kind of manager a man is. We fans can assess the results, but we can't understand what goes on in the dugout and the clubhouse, what a manager does there to make a team tick, because we're not there.

That said, I know Joe extremely well, and I know that he had the full respect of every player who wore a Yankee uniform in the 12 seasons he was at the helm. But I was outside looking in, so I'm going with the guy I knew from inside the clubhouse.

But if Ralph Houk decides he'd prefer to stay in Florida and go fishing every day, then Joe gets the job as manager of my Pinstripe All-Stars in a New York minute.

Trainers

Looking for unsung heroes? Meet JOE SOARES, GENE MONA-HAN, and STEVE DONAHUE, the guys charged with keeping the little things—jammed thumbs, sore ankles, banged-up rib cages—from keeping guys off the field and on the bench. You can't imagine the number of bruises, twists, and strains that develop over the course of a 162-game season.

I remember getting a jammed thumb—one of the most common "little" injuries that won't send you to the DL but still hurts like the dickens—and Gene Monahan taping a sponge to my bat *just so*, some special magical way that deadened the pain when the bat made contact with ball. Another couple of thumbs, another couple of sponges, and I became hooked—after a while, I didn't go up to the plate *without* a "Monahan sponge" taped to my bat.

Thanks to Gene, it became part of my bat.

Clubhouse Manager

PETE SHEEHY spent more years in pinstripes—by far—than any other Yankee in history. Okay, Pete didn't actually *wear* the pinstripes, but he took care of them for almost six decades. Pete joined the Yankees as a clubhouse boy in 1927 (the year a certain Yankee hit 60 home runs); was promoted to clubhouse manager in the 1930s; and ran the show until his death in 1985, taking care of the needs of all the great Yankee players who passed through his clubhouse.

Yes, *his* clubhouse. Until his death in 1985, it was Pete Sheehy's clubhouse—the rest of us were just visiting.

Talk about power!

Pete was the Decider. He decided where your locker was, decided what number you had on your back, decided what special perks you had.

In my case, that meant being assigned to Mickey's old locker when I came back in 1969 after spending 1968–1969 in the U.S. Army.

It meant being assigned number 1 in 1969, after wearing number 17 during my call-up in 1965 and my short stay in 1966. (Bobby Richardson, the previous wearer of number 1, retired after the 1966 season and suggested to Pete that he hold it for me until I returned from military service. Bobby made the suggestion, but Pete made the call.)

And it meant me being allowed to put a rocking chair in front of my locker.

Fact is, Pete was my go-to guy for just about everything except how to deal with a left-hander with a hard slider.

I said to him once, "Pete, you've got so many great stories that you've got to write a book." His answer? "I'll never, *ever* write a book. I'll never, *ever* publicly tell any outsider anything that took place in my clubhouse. I'll take those stories to my grave with me."

And that's what he did.

Bottom line, as anybody who passed through his clubhouse will tell you, Pete Sheehy was one of the most wonderful guys in the world. He was a much beloved member of the Yankee family and would do anything in the world for you. All you had to do was ask him and it was done.

Broadcast Booth

The SCOOTER, of course, is in one chair. And at the risk of appearing immodest, I'm going to take the seat next to him.

As I said, it's my team: the Pinstripe All-Stars, 1969–today.

═══════

Pretty strong outfit, don't you think? Personally, I think they'd trounce any one of the other 29 all-star teams in the majors.

Of course, I'm a little prejudiced.

For me, there's only one team: the New York Yankees. That's been the case for more than 40 years. Truth is, and with due respect to the Giants and the Cubs, and to all the other teams I've watched as a broadcaster over the years, I'm blind to anybody else.

One man, one team.

A WONDERFUL TOWN

here's a very famous verse from the movie musical *On the Town* that's in Kay Murcer's personal Hall of Fame. Musicals aren't exactly my strong suit, but I certainly agree with the sentiment—now.

New York, New York . . .
It's a wonderful town,
The Bronx is up and the Battery's down,
The people ride in a hole in the ground,
New York, New York . . .
It's a wonderful town!

You see, while I've always felt like a *Yankee* for life, Kay and I didn't become *New Yorkers* until after I left the dugout and went up to the broadcast booth and, more important, after our kids, Tori and Todd, flew the coop. Before that, we were a couple of suburbanites raising a pair of kids while I was trying to jack a few homers into the right-field bleachers at Yankee Stadium.

From time to time in the early days, a bunch of us New Jersey–based Yankees would go into New York to see a play or something. The first Broadway show we ever saw in New York was *Jesus Christ Superstar* early in the spring of 1972. The Yankee front office organized it: play tickets, dinner, even transportation. Very exciting for a couple of kids from Oklahoma who had never seen a Broadway show!

But regular theatergoers? Not close. No way we could be. Too many night games.

Kay

We went into the city as often as we could with the Stottlemyres, Mel and Jean, our closest buddies back then. But both couples had small kids, and synchronizing babysitters and off days was a daunting task. Two other close Yankee friends and neighbors in Fort Lee, Stan and Connie Bahnsen, were newlyweds with no children, so they could hit the city lights at the drop of a hat.

If our crowd had its druthers, and we had a free night, we'd make a beeline for one of the new discos that were popping up about then. We especially liked Le Club.

Bobby was—is—a really good dancer. Back in high school, we never missed a sock hop. He was good at the "Shake Your Tail Feathers," but he was really hot when he did the "Mashed Potato."

The guys had their long hair and big sideburns; the girls got all decked out in suede hot pants and shiny patent go-go boots. We were something to see, although pictures from those days make us cringe a little today.

I particularly liked slipping into this green and white checked suit I picked up in Fort Lauderdale and one of my dozen or so brightly colored shirts with the big widespread collars. I drew the line at platform shoes, but I must admit I was partial to my gold chain.

Kay still has pictures from those times, which she trots out when she really wants to embarrass me.

In 1970 we took advantage of the three-day All-Star break—

trust me, I'd rather have been playing—and did what a couple of veterans sold as a very New York thing: we drove up to the Catskills and spent a couple of days at Grossinger's, the famous resort hotel up in the Borscht Belt. The place was jam-packed with folks our parents' age, former New Yorkers trying to recapture what being a New Yorker was like, and a couple of Okies hoping someday to pass for New Yorkers.

Play golf in the morning, eat lunch by the pool, gather in the sunroom for a rousing game of Simon Says led by famous (at least in the Catskills) hotel personality Lou Goldstein, play with Tori and Todd at the kiddie pool, take a nap, eat dinner, and settle back for an evening with Bobby Vinton.

Remember the movie *Dirty Dancing*? Grossinger's to a tee. Except Kay insists that I am—or once was—a better dancer than Patrick Swayze.

Kay's the Broadway nut in our family. Early on, I don't think she ever encountered a Wednesday matinee of a Broadway musical that she couldn't hustle up a babysitter for. Together, we've seen most of the biggies like *Phantom of the Opera* and *The Producers* and *The Lion King*. The ones I've liked best recently are *Jersey Boys* (my era, my music) and Billy Crystal's *700 Sundays*.

———

We became pretty good New Yorkers in the 1990s, thanks to the leadership-bordering-on-bullying of one Tori Keleighn Murcer. A devoted New Yorker herself after finishing school at the Fashion Institute of Technology and going to work in the rag trade, she pushed and prodded me—she didn't have to push and prod her mom—to get out of my rocker and discover the city around me.

About seven years ago, with Tori off my case after marrying a fine young gent named David Witherspoon and moving to Dallas, Kay suggested we make a list of five or so really New Yorky things we'd always talked about doing but never got around to. Only this time we'd *do* them.

Sounded like a plan to me.

So the next thing I know, we're at the top of the Empire State

Building, admiring our domain. All those years, all those friends and family visiting from Oklahoma, and I'd never gone with them. One of the reasons, I admit, is that I'm not a big fan of heights. But I boldly overcame my stark, raving terror at having only a flimsy steel guardrail between me and unforgiving concrete about two miles below, and I went where no male Murcer (except possibly Todd) had ever gone before.

Empire State Building? Check.

Dinner at Windows on the World in the North Tower of the World Trade Center? Check.

Early dinner at the Rainbow Room of the RCA Building at Rockefeller Center following a visit to the observation deck? (I can take heights a lot better if I know I'm going to eat soon.) Check.

Staten Island Ferry to Staten Island and back with an up-close-and-personal look at the Statue of Liberty? Check.

Circle Line around Manhattan? (The best way to get a real feel for Manhattan as an island.) Check.

Catch the Rockettes at Radio City Music Hall? Watch the action on the floor of the New York Stock Exchange? Carriage ride in Central Park?

Check. Check. Check.

Once we got cooking, we moved on from the purely touristy things to the things that make NY, NY so special: its neighborhoods. Spending an afternoon strolling around a neighborhood (Soho), then another afternoon strolling around another (Greenwich Village), then another in Little Italy, and so on.

And our favorite New York neighborhood of all: Central Park.

Think about it. You've got this city, a hustling, bustling, always busy center of finance and theater and fashion and just about everything, all concrete and pavement and tall buildings, a huge, impersonal city that's expensive and sometimes hard to handle.

And smack-dab in the middle of it all you have this big, comfortable backyard, where all the good stuff is free.

On a warm summer afternoon, you've got people playing softball and volleyball and throwing footballs and Frisbees . . . you've got people jogging and walking and doing yoga . . . you've got people lounging around on the Great Lawn and the Sheep

Meadow, reading and talking and taking in a few beneficial rays. You've even got a few people riding horses.

There's a zoo and dozens of playgrounds and, as we discovered once when our granddaughter Sophie was in town for a visit, a carousel.

The best thing about Central Park is that you can just go find your place, be by yourself, take the paper or a book, and spend a whole afternoon in your own space—along with a few thousand other people.

We used to go to early service Sunday morning at the Manhattan Church of Christ on 80th and Madison. After a bite of breakfast, we'd go hang out in the park until it was time for me to go out to the Stadium. (That's another reason why I *love* Sunday night baseball.) We'd stroll around, sit for a while, then stroll around some more. People watching, mostly. Occasionally juggler watching or Zen master watching. Listening to people making music, watching people dancing to it.

Central Park is a nonstop show.

Kay

One afternoon we were sitting on a bench, and this cute older woman came up with her caregiver. She sat down next to us and struck up a conversation with Bobby. People are always striking up conversations with Bobby. There's something about him that invites it.

Anyway, the little 90ish-year-old lady had been in the Ziegfeld Follies. That's right, she was a Ziegfeld Follies girl! She and Bobby started talking, and pretty soon they were singing Broadway show tunes.

Right there in Central Park, Bobby and his new girlfriend were having the time of their lives—and entertaining a few folks around them, as well.

But Central Park wasn't the only show in town that the Murcers loved . . .

The Abyssinian Baptist Church in Harlem was on our to-do list—which, since Miss Kay was in charge, ended up containing way more than five to-dos.

Abyssinian is one of the most famous churches in America. Very historic. By the time the Reverend Adam Clayton Powell, Jr., took over as pastor from his father the mid-1930s, Abyssinian had the largest Protestant congregation in America. The Reverend Calvin Butts, who's been the head pastor there since 1989, is one of the most vocal and respected preachers in America. We always spend Sunday mornings in church anyhow, so why not Abyssinian?

Easier said than done. Tori and David (then her fiancé, now her husband), were with us, and when we got to West 138th Street, the lines were *huge*. I mean, they wrapped all the way around this two-square-block church building. Tour buses with people from all over the country and Europe were parked outside. We'd been to Saint Patrick's Cathedral on a Sunday morning, but it had been nothing like this. We learned only later that it was Homecoming Sunday, one of the biggest special services on the Abyssinian annual calendar.

Well, we stood in line for a little bit, and finally I turned to the girls and said, "Forget about it. Let's go eat lunch."

Uh-uh. Kay wasn't having it. That may be the first time I ever heard her turn down a shot at a good meal.

Kay

I persevered. I walked up to the front of the line. There was a little corps of ushers there, all decked out in white gloves and tails. People had started walking away, because it was the second and last service, and it didn't look like anybody else was going to be getting in. But I approached one of the ushers and cranked up my Southern charm: "Is there any possible chance we could get in? We've come a long way." (Well, it was about 75 city blocks.)

I don't think I batted my eyelashes, but I might have.

"Certainly, ma'am," the gentleman said. "Follow me."

We all four walked in. They took us upstairs to seat us, but when we got there, one of the young ushers looked over and recognized Bobby, and promptly walked us back downstairs and down to the very front of the church.

There he assigned us to four seats right behind a group of women in their big, flowery, colorful hats. Looking around, we were probably 4 of maybe 10 white people in the entire congregation that day.

It was among the most spiritual two hours we've ever spent. First Reverend Butts got up and began reading postcards and letters from members from around the country sending congratulations and greetings on Homecoming Sunday. Then he must have come across a note that our young usher had passed him, because he stopped and said, "Well, well—I am pleased to welcome as our guest the very first New York Yankee we have ever had in the church in the 25 years since I've been pastor. Welcome, Mr. Bobby Murcer. Please stand up and introduce your family."

Everybody started clapping. Not raucous, like a baseball crowd. This was the House of God, after all. But very strong, very extended applause.

So I stood up and introduced Kay, Tori, and David. And then Reverend Butts spoke directly to me, and I responded. He asked where we worshipped, and I told him our home church was in Oklahoma, and he asked if we had a Homecoming Sunday there, and I said yes, one very much like this. I said our congregation was very large, and that we also had two services, and so we felt right at home.

Finally he smiled and said, "We're thrilled to have you and your family here. Praised be the Lord!" I said, "Amen!" and sat down. Then Reverend Butts proceeded to deliver one of the most powerful, moving sermons I had ever heard. After he was done, a huge choir shook the rafters with a magnificent presentation of gospel standards.

It was a special, wonderful day.

After the service was over, we filed out, shaking hands and greeting people. It seemed like a Homecoming Sunday back home, that's how welcome we were made to feel.

One couple stopped us and invited us to have lunch with them at a nearby soul food restaurant down the street called Londel's. (Tori had heard of it and was thrilled.) We joined them and ate a magnificent lunch that included spectacular sausage grits and biscuits, two of my all-time favorite food groups.

It was one of the best days of our entire time in New York.

The absolute New Yorkiest New York thing I did while Kay and I were on our path of discovery was to run the 1988 marathon.

The year before, on the weekend of the 1987 New York City Marathon, some friends of ours from Oklahoma, Jim and Barbie Vervack, were visiting us in the Essex House on Central Park South, where we stayed that summer. On Sunday morning, we strolled over to watch some of the runners, and Jim got all excited and said to me, "We've got to run the marathon, man! We've got to train for a year and run this baby, you and me and some of the guys back home. We've got to do it!"

So then and there we decided we'd do it in 1988. Two other guys and a female friend from Oklahoma City joined up. I went into training. I was running a lot in Central Park already, what with us staying just across the street during that summer, and I was in good shape, so I figured I'd have no problem getting ready.

When I played ball, I hated running. When I retired from baseball, I got into running big-time. The thing that a professional athlete misses most after he or she retires is competing at the highest level. At least that's what *this* professional athlete missed the most. I figured it would be quite an accomplishment to run 26.2 miles, and I'd be competing again—this time against myself.

About four months before the race, I was contacted by Curt Gowdy, Jr., of ABC, which televised the marathon. Curt was the show's producer. He said that he'd heard I'd be running, and he wanted to do a segment on me as a first-time runner. I told him to give me a little more time to make sure I was up to it, and he said fine. A month later, I called him up and told him it was a go.

On race day, because ABC was doing their bit on me, I got to ride out to the starting line on the bus that transfers elite runners. So did the other members of my Sooner pack. Me, a first-timer, on the elite bus? In fact, on the ride over the Verrazano-Narrows Bridge to Staten Island, I sat directly across from Grete Waitz, only the greatest female distance runner in history.

Grete (I figured we'd be on a first-name basis if we ever actually met) didn't look right or left once she got on that bus. She looked straight ahead. She was totally focused. She didn't say a word to anybody. I bet she didn't hear a word, either. I saw her, but she didn't see me. She was completely, utterly, absolutely absorbed in what was ahead of her that afternoon.

In ABC's preproduction meeting earlier in the morning, they prepped me for what I was supposed to do: "We'll pick you up five miles down the road at this doughnut shop. All you have do is run; we'll do the rest. If our race host asks you a question, and you feel like talking, we'd like to hear what you have to say. We'll pick it up. If you don't feel like talking, fine. Just continue to run."

Well, somehow we missed our hookup, and the world was deprived of my observations and insights as a first-time runner. Just as well. That mix-up also spared the world (and my dignity) a TV pan shot of me lying on the side of the road at mile 22 trying to get up enough strength to make it to the finish line.

The first 21 miles went pretty well. Then, on my way into the Bronx I got a cramp in the lower right side, and my whole diaphragm just started folding up. I had to stop running and start walking. (Hey, I was a first-timer, remember?) But once I did that, the lactic acid built up, and my whole body just became one big cramp. Fortunately, Jonathan Giesberg, a serial marathoner (and my pal Suzyn Waldman's husband) recognized my predicament and hung back to help me through my ordeal. Without Jon's help and encouragement, I'd never have finished. As it was, the last few miles went like this: jog a little, lie down on the side of the road . . . jog a little, lie down on the side of the road . . . jog a little . . .

I think you get the picture. Thank goodness, ABC didn't.

I crossed the finish line at 5:00:20. And I *ran* across, like a champion.

My new best friend Grete Waitz? She'd finished a mere 2:32:13 ahead of me to win her ninth New York City Marathon.

She was one of only 19,255 runners to beat me to the finish line.

I was proud of myself for having triumphed over pain, exhaustion, dehydration, and more pain. And I was truly, truly happy—ecstatic, really—that I had completed my first New York City Marathon.

And my last.

Needless to say, the other members of the Boomer Sooner team finished way ahead of me. To their credit, they kept their jokes at my expense to a minimum.

We threw a party afterward at the Essex House. We had a nice big room there, and we had invited some people over to celebrate my triumph. One problem: I was one big cramp. Kay sat me down me in a big easy chair and wrapped a couple of blankets around me. About all I could do was raise my arm just enough to shake hands with all the well-wishers. It even hurt to laugh, so of course all my pals went out of their way to crack a joke or two.

If this was what you had to do to be a real New Yorker, maybe I should have gone back home to Oklahoma.

———

The best memories about the Big Apple are of the many delicious bites of it we've shared over the years. See, Kay and I love to eat out in restaurants, and there's no town in America that whets our appetite more than New York.

I do believe we've eaten in every neighborhood in Manhattan, from Tribeca to Harlem, from Murray Hill to Hell's Kitchen, from East Side to West Side, and all around the town. Fancy places, hot places, little neighborhood places that somebody tipped us off to. Just about every type of food, with a heavy emphasis on Italian. (Must have been those years in the booth with Scooter.) But if I were to start rattling off all the places we've loved over the years, this would turn into a mini-Zagat, and there wouldn't be enough room left for baseball.

So I'm going to talk about just one place, our go-to restaurant in New York: Il Mulino.

Down in Greenwich Village on Third Street, between Thompson and Sullivan, Il Mulino sits right next to one of the old firehouses in New York. A tiny place, with really good Southern Italian food. The best Italian restaurant in New York? I'll give you my answer after I've eaten at all the rest.

Look, it's sometimes hard to pin down why a certain restaurant is your favorite. It's got to do with a lot of things besides the food. The location, the service, the atmosphere, the memories of good times . . .

One such memory of Il Mulino dates to an evening in 1995. Kay and I were waiting to go to our table, when a guy in shorts and a T-shirt came in, spotted us, and walked over.

"Bobby," he said, "I don't know if you remember me, but my name is Frank Tepedino."

Oh my goodness: *Frank Tepedino*!

Never heard of him? That's okay. I'm sure Frank would understand. Let me introduce him to you.

Frank was an outfielder–first baseman who enjoyed a modest eight-year career with the Yankees, Brewers, and Braves (1967–1975).

We first met playing winter ball in Clearwater, Florida, in 1968, just after Uncle Sam cut me loose. Kay and I spent two months in the same little motel complex with Frank and his wife, Karen. Tori was just a few months old, and the Tepedinos had a little baby girl about the same age, so we were pretty much stay-at-motel parents those days. Lots of backyard barbecues, lots of babysitting for each other so one couple could catch a movie, that sort of thing.

We became close, but after Tepi was traded to the Braves in mid-1973, we lost touch.

Well, Frank was now a fireman at the station house right next door to the restaurant, and he'd seen us going in. We exchanged hugs and greetings, and he invited us to stop by the station house after our dinner. We did, and he called Karen, and she and Kay and I caught up with each other for a few minutes while Frank took me around to meet his fellow officers in this very quaint old station house.

We loved it! Every time after that when Kay and I were in the Village, we'd stop by the firehouse to see if Tepi was on duty.

═══════

Tuesday morning, September 11, 2001.

The Yankees had just completed a weekend series at home against the Red Sox. Monday had been an off day. That night they would commence a three-game series against the White Sox. I was scheduled to leave the hotel at 10 A.M. to catch a flight to Milwaukee, where I was going to talk about BAT (Baseball Assistance Team) at the MLB owners' meeting. Kay was back in Oklahoma.

I had just finished breakfast in our suite in our hotel in New York's Murray Hill section. I was working on a second cup of coffee before heading down to the hotel gym for a workout when the news flashed across our TV screen that a plane had crashed against the North Tower of the World Trade Center. I sat there in front of the TV, thinking, What a terrible accident! How could it have happened? Then about 15 minutes later another plane crashed into the South Tower. At 10, the South Tower collapsed. Half an hour later, the North Tower followed it.

The hotel was about 60 blocks north of the World Trade Center. Once I sort of understood what had happened, I left the hotel and started walking south down Lexington Avenue as far as the police would allow people to go. I thought maybe I could help some of the poor souls walking up from the Wall Street area. I saw people covered in ash and looking like zombies. I did what I could to help, if only to offer an arm to lean on.

None of us will ever forget the terrible images of that day.

In all that chaos and horror, I thought of Tepi and prayed he was safe, since I knew his ladder company would be one of the first on the scene because of its proximity to the World Trade

Center. I left him a message on his cell, and he returned my call as soon as he got time to catch his breath—which was about 10 days later. He was safe, thank God.

We talked often during those terrible weeks that followed. His company had lost one young man. And yet Frank and his fellow firefighters barely had time to mourn.

A few weeks later, before the Yankees headed into the playoffs, I spoke to some people in the Yankee front office about a notion I had, and they spoke to Mr. Steinbrenner, who wholeheartedly approved. And so, on October 11, former Yankee and current New York fireman Frank Tepedino threw out the first pitch in game two of the 2001 American League Divisional Championship in Yankee Stadium—exactly one month after 9/11.

Tepi might not have been a star on a championship team back when we were teammates, but the standing ovation he received in Yankee Stadium that night could be heard all the way down at his firehouse.

If there's anything New Yorkers know how to do, it's how to salute their heroes.

NO SMOKING IN THE DUGOUT

I'm proud of my career in baseball.

Proud of the way I played the game. Proud of the way I treated fans. Proud of the respect I showed for the pinstripes I loved so much.

There is, though, one thing in my career that I am not proud of. One thing that I shall regret for the rest of my life. And that blotch on my career is the time I spent as an accomplice of the American tobacco industry in helping them glamorize a product that causes cancer.

For five years, I was a shill for Big Tobacco, exchanging my name and reputation for money to help sell a product that played a huge role in the deaths from lung cancer of my brother, my mother, and millions of others.

Much as I wish I could, I can't undo what I did—namely, use my status as a sports figure to encourage people, especially young people, to use tobacco. All I can do now is apologize to all the fans, especially the young fans, whose trust I betrayed.

Like most American guys who came of age in the early 1960s, I smoked cigarettes when I was a teenager. Not as much as many of my peers, mind you, partly because I couldn't afford it, and partly because Kay rode me pretty hard about it. I almost never smoked when we were together—and we were together a lot.

The main reason that I was a pretty light smoker—less than half a pack a day—was that I was an athlete involved in one sport or another the year around, and there was a general understanding that smoking made you short of breath. Every coach I ever played for had an ironclad rule: no smoking. Get caught by a teacher smoking in the men's room in the morning, and you could count on running extra laps in the afternoon.

But despite the nicknames we had for cigarettes ("coffin nails" and "cancer sticks"), nobody thought that smoking really hurt you. And smoking was certainly socially acceptable. After all, Joe DiMaggio smoked—I remember seeing him smoking Chesterfields in those full-page ads every week in *Life* magazine when I was growing up. So did Mickey Mantle. So did all the top stars that I wanted to be like when I grew up.

The cigarette smokers in baseball—and their number didn't decrease much after the warning started to be put on the packs—had a big problem because the Commissioner's Office prohibited smoking in the dugout. Bad example for kids, you know? So they'd have to go up in the tunnels leading back to the clubhouses. Sometimes you could practically choke to death just walking back there.

Occasionally the TV cameras would catch somebody like Earl Weaver cupping a cigarette in his hand, trying to get away with it without being seen. Even my dear friend Lou Piniella, I hate to admit, has sometimes been caught by TV cameras taking a deep draw, especially in the late innings of a tight game. But they were managers, and they couldn't very well leave the dugout during a game and sneak back to the tunnel to feed their habit.

Players still smoke today, though many, many fewer compared to when I was playing. (I'm happy to report that I can't think of a single current Yankee who smokes.) And while there are still some smokeless tobacco users—Skoal Dippin' Men, God help me— their number is also far fewer than it used to be.

Given all we know today about the link between smoking and cancer, I really, *really* can't understand why *anyone* would touch tobacco. How can you not read the writing on the wall? Or the writing on the cigarette packages and smokeless cans?

———

America led the way with the first warning back in 1965: "Caution: Cigarette Smoking May Be Hazardous to Your Health." And four years later, the surgeon general's warning was even more direct: "Smoking Causes Lung Cancer, Heart Disease, Emphysema, and May Complicate Pregnancy."

But today our country has one of the smallest, least prominent warnings placed on packages and cans of any of the major countries. The typeface and design and placement make the warning blend in with the rest of the pack or can. The message is still there, but it's easier to ignore.

Look, I'm not trying to go holier-than-thou here. As I said, I used to smoke in high school. I smoked my first four or five years in the major leagues. I was addicted to cigarettes. Then I switched over to smokeless tobacco, and I got myself addicted to that.

———

Everybody in my family smoked when I was growing up—my mom, my dad, my older brother DeWayne. When we were young kids, my pals and I smoked grape vines, because we thought that was a cool thing to do and the closest we could come to actually smoking a cigarette.

My dad said to me one time, "You want to smoke?" When I said yes, I do want to smoke, he said. "No, you don't, Bobby Ray. You do *not* want to smoke. Smoking's *bad* for you." So why are you doing it, Dad? Why do you smoke? He didn't have an answer, other than "I'm a grown-up and you're not."

But finally, after about the tenth time I asked him, he said, "Okay, you want to smoke? I'll teach you." And he did. "What you do is you take this cigarette here. You breathe in, real deep. And then you just hold it, kind of swallow the smoke."

I guess he figured that if I did that, I'd start coughing, maybe gag, I might even throw up, and then I'd never ever ask him about smoking a cigarette again.

Didn't work out that way. I didn't *like* it at first—nobody does—but I doggone sure wasn't going to give up just like that. Remember, I wanted to be like my dad. I was 13 or 14, and I had me a goal. By the time I was 15, maybe 16, I had accomplished that goal. I was a smoker.

TV ads helped me get there. My brand was Winston, which was pretty new at the time, and Winston ads were all over the place. I don't recall exactly which TV shows Winston sponsored, but I watched mostly sports, and I sure saw plenty of Winston ads, so I have to believe they were targeting sports fans.

Filtered cigarettes only, please. Not the Camels and Lucky Strikes that the hard guys in school smoked. I mean, I wasn't about to walk a mile for a Camel, and I wasn't moved by the claim that LSMFT—Lucky Strikes Mean Fine Tobacco. And I certainly never answered the "Call for Philip *Mor-ris!*" (Who was that Johnny character in that silly outfit, anyway?)

Winstons were modern. They were cool. The red and white box was sharp. And their filter tips meant they were obviously healthy. No doubt in my teenage mind that Winstons tasted good like a cigarette should.

Funny, I never smoked in front of my parents, because I figured they'd kill me. They smoked, but I knew they didn't want me to smoke, and I wasn't going to test them. But Kay's father smoked, and I did occasionally smoke around her parents.

The most I ever got up to after high school was maybe three-quarters of a pack a day. Then in the early 1970s they started coming out with all those stories about how cigarettes might be bad for you—stories that Big Tobacco denied up one side and down the other, by the way—and a friend of mine told me, "You should get off cigarettes and go to this Copenhagen, you know? Because it's better for you." And he showed me how to use it.

Next thing you know, I stopped smoking cigarettes because

smoking was "bad for you." Not smokeless tobacco, though. No smoke, no fire—that's the way I saw it. From Copenhagen I moved to Skoal. Don't remember why. Doesn't matter, really. What matters is that I was addicted, and didn't know enough to admit it to myself.

It was about then—in the late 1970s—that the United States Tobacco Company came to me and asked me to be a spokesperson for them. Smart move on their part. As a baseball player—a *New York Yankee*, no less—I was something of a celebrity. And I was still young enough to appear credible to the young people they were trying to hook. The money was pretty good—10 grand or so—plus stock options. And there was no heavy lifting involved.

Hey, I used the stuff anyway, why not get paid for the pleasure?

If Kellogg or Nabisco or Chevrolet or somebody like that had offered me the same deal, I'd have jumped on it, too. An athlete's career is short. His earning power drops off the edge of a cliff once he leaves the game. Endorsements helped pay the rent. That was especially true back then, when free agency was in its infancy and player salaries hadn't yet soared off the charts. Like every other ballplayer, I was always just one major injury away from the end of my career and the end my earning power. So I took what I could get while I could still get it.

That's how I became a Skoal Dippin' Man—that is to say, the face of Skoal smokeless tobacco in print ads and TV commercials. And it's how in 1982 I became the driver behind the wheel of their Skoal-Mobile as I tooled around New York.

That's right, a *Skoal-Mobile*.

The United States Tobacco Company got me a brand-new Pontiac, with "Skoal Dippin' Man" and the Skoal logo on the hood, the trunk, and the sides. In retrospect, it's a wonder I wasn't embarrassed to death. It's one thing to take a sponsor's money to appear in his print and TV ads. But to have your own personal car painted up like a NASCAR vehicle and drive it all over the place? Man, that was over the top.

But I did it. Drove that baby to the Stadium. Drove it home. Drove it around my New Jersey neighborhood. Drove it to the mall. Drove it into New York City. Drove it to the ballpark. Drove it just about everywhere. Hey, it was free, including the insurance, the maintenance, and the gas. All it was costing me was my dignity.

How far out of hand did this whole advertising for smokeless tobacco get? Well, for a while there in the 1980s it was such a fad and such a cool thing to do that they were making jeans with the faded circle on the right-hand back pocket, the kind you'd get if you'd been carrying your can of smokeless in that pocket for about two years. Even guys who didn't dip could look like they did, because dippin' was that cool.

Looking back, I can't believe I didn't see all the contradictions built into what I was doing. Most ballplayers, when they leave the ballpark and the public eye, want to escape to their private life, be with their wife and kids, and drive around their own neighborhood where people leave them alone. How can you do that when you're driving this big car with advertisements all over it?

You can't. I turned myself into this big moving billboard for Skoal. I had people following me home, trying to get me to pull over to the side of the road so they could get an autograph.

Kay never drove that car. Not once. She never even rode shotgun. To tell you the truth, I thought tooling around in it was kind of funny at first. She never did.

Finally, after a couple of months, I came to my senses and said to the USTC people, "Forget this deal. Here are the keys."

=====

The United States Tobacco Company had themselves a nice little corral of sports guys for a while. Walt Garrison of the Cowboys. Earl Campbell of the Oilers. Shep Messing, star goalie of the New York Cosmos. Bert Jones of the Colts. And me.

The USTC people treated us like celebrities. They'd invite their endorsers on splashy outings. They'd wine and dine us. Once we were even taken to the Winter Olympics in Lake Placid.

From time to time, they'd take us to Washington, D.C., to lobby the politicians on tobacco's behalf. We didn't testify before congressional committees that dealt with tobacco or anything. We'd just meet individual senators and congressmen, ones who were on those committees. At the end of the day, politicians like to rub shoulders with athletes as much as any other fans.

Big Tobacco is smart.

Or I should say mostly smart.

They once did a commercial with me dipping Skoal on an airplane, only they had this little problem: where was I supposed to spit? You couldn't exactly carry a spittoon on the plane with you back then, even though security wasn't anywhere near as strict as it is today. Didn't make one whit of sense, but they did it anyway. "People will just to have to use their imagination," the executives said.

Kay didn't have to use her imagination. She had plenty on her hands with the nasty reality.

Kay

*Y*ou know, from watching movies when we were growing up, we got the sense that smoking was somehow glamorous, romantic, sexy. But let me tell you, to watch the man you love going from that to spitting into a spittoon was hard to take.

Spitting is most certainly not glamorous. Bobby only used a spittoon at home, of course; he had one sitting next to his rocking chair. In public, he'd put a Kleenex into a paper cup and spit into that, which was even worse.

At the time Bobby was a Skoal Dippin' Man, Todd and Tori were like five and six. And they'd go over to where their daddy was sitting and go, "Oooo! That's gross!"

Didn't stop him.

I made him line the spittoon with a plastic bag so he could tie it up and take it to the garbage and dump it. It was horrible. It was like cleaning up after your dog in the city.

Only worse, because you're doing it in your own living room.

I thought after doing the airplane ad, "They're only looking to sell Skoal to really dumb people." I should have added, "Where does that put me?"

It was right about then that I became a recording artist. While I was shilling for the Skoal people, I cut a record called "Skoal Dippin' Man." That's right, a record.

See, I've always thought I had a half-decent singing voice. Not great, but sneaky good. Anyway, in 1983 a buddy from Oklahoma wrote the music and lyrics to a song about me and Skoal, and . . .

Guess what? "Skoal Dippin' Man" became a hit! At least in New York. According to a friend of mine in the recording industry, it was one of the top 10 most requested songs played on New York–area country & western radio stations for two weeks.

It went a little something like this:

> *Pardon me if I seem just a little bold,*
> *But it's just because I got myself*
> *Another dip of Skoal . . .*
>
> *I'm a Skoal-dippin' soul-dippin' man . . .*
> *I'm a Skoal-dippin' soul-dippin' man . . .*
> *I'm a Skoal-dippin' soul-dippin' man . . .*
> *I'm a Skoal-dippin' soul-dippin' man.*
> . . . . . .

Had enough? I sure have. It goes on a little longer, but I'll spare you the rest. And no, I will *not* sing it for you. Been there, done that. I can stand only so much humiliation.

═══════

Then there was the time in 1978 I had to have a part of my lip cut out.

I had a saliva gland that got stopped up. And at first, I think they thought it might be cancer, because it turned black and blue in that spot. But it was only a clog-up in my saliva plumbing, which they fixed by cutting the saliva gland out of the lower left side of my lip. In the process, they nipped a few nerves, leaving me a lot of numbness in the left side of my face. To this day, I'm still numb on the lower left side of my face and up by my left eye.

All in all, I used smokeless tobacco for 7, 8, 9, maybe 10 years. It's hard to say exactly, because I'd stop for a while, start again, stop, start again, stop—you know, the way an addict does.

The stuff was so addictive that I had it in my mouth almost all the time. I'd load up while I was broadcasting, and I can tell you that some of my partners didn't like one bit my constantly spitting into a paper cup. Occasionally I had so much in my mouth that I could barely speak, or my words would come out a little bit distorted.

Looking back, about the only good thing you can say about smokeless is that it's marginally less disgusting than a big chaw of tobacco. A few players, especially the older guys, would jam a big old wad of Beechnut in their jaws just before the first pitch and spend the whole game splattering the stuff all over the dugout floor.

You think spitting into a spittoon in your living room is disgusting?

———

Some years after I came to my senses and stopped using tobacco in any form, I used to go over to the state capitol in Oklahoma City and talk to the politicians there about toughening up laws against smoking in public places. This was the core of my standard stump speech:

> *Tell you what, all I want you to do is just tell me one tiny little positive thing about tobacco. Any tobacco, any strength, in whatever form. You were elected to do what is best for the people of the State of Oklahoma. And if you've got an issue in front of you and you can't find anything that is positive or good about it, how can you possibly vote for it?*

In 1997, the Oklahoma State Senate passed Senate Bill 619 to "beef up local regulation of tobacco sales to minors." Called the Bobby Murcer Tobacco Addiction Prevention Bill, it was subsequently passed by the Oklahoma House and signed into law. It's a small step in a long, hard march, and I'm proud of it.

Kay gives me some credit for *finally* getting Oklahoma City— on March 1, 2006—to ban smoking in most restaurants here. It was a community effort, of course, and I wish it hadn't taken so long, but I sure am pleased that now when we go out to restaurants we don't have to worry where we sit. We just get to enjoy our food.

———

"Caution: Cigarette Smoking May Be Hazardous to Your Health."

Big Tobacco knew when they were forced to put that *first* warning on cigarette packs back in 1965 that there was no "May Be" about it.

Tobacco kills. Period.

My older brother died of lung cancer. He died a slow, horrible death, with a great deal of pain and suffering. He was 47.

My mother died of lung cancer. She had suffered many, many years with emphysema brought on by smoking. She was 72.

Years ago, there was a hospital in Oklahoma City that had a special smoking room for those on the respiratory illness floor. People with terminal respiratory disease would literally be unhooked from their oxygen and wheeled from their rooms—from their deathbeds—to the smoking room, so that they could have two or three last drags on a cigarette. You could hardly see in that room because the smoke was so thick.

I know that firsthand, because my mother was one of those poor souls.

Do I need any more reasons for hating tobacco?

———

As I said at the beginning of this chapter, I'm proud of my career in baseball. But I have this one giant regret, and it is that I used my celebrity to try to influence people—especially young people—to use tobacco.

That was a terrible error of judgment, and after realizing this, I vowed to do everything I could to make amends. Though I can't change my past, I would love to be remembered as a guy who helped change the future by trying to build a tobacco-free environment.

PIECE OF CAKE!

t's Christmas Day 2006, and instead of decking the halls, we're looking for a brain surgeon.

You can't just let your fingers do the walking in the Yellow Pages.

And you can't count on friends having a line on somebody they've had firsthand experience with. If I'd needed a knee replaced or a shoulder scoped or an elbow fixed, I could have had a dozen referrals in 15 minutes. But how many people do you know who've had brain surgery?

Remember that line in the old Woody Allen movie when he refers to his brain as his "second favorite organ"? Well, mine ranks pretty high up on my list, too, so I was still reeling from my Christmas Eve message: "Bobby, you have a brain tumor."

Then there was that third, unspoken word that comes immediately to mind when you hear the words "brain" and "tumor" linked together.

That word, of course, is "cancer."

Nobody talked about cancer when I was growing up. People tried not even to say the word. It was the "Big C" or the "Big Casino." That's because up until the last few decades, a diagnosis of cancer—just about any type of cancer—was pretty much a death sentence.

It's a lot different today.

Cancer's still a big killer, of course—number two in our country, next to heart disease. But huge strides have been made in treating it, and as a consequence people are a lot more open about it. People don't lower their voices to a hush when they say the word anymore. They treat it more like what it really is—not some supernatural, so-dreaded-you-must-never-utter-its-name kind of deal, but a disease.

It can be nasty, it can be devastating, but it's still just a disease, not a death sentence.

And if it's a disease, we can fight it. The key is to never, ever give up the battle. Be positive. Have faith. Keep fighting. And—this is going to sound kind of funny—maintain your ability to laugh.

Cancer's no laughing matter, of course. But Kay and I are true believers in laughter—we've been making each other laugh for 50 years—and we haven't seen any reason to stop just because of this bump in the road.

But I'm getting ahead of myself.

I haven't even picked a surgeon yet . . .

So, as I asked earlier, how *do* you go about finding a brain surgeon—on Christmas Eve?

First, and I believe this with all my heart, you have to be blessed by the grace of God. Every step I've taken since 1 in the afternoon on December 24, 2006, I have had a great guide. The greatest. If Kay and I are absolutely certain of one thing in this world, it's that God has guided us on this journey. I don't even want to think where we would be right now without Him.

Second, and I also believe this with all my heart, you need

the total support of people who care for you. In my case, a loving family, dear friends, many fans, and—have I mentioned her before?—my sweetheart, Kay Murcer.

Third, an unwavering faith in the first two.

It was Christmas Eve afternoon when we got the news, remember. Not the best time to embark on a search for a brain surgeon. And yet surgery to remove a brain tumor—C word or no C word—is not something you want to put off until after the Super Bowl.

So we got on the horn.

A good friend with strong New York connections, Barbara Cohen, suggested a major brain surgeon whom she could call on our behalf, a Dr. Patrick Kelly, the chairman of the Department of Neurological Surgery at the NYU Medical Center. But flying to New York was out because of the edema I had, so Dr. Kelly wasn't an option.

Next up was our dear friend Kay Oliver, who was, fortunately, at home when we called. Kay's the director of the Mercy Foundation, the fund-raising arm of the Mercy Health Center in Oklahoma City. We'd gotten to know her over the years, first as a neighbor—her son and our Todd were on the golf team together in high school—and then through our membership on the Mercy Health Center Foundation Board of Directors. Kay's official title is director, but we've come to think of her as our "go-to girl" for any tough problem that needs solving.

Kay picked up on the second ring. She heard us out, and then, without wasting breath on commiserating and hand wringing, clicked off and went to work. Two hours later, she had put together a conference call with our Dr. Saadah and three top doctors at Mercy to discuss my MRI and other lab tests.

("God must really love you two," Kay said later. "I still cannot believe I was able to find these people available and bring them together for a conference call on such short notice on Christmas Eve. It was a minor miracle.")

Their unanimous recommendation: go straight down to M. D. Anderson Cancer Hospital in Houston and get the work done there.

It wasn't until weeks later that we began to realize that this call might have been the beginning of our God-led journey. Do you know Carrie Underwood's big hit single, "Jesus, Take the Wheel"? Well, Kay and I know that He's been driving our bus for quite a while now, and we like that just fine.

My days of micromanaging ended then and there. Somebody else's hands were on the wheel, and He knew where we were going and how best to get there.

Guidance from God. Support from friends and loved ones. Faith in both.

Hey, everything was going my way.

———

So many decisions to make, so many things to do, so little time.

We made arrangements with the M. D. Anderson Cancer Center to come down the day after Christmas. We celebrated Christmas Day at home, quietly, with our Oklahoma City family, then spent the afternoon and early evening packing for our trip the next day and calling a few friends.

Kay's sister, Cindy, called to say that she was going to drive us to Houston. I told her that wouldn't be necessary, but she said it was all settled. Technically Cindy's my sister-in-law, but for as long as I can remember, I've thought of her as the sister I never had. And I knew her well enough to know that if she said she was driving, then she was driving, period.

On Christmas Day, our own Dr. Saadah in Oklahoma City had spoken to his friend Dr. Raymond Sawaya, who said he would be glad to see me. This Dr. Sawaya's titles must have required a special oversize business card: Professor and Chairman, Department of Neurosurgery; the Anne C. Brooks and Anthony Bullock III Distinguished Chair in Neurosurgery; and Director, Brain Tumor Center.

Great! I was going to be taken care of by the Top Gun himself!

We were in good hands.

———

On the way down to Houston on the 26th, I did the dumbest thing I've ever done in my life.

After stopping in Dallas for a bite to eat, I jumped behind the wheel and drove the rest of the way. Hey, I was hopped up on steroids, and I was feeling no pain. Kay and Cindy tried to talk me out of it, but I said, No, no, I feel fine. Just get in the car and let's get going.

Of course, I learned later that I could have had a seizure at any moment—that seizures are common in people with brain tumors—and that I could have killed all three of us right there on I–45.

Lucky? No, blessed.

The admissions process on the evening of the 26th was a little bumpy at first, because we had trouble finding the emergency room. As walk-ins, we'd been told to report to the ER for pre-screening prior to admission. I know: ERs tend to have big neon signs that say "Emergency Room," but we arrived around 9 P.M. and drove around the place a couple of times—the Houston Medical Center, where Anderson is located, feels bigger than Rhode Island—before we finally found it.

Finally, we got to where we were supposed to be, parked the car, and went in to get me admitted. There I filled out a bunch of forms and presented myself before the admitting nurse, who scanned them and began to grill me.

HER: "Mr. Murcer, what type of cancer do you have?"

ME: "Ma'am, I have a brain tumor. I don't have cancer." (That was technically honest: I *didn't* know, not for sure, that my tumor was malignant.)

She didn't *exactly* roll her eyes, but she might as well have. After all, you don't go to M. D. Anderson unless you *do* have cancer.

HER: "Do you want DNR?"

ME: "Beg pardon?"

HER: "Do Not Resuscitate. Do you want Do Not Resuscitate—DNR? You know . . . *Pump, Pump. Pump!*" (And she motioned her hands up and down.) "Do you want DNR?"

ME: "Heck, no. I definitely want to be resuscitated!"

As far as I knew, I was just checking in to get a biopsy and a second opinion. What part of an exam requires resuscitation? I told Kay as we walked back to our seats in the waiting room that I was pretty sure they weren't going to pull any punches around here.

Next I got a preliminary checking out from a couple of doctors and nurses there in the ER. I'd brought along all my medical records from Oklahoma City, including my MRI pictures. They drew some blood, took all my vital signs ("normal but nervous," was how I read them), and asked a few questions. Then one of the docs, a neurosurgeon, asked if I'd like to see my MRI. Sure, why not. I'd never seen one before. She put it up on the screen and there, on the right side, was what the doc described as "a mass with edema."

To me, what it looked like was a satellite picture of a category five hurricane.

A few more questions, and we were done. Good thing, because all us Oklahoma people were running on empty. Next thing I knew, Kay was tucking me in at our room at the Marriott Medical Center across the street from the hospital. We got to sleep about 2 A.M.

It had been a long drive, a long day.

═══

The first order of business on the morning of December 27 was to meet Dr. Sawaya at the Brain and Spine Center and get this show on the road. But when I showed up as directed at 9 A.M. on December 27, I was told that Dr. Sawaya wasn't in the office that day, and that I had been assigned to a Dr. Jeffrey Weinberg.

Who? All the docs I knew personally were a state away, the doc I'd driven all the way down to Houston to see wasn't around, and

I was being turned over to someone whose name had never even surfaced in the conversations of the last 48 hours.

Who was this Dr. Weinberg anyway?

For starters, he was on the young side, late 30s, which I took as a good sign. It meant to me that he was likely to know all the new tricks of the trade. But we explained to him our situation: that we had come down to see Dr. Sawaya.

Dr. Weinberg said he appreciated my frustration, and that he would certainly understand if I preferred to wait for Dr. Sawaya. But he was very straightforward about the need to move fast. We couldn't pussyfoot around; this thing had to come out.

Do I wait around for Dr. Sawaya, who wasn't available right now, to do the job? Or do I let this Dr. Weinberg cut out my category five hurricane the next day?

Big decision. Biggest decision I'd had to make since Mr. Steinbrenner put me on the spot back in 1983—and then even he had given me more time.

Kay and I explained to Dr. Weinberg how confused we were about making that choice. We told him that a friend, Barbara Cohen, had given us the name of one other brain surgeon she had heard was the best in the business, but unfortunately he was in New York City—Dr. Patrick Kelly. As soon as we said Dr. Kelly's name, Dr. Weinberg smiled: "He was my mentor for seven years while I was at NYU. And you're right. He'd be your man if you were in New York for this surgery."

Well, that was all we needed to hear. We both had tears of gratitude in our eyes at this wonderful "coincidence." This was when we finally saw the pieces of our puzzle coming together. We saw that God seemed to be setting up the board, as in a chess game. People were moved out of the way, others (Dr. Weinberg!) put in our path. It all became very clear to Kay and to me that there was a plan, and that we had a Leader, and we would know just what to do.

We decided on the spot: Dr. Jeffrey Weinberg was our guy.

But still, I'd never seen him work, so I asked him one more question.

"Do you have a ball and glove around here, by any chance?"

"Uh, no, I don't. Why do you ask?"

"Oh, I just thought we might go out to the parking lot, have a little catch. Give me a chance to check out your eye-hand coordination."

To his credit, he smiled. I'm guessing he sensed I was fighting a bunch of butterflies in my stomach and trying to joke them into calming down. I got the feeling that he understood. I also got the feeling that he was pretty confident in his eye-hand coordination.

Finally I popped the question that Kay and I had been putting off since we got the brain tumor news in the restaurant parking lot just three days earlier—it felt more like three years—back in Oklahoma City:

"Is it malignant?"

We both pretty much knew what the answer would be. After all, this was the M. D. Anderson *Cancer* Center. But I know I wasn't prepared for the certainty in his voice.

"Yes. Definitely."

My gut response, which I kept to myself, was "Can I get a second opinion?"

Instead I asked him, "So how bad is it?"

"No way to tell at this point," Dr. Weinberg said. "First we need to remove it, then we need to get a pathology report, and then we'll know where we are and exactly how to proceed. Let's just take it one step at a time."

Good by me.

As soon as we told Jeff that he was our guy—you want to be on a first-name basis with somebody who's going to hold your life in his hands, don't you?—he sent me off on a marathon of tests. I was at it from 10 A.M. until 9 P.M.—no food, no breaks—and let me tell you, it was as exhausting a day as I'd ever spent.

After the last MRI when we were finally back at the hotel, Jeff called to tell me that there was no cancer anywhere else. At least we could have that comfort going into surgery the next morning.

I thought about suggesting to Dr. W. that he read a book by a former colleague and good buddy, *Tim McCarver's Baseball for Brain Surgeons and Other Fans.* You never know, I might want to quiz him again the next morning before he started cutting.

But I decided that it was more important that he get a good night's sleep.

═══

Kay and I reported back to M. D. Anderson at 5 A.M. on the morning of December 28 as instructed. Our son, Todd, and our daughter, Tori, were with us. We had no idea what to expect. We had only just the day before met the surgeon who would be cutting open my skull. We'd been told that the operation would take place at 6:30 or 7 in the morning, but that we had to be there at 5 A.M. So we got there exactly at 5.

Don't want to be late for your own brain surgery, right?

When Kay and I described to close friends later how all this was going down, and how we were reacting to it, a few of them said flat-out that we must have been in full denial, that we had to have been going crazy with fear and anxiety.

Well, we weren't.

You have to understand that I've never been a worrier, what Kay calls a "hand wringer." Neither has she. I've always felt that I could overcome anything. A problem presents itself, you map out a plan of action, and you take the problem on, one step at a time.

That's just the way I am. That's the way *we* are.

The night before, we'd all come together as a family in our room across the street at the Marriott: me; Kay; Todd; Tori; Cindy; her husband, Calvin; Kay's brother Dwaine; his wife, Phyllis; and Kay's parents. There Dwaine led the family in a devotional based on Deuteronomy 31:6, in which Moses assures Israel of the presence of God within them:

> *Be strong and courageous. Do not be afraid or terrified because of them, for the Lord your God goes with you. He will never leave you nor forsake you.*

That verse has carried me through each day since then. It's sort of become my personal mantra.

That moment together the night before my surgery was the start of the peace and calm that has continued to this day. Pretty darn powerful. A small moment really, but it changed us all as a family.

Sure, we all got a little emotional, we all cried some. But we bolstered one another, gave strength to one another. We hugged a lot, and we spoke of our conviction that we were doing what we could do, and we shared our belief that God would take care of us.

We all knew that I wasn't going into this thing alone.

So there we were at 5 o'clock in the morning in this big room with about 20 other patients and their families. Not a lot of small talk going on there, I tell you. But there wasn't time for any, because pretty soon this nurse was up in front of what felt like a classroom telling us that we were going to be taken down to the pre-op area, where each of us would be assigned a cubicle.

You almost felt like you ought to be taking notes so that you got everything right.

I looked around, sort of curious, and there were people of all ages—no, make that *adults* of all ages. No kids. Thank goodness. Kay and I and Tori and Todd were hanging tough, but I think if there'd been little kids in there, too, we'd all have lost it for sure.

People of all ages and all colors and, from the look of it, from all over the world. Kind of a mini-UN of people getting ready for cancer operations.

The nurse started calling out names, kind of like a roll call, then she said, "Follow me," and everybody marched out behind her to this huge elevator. I didn't see how they were going to get everybody on, but I guess they'd done this a time or two before.

The elevator took us down to the pre-op area, which was a big, L-shaped room with a wide aisle down the middle and cubicles on either side. There were about 20 cubicles containing pre-oppers like me that morning, with one family member allowed to provide moral support. They had curtains for privacy, but you could hear everybody around you talking, carrying on semiprivate conversations.

The nurse then began calling out names and numbers of our cubicle assignments. I was toward the end of her list: "Mr. Murcer, number 15."

Number 15? Kay and I looked at each other and smiled: 15 was the number worn for 11 seasons by our dear friend Thurman Munson. That *had* to be a good omen. Cubicle 15 was at the far end, at the tip of the L, which meant I had a neighbor on just one side, and thus a bit more privacy.

Every patient was here for one sort of cancer operation or another, of course, but you sure couldn't tell it from the subdued talk going on all around us. I heard no crying, no raised voices, no sense of tension in the air. I think it was probably because everybody was trying so hard to keep their own emotions in check so as not to trigger anxiety in a family member.

After a while, a nurse came and told me to get undressed and put on this gown affair and surgical hose. All new gear to me. Kay stayed with me. We weren't despondent or weepy, but neither did we display any false cheerfulness in my cubicle. Serious business, yes.

I got undressed and put on my gown and surgical hose. I gave Kay my watch and billfold and stuff. But I kept on my underpants. Hey, I didn't know any of these people, right? Sounds silly, looking back, but nobody told me I had to take off my shorts, so I didn't.

That morning, before heading out to the hospital, I'd looked in the mirror and said, "Goodbye, cowlick." I figured they were going to shave my head. Don't they always shave your head bald before brain surgery?

My nurse then said that my anesthesiologists would be coming in a couple of minutes to give me some instructions and "to answer any questions you might have."

Questions? How much time do we have? For starters, I'd never met the anesthesiologists, didn't know their names or anything. I'd met my surgeon just the day before, but these were the people who were going to put me under and, at some time or other, bring me back up, and I didn't know a thing about them.

Were they rookies? Veterans? Stars? Journeymen? For somebody with my mind-set, not knowing is *always* unnerving. I like to know who everybody is and what their assignments are. Kay says I like to micromanage sometimes, and I suppose she's right.

Finally—it seemed like a long time but was minutes at most—the anesthesiologists came in and introduced themselves. Young man by the name of Tom Rahlfs, young woman by the name of Julie Gayle. They started telling me who they were and what they were going to do and what the anesthesia was going to be like. That made me feel a little better. Times like that, just having concrete information is soothing.

Next thing I knew, Julie was sticking needles in my arm and capping them with IV ports they were going to need later. I asked her, "Do I need to take my shorts off now?" She said, "No, you don't have to right now if you don't want to. We'll take care of them right before surgery."

Good.

Got to keep on what I was now thinking of as my lucky shorts.

Kay left so that Tori could come in and talk for a little spell. Then she left and Todd came in. Then Kay's sister, Cindy, and so on, around the horn again. Shuttling well-wishers.

Funny, it was extremely comforting to hear people I love tell me they loved me and give my hand a little squeeze or something. On the other hand, considering the conditions, and what was coming next, it was a little spooky, as though we all knew what nobody was going to say: that this might be the last time.

Gives me chills just thinking back on it.

KAY: "But Bobby was very calm."

BOBBY: "You know, you're right. I did feel calm. Go figure."

KAY: "He was calm and reassuring to all of the rest of us. Very much in control . . ."

BOBBY: "Shoot, I hadn't had any sleep all night. I was looking forward to getting a little shut-eye."

My family and I were together, with me all prepped and ready to go, for about 40 minutes, I imagine. Nobody was feeling too chipper, but there were no tears. I have to say that helped.

Just before they carted me off, Tori and Todd came back into the little dressing room. Tori was wearing bright red lipstick. She said, "Lean over here, Daddy. I want to kiss that tumor goodbye." And she planted a big, bright kiss on my forehead. Then Kay stepped back in, and I said, "Honey, kiss this tumor goodbye like Tori did."

Well, she kissed me all right, but on the left side. That wasn't going to cut it. The surgeon had told us he was going in on the right side, and I didn't want any confusion. "Not the left side, honey," I said. "It's on the right side." So she wiped away that first kiss and gave me a big red smack on the right side, overlapping Tori's.

"Perfect," I said. "They won't be able to miss that sucker now."

"It's time," a nurse said, and so Kay gave my hand another squeeze and left, a big smile on her face. Next, an orderly appeared, introduced himself, and wheeled me away on my gurney off down the hall. I was looking left and right, trying to observe everything that was going on. They hadn't given me any sedatives prior to this, so I was still very much alert.

(Probably nothing in the world makes you more alert than impending brain surgery.)

We got on an elevator, and the next thing I know the orderly's wheeling me into the operating room. Now I was *really* paying attention. I was looking at everything in that OR, trying to get a good picture of everything, making sure it looked like it was clean enough.

Frankly, I wasn't impressed. I thought it was going to be all modern and shiny with plenty of stainless steel. No, it was just this small, square room with light gray walls. Reminded me of Dr. Frankenstein's lab where Gene Wilder put his monster together.

"Here, Mr. Murcer," the orderly said as he parked my gurney next to the operating table in the middle of the room. "Hop off and climb up on this table, will you sir?"

Did I have any choice?

I got situated—not exactly comfortably; I could have used a pillow—but situated enough, and people started plugging in IV lines to the ports that Julie had stuck in me earlier.

I craned my neck left and right, looking for saws and hammers and other instruments of torture. Tom was standing at the table next to me, and I said, "Now, Tom, don't put me to sleep just yet. I've got some things I need to ask you, and . . ."

Tom interrupted me: "Just relax."

Those were the very last words I remember hearing until I came to and a different orderly was wheeling me out of the OR, and he said, "How you feeling, Mr. Murcer?"

Five hours.

The total elapsed time between "Just relax" and "How you feeling, Mr. Murcer?" had been just shy of five hours.

Five hours?

Think extra-inning game plus a couple of rain delays. Back in the day, Scooter would have been long gone.

Five hours?

The New York City Marathon I ran in 1988 had been 5 hours, 20 seconds, and believe me, the last five miles of that sucker had been absolutely brutal.

By comparison, this had been a piece of cake, particularly since I got to sleep through it.

Kay

*A*fter they carted Bobby off, the rest of us congregated in the waiting room.

This was unlike any hospital waiting room I had ever seen before. A big, airy space, with sofas and comfortable chairs and coffee tables. There were a couple of computer stations for people to check their e-mail or whatever. A few floors below was a cafeteria.

We'd been told the operation would take about five hours, and I have to tell you I was expecting your usual uncomfortable waiting room. This was a pleasant surprise.

About three hours into our vigil, volunteers from the MDA Wellness

Institute came around and asked if any of us would like a 10-minute chair massage. Cindy and I looked at each other, and we were like, "Why, yes, thank you, that would be very nice."

You could use your cell phones in there, and while we were waiting we got calls from Lou and Anita, Yogi, and a few other friends we'd clued into what was going on.

I won't say that the MDA waiting room made time fly, but it certainly made the ordeal more manageable for family members than it might have been.

From the OR, they took me up to the ICU, which everybody who watches any TV at all knows stands for intensive care unit, with me chattering away the whole trip. I was wide-awake, and I stayed awake that whole night.

(Later, I found out that was because I was so hopped up on steroids. I'd never have passed an MLB urine test.)

Funny the little things you remember. As I was being wheeled into my room in the ICU, I noticed there was a window, and I thought, Oh, good, I'm going to be able to look outside, going to see some sunshine, some bright lights. I always like to be in a place where I can look outside.

But they parked my gurney so I was facing the nursing station and the window was behind me. The only way I could have seen out would have been to get up and turn around, and that wasn't in the cards just yet.

But I figured out a partial solution. A little later, I borrowed Tori's compact, and I used the mirror to sneak peeks at the window. It also allowed me to monitor the equipment behind the bed that was monitoring me—BP, pulse rate, that sort of thing. It took me a few minutes to get a handle on the reverse image thing, but after a little while I could tell the nurses who stopped by periodically to check on me everything they needed to know by the time they got through the door.

Nurses started giving me drugs and hooking me up to all kinds of monitors and machines. All those IV ports came in handy again.

One of the other things I noticed in the ICU when they first took me in was a clock on the wall. Various doctors and nurses were fussing with me, doing this and that, when Tom, my anesthesiologist, came in and said to me in this very slow, deliberate voice, "Now, Bobby, the operation is over. You're in the ICU. We're just going to do a few things here, and—"

"Tom," I interrupted him, "I've been in here already for 20 minutes."

"How did you know that?" he asked.

"I see the clock up there," I told him. "I saw it when I came in, 20 minutes ago."

He said, "Well, I guess I can report that you're alert."

"Oh, one more thing," I said. "Where are my shorts?"

Kay

*D*r. Weinberg came into the waiting room after the surgery was over. I was there with Tori and Todd, my mom and dad, my brother and sister and their spouses, and three friends from home—12 of us altogether.

Dr. Weinberg called me aside: "I want to talk to you and tell you how it went."

And I asked him, "Will you tell all of us here?"

"I will if you wish me to," he said. "Do you want everybody to know?" I said yes.

Dr. Weinberg told me that he wouldn't be going into any pathology news at that time; he would just talk about how the operation went.

Fine, I told him, because none of the others knew yet that it was malignant.

Bobby and I had talked about this the night before, and we didn't want the family speculating about this or that until we knew the situation for sure. We didn't want it revealed to them that it was malignant until we knew 100 percent what type of malignancy it was.

One step at a time.

So Dr. Weinberg took us all back to a little family room and sat us down.

"The surgery went great. It lasted just under five hours. The tumor was 3.5 centimeters in diameter, a little bigger than a golf ball, and it lifted out in one piece just like you were removing a golf ball out of the rough."

(Bobby said later that he'd lost his share of golf balls in his life, but this was the first one he'd ever been happy to lose.)

Dr. Weinberg said that Bobby was talking, that he was alert, that he'd come out of the general anesthesia really fast. And then he said he'd take me to see him, and that we could eventually all go, but one by one.

The first thing I noticed when I walked into his room was that Bobby had hair peeking out on both sides of this little turban wrapper he was wearing. We all had thought they would shave his head for the operation.

"Oh no," said one of the nurses. "We don't shave his whole head. We only shave a little area at the front. He's still got his hair."

There was a line of little bitty staples running from just in front of his right ear up along his hairline to where his widow's peak would be, if he had one. It was like he had a tiny little railroad track going up from his ear to the center of his forehead.

When Kay walked in, Tom, our anesthesiologist, was there, and he started bubbling: "The minute he came out from under the anesthesia, he looked at me and called me by name and started talking to me. He started asking me questions about the surgery. I've worked here 16 years, and I don't remember seeing anybody coming out of brain surgery so fast!"

Kay

That first time I saw Bobby in the ICU, I thought he looked and acted absolutely fine. He seemed great. It was such a huge relief. I thought, Thank goodness that's out of there. The rest of the family had the same reaction when they got to see him.

We were all pretty high at that time because we hadn't been told exactly what kind of tumor it was.

The next day, after they'd removed his turban and he was set up in a private room, a nurse walked in expecting to find a post-op patient, saw this dapper gentleman sitting in a chair by the window, decided she was in the wrong place, and walked out.

Really, he didn't look at all like a patient. We took a picture of him that I sent out to friends and family about three days after his surgery. You would have never known that Bobby had just had brain surgery.

The way Kay and I looked at it at the time, those first few hours after the operation everything was over and done with. It was a tumor, a cancerous tumor, but they'd taken it out. It was gone. The hard part was over.

Then the kids and the rest of the family started coming in, one by one. I could tell by the looks and smiles on their faces that everybody was as relieved as I was.

Piece of cake.

H ey, Carm," Yogi yelled over his shoulder to his beloved Carmen. "It's Mel on the phone. He wants to know if we've heard anything about Bobby's autopsy down in Houston."

"*Biopsy*, Yogi!" Carmen shrieked in the background. "*Biopsy!* Bobby went to Houston to have a *biopsy*, not an *autopsy*!"

Yogi wasn't being premature. He was trying to protect me.

In his answer to a question from Mel Stottlemyre, 10 days or so after my surgery, Yogi was just taking it upon himself to be our gatekeeper, shielding us until we were ready to go public with our diagnosis.

See, initially all I told friends was that we were going down to the M. D. Anderson Cancer Center in Houston for a biopsy and a bunch of tests. We kept the surgery part within the family.

After the joint press release by the YES Network and the Yankees, of course, everybody knew about the surgery to remove a brain tumor. But when Kay and I got the exact diagnosis, we decided to keep it within the family for a while to give us time to absorb it.

I shared our otherwise private news with Yogi because he has become sort of like a favorite uncle to the two of us. Yogi and I have become very close over the last decade or so, ever since he and Carmen started coming out to Southern California in the winter.

So when Mel called, Yogi wanted to be sure not to talk about anything that I had told him in confidence. And in the process, he committed a classic Yogism.

But let me state for the record about my trip to Houston: they did a bunch of things to me, but they did *not* perform an autopsy.

─────

"Glioblastoma multiforme, grade 4."

Those words, when Dr. Weinberg uttered them on Friday, December 29, 2006, had no meaning whatsoever to Kay or to me. The pathology report was in, and we knew my tumor had been malignant, but "glioblastoma multiforme, grade 4"?

We held hands there in my hospital room as Dr. Weinberg quietly explained that a glioblastoma multiforme is a malignant brain tumor—we had figured that one out—that it is the worst type of brain cancer you can have.

"The worst?"

"Yes, I'm afraid it is."

Kay and I squeezed each other a little tighter.

"Well, you got it all, didn't you?"

The day before he had told us, and then our family, that he had successfully removed a tumor the size of a golf ball from my right frontal lobe, and that he had gotten *all* of it.

That had been comforting news then. Today, though, when Dr. Weinberg carefully explained the nature of a GBM—we caught on to the lingo pretty fast—that comfort quickly faded away.

It turns out that even after successful removal of a GBM, the surrounding healthy, functioning tissue still contains live cancer cells. Chemotherapy and radiation are then administered to destroy those cancer cells that cannot be removed with surgery. Unfortunately, these therapies are unable to destroy *all* the cancer cells, so, in time, they cause the tumor to regrow.

What Dr. Weinberg was telling us is that I have terminal cancer.

＝＝＝＝＝

It took me a few moments to formulate the next, pretty obvious follow-up question: "So tell me, Doc. How much time do I have?"

There was a barely perceptible shift in the tone of Dr. Weinberg's voice. Slightly more "mechanical," as if he were reciting by rote something that he'd memorized. This was clearly the hard part of doing what he does. He'd delivered this news goodness knows how many times before, but it was obviously still difficult for him.

"The bell curve of life expectancy following successful surgery to remove a tumor of this type is 14 months."

Whoa, there—*14 months*? C'mon, Dr. Weinberg, can't you sugarcoat that pill a little? *Fourteen months?*

"Well," I finally said, "that's not *my* bell curve. So what do we do next?"

Dr. Weinberg laid it out for us. Back home to Oklahoma to rest. Return to Houston in a week to commence seven weeks of chemotherapy and radiation. Later on, enroll in a "cancer trial"—that is, a meticulously designed treatment program for my type of cancer, which would require monthly monitoring and tests at MDA.

Kay and I relaxed our grips on each other's hands a little. News like what we'd just heard isn't exactly conducive to relaxation— but now we had a *plan*. We had a problem on our hands, a big one, but we had a strategy to deal with it.

Let's get on with it.

＝＝＝＝＝

The crying came later.

The crying came when we brought in the family, and Dr. Weinberg told them what he had just told us. They were as stunned as we had been, but Kay and I had progressed a little beyond, and we found ourselves comforting them.

For the first time, Kay and I allowed ourselves to cry.

After Dr. Weinberg left, there were more tears, and rounds of hugs, as the news sank in.

We'll get through this, Kay said.

We'll get through this *together*, I said.

We'll get through this because we have God's strength to guide us, we both knew.

<hr/>

They wanted to release me from the hospital the next morning, December 30. Twenty-four hours after I'd received this—how else to put it?—"death sentence," the hospital wanted to kick me out in the street!

I was feeling fine, even charged up. (Thank you, steroids.) I was in complete command of my faculties, such as they are. I could walk unassisted. I could talk. A little weak, maybe, but nothing a little rest wouldn't cure.

Rest! How about another day here, folks? The bed's comfortable, the service is good, and I'm not all that hungry, so the food doesn't matter.

Sure, they said. Does that bed need a little adjusting? And so I checked out on the morning of December 31 and moved right across the street to the Marriott.

New Year's Eve!

Just three days before, I'd had brain surgery to remove a malignant tumor. Just two days before, I'd learned that it was the worst possible form of brain cancer. Just that morning, I'd been released from the hospital. Now what did I do?

Happy New Year!

That's right. The Murcer family had themselves a New Year's Eve party right there in our room in the Marriott across from the hospital. Tori bought silly hats and horns and noisemakers. Todd went to the Central Market and bought a ton of food. We watched the ball drop in Times Square at midnight EST on TV. Thank goodness New York's an hour ahead of Houston, because I was flat-out pooped—and I confess I didn't make it till *our* midnight.

Brain surgery really takes it out of you.

We had to eat black-eyed peas and watch football the next day, of course, because that's what you do in our part of the world on New Year's Day. Every black-eyed pea you eat gives you one day of good luck in the New Year, and Oklahoma was playing Boise State in the Fiesta Bowl.

It was a great game, some say the greatest bowl game ever. It won two ESPYs (Best Play, Best Game in college football). It topped ESPN SportsCenter's Top 10 Games of the Year list. And it doggone near drove Kay Murcer bonkers: "Bobby, did you see that! . . . No! . . . Ooooh! . . . Yes! Yes! Can you believe this game? . . . Oh my goodness!"

Down 18 points in the third quarter, OU fought back to tie it at 28–28 with 1:26 left. Then we scored. Then they scored. OT. We scored in OT to lead 42–35. Then they scored to make it 42–41. And then—the knife in every Sooner heart—they went for two and made it on a wacky Statue of Liberty play.

Boise State 43, Oklahoma 42.

Obviously, I should have had another bowl of black-eyed peas.

I nodded off early in the fourth quarter. Probably a good thing. So soon after brain surgery, I might have had a heart attack.

On January 2, Kay's sister, Cindy, and her husband, Calvin, surprised us by getting a friend who owned a plane to fly them down to Houston so they could pick us up and bring us home. Cindy figured that if I got a hankering to take over the wheel the way I had on the drive to Houston six days earlier, she'd be able to remind me that I didn't have a pilot's license.

The next seven days were pure R&R: rest and reflection. A lot had happened to the Murcers' world since Christmas Eve, and it took us a while to wrap our minds around the events that had taken us from a restaurant parking lot in Oklahoma City to a hospital room in Houston and back to Oklahoma.

We were scared, no two ways about it. Not shaking-all-over scared, but scared. We had a plan, which was good, but there were a whole mess of unknowns running around out there.

The week crawled by. I spent a lot of time napping. Kay spent a bunch of time on the Internet becoming an expert on GBMs. We talked to our kids and our grandkids every day. We saw Cindy and Kay's parents almost every day. We made lists of questions we wanted to ask when we got back to MDA. And, most important to our peace of mind, we spent a lot of time reading devotionals and the Bible and reflecting on our great good fortune that we could count on God to guide us.

By the end of that first week at home, I was feeling . . . well, not 100 percent myself, but a lot better physically than I had expected. And crisper mentally. At least I now understood what I faced. I knew what cards had been dealt me. Bad odds, but the game wasn't over.

Just one nagging question: where were my lucky shorts?

Better get on back down to Houston and look for them.

———

"Bobby, you have a mutant receptor gene."

Oh man, on top of everything else, I have something—a gene that catches passes?—and it's gone mutant on me. When it rains, it pours . . .

"No, that's a good thing," said Dr. Amy Heimberger, an associate professor in the Department of Neurosurgery at the University of Texas–M. D. Anderson Cancer Center. She specializes in immunotherapy for brain tumors. Kay and I were meeting with her in Dr. Gilbert's office in January, just after my return to Houston to begin chemo and radiation treatment. "Only about 25 percent of GBM patients have a mutant receptor gene, and it's necessary to join the Double Whammy trial."

Once more, Doc. This time in English.

Dr. Heimberger had previously explained that it was important that anyone with a deadly form of cancer like GBM take part in a clinical trial because "that's where the cutting-edge medical therapy is."

Fine. Count me in. But what's this Double Whammy business?

Next, she explained that she and her research partner had developed a vaccine that, in GBM grade 4 patients with that mutant gene, almost doubles life expectancy compared with that of GBM patients who receive only chemotherapy.

I was ready to roll up my sleeves and get to it then and there, but she said we'd have to wait until my first MRI, which they'd do about a month after my chemo and radiation. If it was clean—no tumors—I could enroll in the program.

Okay. Good. I understand. Put me on the waiting list.

But what about this Double Whammy business?

The Double Whammy clinical trial got liftoff (and its name) because Dr. Sam Hassenbusch, a prominent brain surgeon there at MDA, had a GBM of his own removed in May 2005. When it came time for his treatment, Dr. Heimberger said, the question came down to a vaccine (which is a form of immunotherapy) or chemo, the two traditional forms of treating GBMs.

Why not both? Dr. Sam asked.

(That's what everybody at MDA called him. That's what we started calling him when we met him a little later that day. Tori had read about Dr. Sam in *Newsweek* back in December, and had urged us to try to meet him when we went back in January after surgery.)

Nobody's ever done both, Dr. Heimberger told him. The combination could kill you.

Dr. Sam's response, as reported in a March 2007 CBS interview with Katie Couric, was typical of the kind of guy we found him to be: "Don't worry about it. Look, just think of me as a six-foot-tall research rat. And go ahead and do whatever you would do to a rat."

Then he explained in a more serious vein why he was willing to serve as a research rat: "Try it on me. If it works, that's great. If it doesn't, well, that's why I've devoted my life to medicine."

And that's how Dr. Sam became enrollee number one in what he and Dr. Heimberger dubbed the Double Whammy trial.

That was back in August 2005. When Kay and I met him in January 2007, he was serving as a consultant at MDA. The man exuded unbelievable enthusiasm for life. We agreed after our first meeting with him that he was one of the most charismatic persons that we had ever met.

So after getting a clear MRI a month after completing my seven-week chemo-radiation treatment cycle, I became enrollee number six in the Double Whammy. As you know, I've always been partial to number one, but I respectfully tip my Yankee cap to the man who earned that distinction in the Double Whammy: Dr. Sam Hassenbusch.

There are about 20 people enrolled in the Double Whammy trial that I'm participating in. Kay and I have been in touch with most of them. And here's a bulletin from the It's a Small World Bureau—Bob Sheppard's daughter, Barbara Derenowski, who lives in Arizona, is also in the Double Whammy trial. She enrolled five months before I did.

———

Chemo and radiation.

You hear the words all the time when you learn somebody has cancer, but if you're like I was, you don't have a clue what they involve.

For instance, I assumed that the chemo (or was it the radiation?) would cause all my hair to fall out, like, overnight. That was no big deal. I hadn't worn my hair long since the 1970s, when I had muttonchops and bangs and a thick mat that almost touched my collar. (Almost but not quite: Mr. Steinbrenner had a rule about hair touching your collar, remember?)

The chemo cocktail (five capsules of a cancer-fighting drug called Temodar) that I took every night for seven weeks had two side effects, one minor and one major: a little mild nausea (*No problema!*) and a lot of serious constipation (*Problema!*). I asked my nurse what was in the doggone pills. Her reply: "Concrete."

(Dr. Mark Gilbert, my oncologist, explained that the German word for Temodar was *Farfrompoopin'*. One of the great things about Mark that helped us get through our ordeal was his sense of humor.)

The radiation treatments took place at nine every morning and lasted about 20 minutes. I'd lie down on a table and they'd put a contraption that looked like a fencing mask on my head, which they then locked to the table so my head couldn't move. Then this sci fi–looking machine would revolve around and zap me.

I didn't feel a thing while the zapping was going on, other than the anxiety that comes from knowing you couldn't move your head a millimeter even if you wanted to.

The first couple of weeks into treatment I experienced no pain or discomfort at all, so I'm going, What's the big deal? We had a lot of free time, so we checked out different Houston restaurants (the Murcers' default mode of entertainment is always eating), and we took long walks through Memorial Park, Rice Village, and the Galleria. Friends came to visit from New York, Florida, Oklahoma, and Arkansas. We had plenty to do, but we also had to make sure that I got lots of rest. In a weird way, it was almost like an extended vacation.

After about three weeks, the radiation kicked in, and my hair started falling out. Hey, so what? As longtime New York sportswriter Maury Allen wrote to me in February, "It's not the hair. It's the here." Thanks, Maury—truer words were never written.

Then, over the course of treatment, they upped the zappage, and toward the end of the treatment period I became very fatigued. Taking a shower was an ordeal, and then I'd have to lie down and rest for a while before getting up the strength to put on my clothes.

One thing that Kay and I found a little surprising is that the chemo and radiation operation closed up shop on weekends. We were like, What's wrong with this picture? Does cancer take weekends off?

Actually, that was a blessing in disguise, because on Friday, January 26, our daughter-in-law, Lynne, went into labor. Kay and I skipped town early Friday afternoon right after radiation and drove straight to Dallas. We arrived minutes after the twins,

Holden and Ava, arrived in the nursery. Todd, the proud papa, took a great photo of Kay and me holding them. I'm the one with the biggest grin.

That weekend in Dallas was, I must say, an enormous boost to our spirits. All our family and a number of friends came in, and it was a great reunion and celebration of new life. Just the tonic I needed to go with all the chemo and radiation I was getting.

At M. D. Anderson they have a tradition called the "ringing out" ceremony when a patient completes radiation treatment. Mine took place on February 27, 2007.

Since my surgery, Kay had been keeping in touch with family and friends via e-mail. Here's a poem that she sent around just before my "ringing out" ceremony to commemorate the completion of my seven weeks of chemo and radiation treatment.

> The end's in sight, and so tonight,
> our greeting's sent with glee.
> With 7 "zaps" and cute skull caps,
> from Houston we'll soon flee.
>
> Our long home fix, was such a mix
> of family, friends, and fun . . .
> It did the trick! We don't feel sick,
> just ready to be done.
>
> B's appetite returned with might . . .
> His taste buds are a' bloomin'!
> His strength, once sapped, is no longer trapped.
> In fact, it's finally zoomin'!
>
> The corner's rounded. He's rebounded.
> We're in the bell lap trot.
> You're all such dears . . . your love, your cheers,
> your prayers have meant a lot.
>
> So off we go. But you must know
> our blessings still are many.

We're grateful, cheerful, and occasionally tearful . . .
But fears? We haven't any.

Immediately after my last radiation treatment, I got off the table and walked a few steps to a nearby waiting room, where my techs, T.O. and Lacey, had assembled with Kay and Dr. Sam. There I rang a small brass bell that looked like the kind you'd see on board a ship at sea. Next to it is a plaque with the following inscription:

Ring this bell
Three times well
Its toll to clearly say,
My treatments done,
This course I've run,
And now I'm on my way!

As I rang away, cheering could be heard throughout the area from other patients and medical staff, all of them pleased to help me celebrate this moving-on ritual. We had cheered for many others before this day came for me, and it was great to feel such an outpouring of support as I left the radiation treatment area for the last time.

It wasn't a Yankee Stadium ovation following a big home run or anything . . . but in many ways it was better.

═══

Calories and goals, Dr. Sam said. Calories and goals.

That was back in January, when we met him after learning about the Double Whammy from Dr. Heimberger.

"Eat a lot," he said. "Eat even when you're not hungry. Calories, calories, calories! I can't stress enough how important it is for you to eat."

Music to my ears, Doc. I'm assuming that we're talking here about chicken-fried steak and creamed gravy? Hot biscuits? Turkey meatballs and red beans and cornbread, and . . .

I could have kept on going here for a while, but Dr. Sam was nodding, yes, you have to really pile on the calories.

"The next thing I want to stress is the importance of setting goals," Dr. Sam said. "Short-term goals and long-term goals. Realistic goals. Short-term *and* long-term."

He didn't explain why. He didn't have to. I'd been diagnosed with incurable cancer. Having goals, like chemo and radiation, was part of my treatment package. Look ahead. Look at the positive things you can accomplish.

As Satchel Paige once said, "Don't look back. Somethin' might be gainin' on you."

═══

Sadly, something *was* gaining on Dr. Sam: brain cancer.

Dr. Samuel Jack Hassenbusch III died on February 25, 2008.

Up until near the end of his extraordinary life, he remained active at M. D. Anderson, inspiring cancer survivors by his own heroic example to fight this insidious disease—"Calories and goals, Bobby, calories and goals"—to make every moment count . . . to embrace life.

Dr. Sam never looked back.

═══

Less than a month after my surgery, I went on Michael Kay's radio show on ESPN to talk to Yankee fans. It was Michael's idea, and I was a little nervous, a little emotional about the idea of it. What I mean is, I didn't want to go on radio and start talking and break down. Kay pushed me. She said I could do it. She said this could be one of those short-term goals Dr. Sam had been talking about. And so I did.

The way we did it was that Michael interviewed me, throwing me BP pitches about how I was feeling, about the support I had received from fans, and that sort of thing. Michael and I had a little back-and-forth, some about health issues and a little about Yankee winter moves. And then we took a few phone calls from listeners. I finished by speaking directly to the fans who had tuned in:

> *Michael, I want to thank you very much for giving me this forum to tell Yankee fans that even though this looks bad, I'm doing great. I really am. I'm in a great place. God has given me peace, and the overwhelming outpouring of love and prayers from all you fans out there has been unbelievable. I can feel your thoughts and your prayers, and I am so happy for this opportunity to tell you all how much I love you.*

My next goal, once treatment was over and we were home, was to go back to Yankee Stadium. Kay said, How about Opening Day? I said I didn't think I could handle that just yet, that it would be too emotional. She said, Bobby, it's going to be emotional whenever you return. Putting if off could just build up the pressure and make it harder. Let's do it.

And so we did.

Opening Day, April 2, 2007: Tampa Bay Devil Rays vs. New York Yankees at Yankee Stadium.

I knew I couldn't handle any on-field introduction. I'd have broken down for sure. So I came in under the radar, went up to the booth, and worked the third inning with my YES Network colleagues (Michael Kay, Ken Singleton, Joe Girardi).

After I'd done my inning, the scoreboard in right-center flashed out the news that Bobby Murcer was in the house, and I received the loudest, most thrilling standing ovation I have ever heard from the 55,031 Yankee fans in attendance. The giant scoreboard video screen flashed an image of me waving from the booth, and they cheered even louder. I waved again, and they cheered even more. Then Joe Torre and all the guys came out of the dugout, and all the guys in the bullpen came out onto the outfield grass, and they all waved and clapped and took off their caps.

That's when I cried.

It was a great game. We fell behind 5–3 after five, but came back to win 9–5. A-Rod and Jorge hit homers, Derek drove in two runs, and Mariano—of course—pitched a scoreless ninth.

Exactly the way you want to begin a new season.

MY NEW TEAM

s I mentioned, we informed the Yankees and the YES
Network of what was going on shortly after my surgery—can't go on sick leave without telling your bosses,
right?—and they issued a joint press release that incorporated a
plea from Kay that our family's privacy be respected at this difficult time:

> *Since Christmas Eve, when we first learned of Bobby's brain tumor,
> we have been thrown into a situation that has required as much total
> focus as we can muster.*
>
> *Today, with the surgery over, we are now needing to expend all our
> energies on decisions that will benefit Bobby's full recovery.*
>
> *Hundreds of you have asked, "What can we do to help?"*
>
> *If you truly mean it, we do have one request. Please allow us, as a
> family, to have the time we need to face these new challenges.*
>
> *We respect the fact that the media have their jobs to do, but we
> cannot be distracted from our goal here in Houston.*

Bobby is gaining so much encouragement from all the emails, calls, and overwhelming outpouring of love, and he looks forward to sharing in a Q&A as soon as his doctors allow.

Until then, we would appreciate your continued prayers and patience.

Thank you.
—KAY MURCER

Even so, the news triggered what the hospital said later was an avalanche of letters and cards and flowers that came in addressed to me.

Kay and I and our family truly appreciated this outpouring of support, but we had a lot of things on our plate, a lot of things to think about, a lot of things that really demanded our attention. Like all hospitals, M. D. Anderson Cancer Center goes to great lengths to protect the privacy of people in the public eye who come to them for treatment. So during the week we were back home before returning to Anderson for seven weeks of chemotherapy and radiation therapy, the hospital sent back everything that came in, insofar as it was possible to do so.

Make that *almost* everything.

━━━

A few days after news of my little trip to M. D. Anderson was made public, I got the following letter from a young man in Weston, Connecticut:

Dear Mr. Murcer,
Hello, my name is Aaron Gaberman. I read the article about you going to M. D. Anderson to have surgery for a brain tumor. M. D. Anderson is a great place to get surgery! My cousin Ronnie's friend, Murray, works at the Cancer Center as an oncologist. He gave me a list of vitamins to take after radiation. I know that you will be okay because I had two brain tumors when I was 10 years old. Dr. Allen at

NYU treated my tumors with chemo and radiation. The tumors went away after two cycles of chemo. But I had to get all six cycles and six weeks of radiation in Boston. It is now one year after my treatments, and I am cancer free. I start growth hormones in January at NYU so I can grow.

Here is a list of the things that helped me through my journey with cancer, and I hope they will help you get better from your surgery:

1. *Listen to peaceful music. I've sent you a CD made by a brain tumor survivor (just like us) for you to listen to.*

2. *Be brave . . . just like the New York Yankees!*

3. *Never give up. (This I learned from Lou Gehrig and Derek Jeter.)*

4. *Have a positive attitude.*

5. *Always pray to God to help you get better.*

6. *Watch the YES Network and Yankee games.*

7. *Play baseball and golf.*

8. *Don't worry, your hair will grow back . . .*

9. *Always have fun with your friends and family.*

Best wishes for a quick recovery.

Your Friend,
AARON GABERMAN
    Cancer Survivor, Age 11

P.S. Get well soon!

Most likely, Aaron's letter would have been sent back like all the rest of them, or trashed if it had no return address, except that the envelope it came in didn't say "Bobby Murcer" on the outer envelope. It just said "Yankees" and "M. D. Anderson" and "Houston, Texas" on it. So someone in the public relations office opened it, decided it was something I would want to see, and had it brought to Kay and me.

Like so many wonderful, inspiring things that have happened to me, this was—Kay and I believe with all our hearts—simply meant to be.

Kay

_A_fter Bobby's surgery, a lot of little miracles began to happen. Aaron's letter getting through was one of them. Our faith has played such an important role in our lives, and now we felt like we were being God-led. Our faith had been given this huge booster shot, and we've just sort of climbed this ladder right up the steps, as we've been supposed to do.

Kay and I read Aaron's letter, cried some, and decided that I would try to get in touch with him. You can see why. The bravery, the strength, the positive attitude conveyed in his letter bowled us over. Maybe he was only 11, and I was 60, but I knew I could learn from him.

Kay

_T_he minute Bobby and I read Aaron's letter, we were both reminded of a young man we had met nine years earlier, Seth Zimolzak, from Shickshinny, Pennsylvania. (I just love that name.) Seth and his parents, Sue and Lon, were staying at the same New York City hotel Bobby and I were in. Bobby was in town to work a Yankee home stand, the Zimolzaks so that Seth, then 18, could undergo his chemo and radiation treatments for cancer.

We struck up a friendship, and took them out to dinner. Seth was bald at the time from the chemo, so Bobby gave him a Yankee hat.

We stayed buddies with Seth and his parents through the following year, when Seth died. Afterward, we stayed in contact with his mom and dad for a while, but after a time we lost touch.

But that morning in January 2007 when we read Aaron's letter, and looked at the baseball card he'd enclosed—him with his little bald head and baseball cap and brave smile—it brought back memories of Seth from nine years before.

And guess what? When we got back up to our hotel room, the phone rang and it was Sue Zimolzak! We hadn't talked in a couple of years, but she had heard about Bobby's surgery, and she was calling to see how he was doing. I told her we'd just been talking about Seth not 15 minutes earlier. She laughed and said that very day would have been Seth's 26th birthday.

That made the hair stand up on my arms.

And it made me begin to believe that everything that was happening to us was meant to be.

I called Aaron's home number in Weston, Connecticut, but no one was home, so I left a message telling him that I would try him again in a couple of days. Two days later, I called back, only this time I was greeted by a different message on the answering machine: "Hi, this is Aaron Gaberman. If this is Mr. Murcer, please call me. I'm in Boston getting my treatment."

Kay and I got a kick out of that, so we called him on his mother's cell phone number, and Aaron and I had a great conversation. It was the beginning of a wonderful friendship.

As with the Zimolzaks, Kay and I felt there was a connection, some reason we were supposed to know Aaron and his family.

In the summer of 2007, when the Gabermans came down to Yankee Stadium, we had a heckuva good time. I brought Aaron up to the booth. We took some great pictures, and laughed a lot. He's 12 years old now, a *huge* Yankee fan, and a Notre Dame fan as well. My birthday's May 20; his is May 21. We call and e-mail each other. He keeps me posted on how his golf game is coming around; I tell him to hang in there, that the Yankees are going all the way this year.

Manny Ramirez and David Ortiz? Yeah, they're pretty good, but when it comes to a 3–4 combo, I'll take Bobby Murcer and Aaron Gaberman any day.

═══════

My journey—our journey—since December 2006 has opened up a wonderful new world to Kay and me. We've met a whole new community of extraordinary people we'd never have known had it not been for this cancer.

I'm talking about our very own Club Med at M. D. Anderson, the doctors and technicians whom we respect so highly and who have become fast friends and reliable teammates:

- **DR. SAM HASSENBUSCH.** A veteran neurosurgeon who became a GBM patient himself, Dr. Sam was lab rat *número uno* for the Double Whammy vaccine trial program that I am currently going through. He led the way, which is understandable because he was such a natural leader.

- **DR. JEFFREY WEINBERG.** My neurosurgeon. Still don't know how he'd do with a ball and glove, but I can attest that he knows his way around brains. A young (40) New York guy and, of course, a Yankee fan.

- **DR. MARK GILBERT.** My oncologist. Another New Yorker. I have a sneaky feeling that he favors the Mets, but I don't hold that against him. Much.

- **DR. CHRIS PELLOSKI.** My oncology radiologist. He was responsible for making me bald, but it was only temporary.

- **DR. AMY HEIMBERGER.** A neurosurgeon and immunologist, she was in charge of the vaccine trial when I was admitted. Speaks in a lingo that you'd need a Ph.D. to interpret, but we get along okay with hand signals.

• **LAMONNE CRUTCHER, R.N.** A research nurse with the Heimberger Team, Lamonne assists with all the procedures that I get done every month, from the blood draws through the vaccine shot.

• **VIRGIL FRY.** The executive director of Lifeline Chaplaincy at M. D. Anderson, Virgil paid me a visit right after I came out of surgery. He has remained a friend and a great source of inspiration. During those seven weeks when I was undergoing radiation and chemo, we started attending the same church as Virgil in Sugarland, Texas, a sprawling suburb, where he introduced us to a terrific bunch of folks who remain our friends to this day. If I ever write a handbook, *A Dummy's Guide to Surviving Brain Cancer,* I'm going to recommend that the patient find a wonderful church in the community where he or she is taking treatment and get involved in it.

And then there are the great people at the Tug McGraw Foundation, the outfit started by the slightly wacky but wonderful former Mets and Phillies relief pitcher in 2003 to help people with brain cancer. (His son, Tim, has carried the lead since Tug's death in 2004.) The McGraw Foundation supports research that focuses on devising strategies for dealing with the social, emotional, and spiritual impact of the disease.

(As Tug used to say, "Ya gotta believe!")

And I have to mention what I call my Expansion Team, 25 to 30 other brain tumor patients like me, some of whom are in MDA's Double Whammy trial. We're from all over the map, and from all walks of life, but we have one thing in common: we used to have brain tumors (most of them GBMs, like mine). We stay in touch, we lean on one another for support, and we have become a tight, close-knit team.

Membership includes its own special language, a sort of "chemo lingo" of our own, in which we share details about different treatments and coping mechanisms. Early on, I got the distinct feeling that other club members were going out of their way to bring the new rookie along, to soothe his anxiety, to help him focus on positive values, and to avoid the natural inclination to wallow in self-pity.

It's incredibly helpful, beyond anything I might have imagined, to connect with others in the same boat, especially the veteran survivors whose example made the ordeal seem manageable. I'm now very comfortable calling up a total stranger, newly diagnosed, to talk through any questions he or she might have, to offer an understanding ear, and to pass on possibly useful tips.

Hey, we're teammates, and teammates have to help each other out.

Not so long ago, I personally knew very few cancer survivors. Unfortunately, Kay and I now probably have more friends than not who have weathered bouts of cancer and are in some kind of treatment.

Look at my longtime Yankee buddies, Joe Torre and Mel Stottlemyre. Both have come through some pretty rough times with their own cancers—Joe, prostate; and Mel, multiple myeloma. They're both now in remission, but over the last year or so we've shared talks about stem cell transplants, leukapheresis blood draws, the benefits of flax seed, MRI results . . . not exactly your typical clubhouse banter. Despite having served time with other organizations, we three are Yankees through and through, but now all three of us are members of another team as well.

Kay and I also hooked up with unexpected supporters like Colonel Doug Wheelock, the astronaut, who in the fall of 2007 spent 14 glorious days orbiting the earth 219 times and flying 5.8 million miles in the space shuttle *Discovery*. Doug, who was born in 1960 in Binghamton, New York, became a big fan of the Yankees about the same time I was first earning my pinstripes. He listened to all the Yankee games on his transistor radio, which he would take to bed with him with the volume turned down low for night games. He says his mom used to catch him with it on late, long after he was supposed to be sleeping.

Doug used to tell her that he wanted to be an astronaut one day, and that if he ever did get a chance to blast off on a mission, he would try to find me, his favorite Yankee, and invite me to his launch. Almost 40 years later, Doug's mother heard about me taking my cancer treatment in Houston, 30 minutes from NASA, where Doug was in training for his mission. She suggested to her son that since we were both spending a lot of time in Houston, he ought to get in touch with his old baseball hero.

Well, he did, and he and Kay and I had dinner several times when we were in Houston for my monthly checkups. We'd talk baseball and outer space, my world and his. Then, in the fall of 2007, when he blasted off from Cape Canaveral on the space shuttle *Discovery*, the Murcers were there as his guests to witness the launch—me, Kay, my son and daughter, and their families. It was way more spectacular than TV can possibly portray.

And get this: Doug carried my old Yankee jersey and a few of my baseball cards with him into space and back so when our grandkids grow up and go to school, they'll have officially certified space memorabilia to take to show-and-tell!

Meeting Doug Wheelock was one of the many unexpected blessings I encountered during the very surreal year of 2007.

I also have received a ton of support from members of my extended sports family who got in touch with me in those early, tough weeks after I had my head sawed open. Guys I played with. Guys I played against. Guys in other sports I met over the years.

Also a part of my team, of course, are the *million-plus fans* who logged onto the Yankee Web site to express their concern and support after we went public in January with my diagnosis.

———

Funny how cancer focuses your attention.

I used to be a hall of famer at wasting time. I played a lot of golf, a lot of gin games at the club. Spent a lot of energy trying to figure out ways of making more money so I could have more leisure time to waste.

Several years ago, I discovered that I got much more enjoyment from contributing to the community with my efforts than just plain hanging out. After my brother DeWayne died in 1989, Kay and I started a foundation in his name and joined with the American Cancer Society in Oklahoma City to raise awareness and money for cancer treatment and research. We got friends and some businesses to join forces with us, and we ran about a dozen annual golf events. That eventually got to be more than we could handle, so we took a couple of years off.

Even before my diagnosis, we had been involved in a charity venture with the Oklahoma Children's Medical Research team. With the support of friends and the local community, we've helped establish a $1 million chair in pediatric cancer research in the Murcer family name.

Now that I have a little bit of experience with this business of being a cancer survivor, we're beginning to meet with several brain tumor foundations to see if we can assist with their efforts to increase awareness and raise more funds for treatment and research.

I still work about 50 Yankee games a season for the YES Network, which I plan to continue to do until they pry my cold hands off the mike. But I spend more of my off-season time now helping raise money for cancer research and treatment, especially for kids. (I have Aaron to thank for showing me the way.)

Family get-togethers have taken on a whole new importance: Kay and I spend more and more time with our kids and grandkids.

And I also try to respond to every single well-wisher, every fan, every person who's become a member of my new team since December 29, 2006. I'm told there were more than 1 *million* posts on the Yankee/MLB Web site wishing me well in the first two months after my surgery, so getting back to each of them is going to keep me busy.

Hey, this cancer survivor business is a full-time job!

21

A WHOLE NEW BALL GAME

*H*ad enough cancer talk?
Me too.
Let's talk a little baseball.

Baseball fans talk more about their favorite game than do fans of any other sport. Is that a rock-solid fact backed up by a bunch of think-tank survey research? No, but I know in my heart that it's true. Can you name another sport that has a name—the "Hot Stove League"—for the conversation that takes place between the last out of the World Series and Opening Day?

I rest my case.

Baseball talk is extremely wide-ranging, probably because the game has so many levels, so many nooks and crannies that fans like to bore into. You talk mainly about "your" team, for sure, but over the course of the Hot Stove League season, you talk about what's going on with other teams as well.

Even Red Sox fans, for example, have been known on occasion to take a timeout from waxing poetic about their Green Monster to consider other things in baseball. Sometimes they'll change the subject to the 2004 season or the 2007 season.

But wasn't baseball a better game before hyper-inflation of salaries and oversaturation by media and steroids and . . .

Stop. There are many disturbing, repugnant things about big-time sports in America today. It's one thing to feel all warm and tingly about the "olden, golden days," but it's quite another thing to think that the quality of baseball—the game on the field—"back then" was better than it is today. It wasn't.

So now I'm going to offer up a few unsolicited opinions about the game *today*—and the game *tomorrow*—with only an occasional look back at the game *yesterday*. And I'm going to frame them as responses to the sorts of questions that people actually come up to me and ask me in airports, in restaurants, wherever else we bump into each other during the Hot Stove League season.

What Did You Think of Mayor Giuliani Wearing a Red Sox Cap and Rooting for Boston During the 2007 World Series?

Traitor! Boo! Getouttahere!

Just kidding. I said back then that I was just happy that Mayor Giuliani, one of the all-time great Yankee fans, was rooting for the American League champion.

I might add that when Mayor Giuliani visited Oklahoma in December 2007 during the presidential nomination campaign (talk about a long season!), we had a little fireside chat about that Red Sox rooting business, and I was pleased to have reconfirmed that Mayor Giuliani remains, in his heart of hearts, a true-blue Yankee fan.

I was also relieved to hear from him that the photo of him in that Red Sox cap that the New York tabloids splashed around town had been doctored; the cap had been superimposed on his head.

This news was a huge relief. After all, it would be one thing to root for the Red Sox because they represented the American League; it's a totally different thing to wear their gear.

After all, back in the day Mayor Giuliani used to wear his

Yankee cap to City Hall on occasion, not showing much concern that the Mets also played in New York. He was that much of a Yankee fan.

So I can forgive him for rooting for the Red Sox this one time.

Time will tell whether the folks in Yankee Stadium will.

Do You Think Barry Bonds Should Get an Asterisk?

No, I do not.

Do I believe he used performance-enhancing drugs?

Yes, I do.

Do I think it's likely that we will ever see concrete proof of such usage that will stand up in a court of law?

No, I do not.

But even if it were to be proven beyond a reasonable doubt in a court of law that Barry Bonds used illegal performance-enhancing drugs at some time(s) in his 22-season career, what good would it do to slap an asterisk on any of his accomplishments?

Bonds still hit those 73 home runs in 2001 and those 762 through 2007. There would be absolutely no way to determine which ones he might have hit while "under the influence" of illegal PEDs and which ones he might have hit when he was "clean."

But what if you *could*?

What if you could determine beyond a reasonable doubt that Bonds began using PEDs sometime *after* the 2000 season, when he hit a career-high (to that point) 49 home runs, and *before* the beginning of the 2001 season, when he hit 73 homers to break Mark McGwire's 1998 record of 70? And that he continued using PEDs at least until August 7, 2007, when he swatted HR number 756 to break Hank Aaron's record?

If you were the Commissioner of Baseball, would you move to "invalidate" those PED-aided round-trippers on the grounds that they weren't legally hit home runs and therefore shouldn't count?

Let me illustrate how preposterous that notion is.

The Giants swept the Braves in 2003 in a three-game series for the first time since 1990. Bonds won the first and third games with walk-off home runs in the 10th inning, his 38th and 39th on the way to 45 on the season.

If those two home runs shouldn't count, because Bonds was using illegal PEDs, then neither should those two Giants wins, right? Retroactively, Giants forfeit; Braves win series, two games to one.

Now, let's look at how many other games the Giants have won because (or even primarily because) of Bonds's HRs since Opening Day, 2001 . . .

As I said, preposterous.

And yet, I do believe an asterisk *is* called for.

Not for Bonds's accomplishments.

No, the asterisk I'm talking about should be applied to the last two decades, from the time the Bash Brothers—José Canseco and Mark McGwire—started flexing their muscles in the late 1980s.

The *whole era* should get an asterisk.

An asterisk wouldn't have any tangible effect retroactively on W-L marks or records (individual or team). But it would be a permanent symbol of the most shameful time in baseball history since the 1919 Black Sox Scandal.

Let's call it the Asterisk Era.

What About the Individual Players Named in the Mitchell Report in December 2007?

The key word there is "named."

President George W. Bush, who owned a piece of the Texas Rangers in the 1990s, had it exactly right a few days after the report came out:

> *As you know, I'm a baseball fan. I love the sport. I think it's best that all of us not jump to any conclusions on any individual players named, but we can jump to this conclusion: performance-enhancing drugs are a major, hard-to-exaggerate threat to the fundamental integrity of the game.*

How Widespread Do **You** Think the Use of Performance-Enhancing Drugs Has Been?

Very widespread.

As a broadcaster, I've heard rumors for years about first this player being on steroids, and then that player using HGH, and some other player being on who-knows-what type of PED. That's all they've been: rumors. I've never been told by a single player that he used PEDs, and only a couple of players (José Canseco, Jason Giambi) have admitted it.

Do I *think* a lot of players have used illegal performance-enhancing drugs over the last 15 years or so?

Yes, absolutely. A whole lot more than the ones named in the Mitchell Report.

Do I *know* this to be true—as in, do I have proof?

No.

But I believe that it would be naïve to think otherwise.

The stakes for a baseball player are huge. His window of opportunity is small. The payoff is immense, both for the minor leaguer trying to make the leap to the majors and for the star hoping to lock down a multimillion-dollar contract that will provide for him and his extended family for life.

The *minimum* annual salary in baseball today is $390,000.

The *average* annual salary in baseball in 2008 will crack the $3 million barrier. (It was $2.9 million in 2007.)

That's all you need to know to understand why a ballplayer in today's game will look for every possible edge he can get. He's willing to risk just about anything, including his health, for the prize, especially when he sees other players bending, stretching, breaking the rules to gain an edge over him.

Major League Baseball and the Major League Baseball Players Association have been adversaries, not allies, in addressing the problem. Until they figure out how to pull together, the game will continue to be torn apart by the PED issue.

The fans will be judge and jury. Maybe they'll push MLB and the MLBPA to do more to rid the game of illegal drugs. Or maybe they'll decide it's okay for players to juice if that's what it takes to produce all those home runs.

If MLB and the MLBPA don't get their act together and put in place a comprehensive, concrete program to end the Asterisk Era, then that verdict might be harsh.

But you know what? My prediction is that the judge and jury—the fans—will let baseball off with a rap on the wrist, if that.

They'll boo some, maybe a lot at first, as certain players come to bat or take the mound.

And beyond that? I don't see a sharp drop in attendance or a steep decline in TV ratings. Looking at my crystal ball, I don't see a fan revolt based on repulsion at the prevalence of PEDs.

Back in the day, Yankee Stadium fans would chant "Ste-*roids!* Ste-*roids!*" every time Canseco came to the plate. He'd stand there, let it wash over him, for a few seconds, then look up toward the grandstand and slowly flex that huge right arm of his in response. They'd boo some more, but there weren't a bunch of walkouts in protest, and there certainly wasn't any boycotting of games when the A's came to town. To the fans, José was just part of the show.

My prediction is that fans will still come out to the ballpark, buy some peanuts and Cracker Jack, and root-root-root for the home team, just like they always have.

Fans have "known" about the prevalence of PEDs in baseball for many years. How could they not? And their response so far has been . . . well, have you checked major league attendance figures over the past decade and a half or so, the years that the use of PEDs took off?

Average attendance per team: *up* 26 percent since 1990.

Average home runs per team: *up* 29 percent since 1990.

Maybe they'll change their minds, but I think baseball fans may already have reached their verdict.

That leaves it up to the owners and the players to get their house in order and put in place a comprehensive, concrete program to end the Asterisk Era. Not because the fans demand it (or not), but because it's the right thing to do.

What Do You Think About the Designated Hitter?

Talk about your medium fastball right down the middle.

That's how I made my living the last few years I was in the game. I love the DH. I've loved it since former teammate Ron Blomberg showed us the way by drawing a walk from Luís Tiant in Fenway Park on April 6, 1973.

Yes, I'm a traditionalist, and I realize that guys like DiMaggio and Mantle and Mays and Aaron did just fine without the DH.

But I also believe in progress, and I believe in entertaining the people who pay our salaries. As long as the fans like the DH, and they obviously have ever since Bloomie stepped up the plate instead of Mel Stottlemyre in 1973, then how could I be against it?

The DH extends the careers of great, popular players who couldn't stay in the game otherwise.

Take Frank Thomas. The Big Hurt hit 26 homers and drove in 95 runs in 2007. That's a lot of offense. And he's 39 years old! Except for a handful of games at first base, Frank has been a full-time DH for the last nine years. He has 513 home runs and counting. Personally, I like to see him stride up to the plate and take his cuts. Pitchers don't, but I sure do. And so do fans.

See, that's the key. Fans like the DH because they prefer offense to defense, high-scoring games to low-scoring games. They want to see the ball leaving the ballpark; they want to see runners running around bases. It's all right to see a good, well-pitched 2–1 game every once in a while, but if you saw it every day, every game, it would get boring pretty fast.

Now the one big problem with the DH is that more runs equals longer games. Sometimes much longer. The American League definitely has a problem with games that run too long. A game hits the 3:30 mark and it's just the seventh inning, and I'm looking at my watch and thinking about dinner.

Much as I like the DH, I'm not a big advocate of extending the DH to the National League. You heard me right. Isn't variety the spice of life? I think it's good that there are differences between the leagues. For one thing, it makes the World Series more interesting. Plus baseball fans love to argue about their game. Extend the DH to the National League and there'd be one less thing on the Hot Stove League agenda.

What Are the Five Biggest Changes in Baseball Since You Broke In?

That's a toughie, because there have been a lot of them, from more fan-friendly ballparks to improvements in ballpark lighting to the retreat from artificial turf to a huge increase in home runs to much higher attendance to . . . How much time do you have?

1. Better Conditioning

The difference is night and day.

For starters, nobody worked out with weights when I came up. It wasn't that we were lazy. It was that weights were supposed to be bad for you: they "tightened you up." Contracts in the "good old days" only a little before my time contained provisions that specifically prohibited certain activities: no football, no boxing or wrestling—and no working with weights. I don't recall whether any of my first contracts had such a provision, but I wouldn't have considered going to the gym and lifting so much as a five-pound barbell. That's how strong the fear of working with weights was ingrained in players in my era.

Nowadays, all ballplayers work with weights, typically under special supervision by their own highly qualified personal trainers. Strength training has become as essential as aerobic training, and way more sophisticated than anything we could have dreamed of.

Speaking of which, I never even knew what the word "aerobics" meant until the early 1980s, and I was an early adopter to just about everything having to do with physical fitness. You could hardly call the sprints (for position players) and laps (for pitchers) we coasted through during spring training in the 1960s and 1970s "aerobic." We certainly never did anything but loosen up before games.

And off days? Why do you think they call them "off" days? Neither I nor anybody I ever played with would have been caught dead near a gym on an off day.

Don't forget nutrition. Looking back, I'm appalled at the stuff that dominated clubhouse spreads, and how we all wolfed it down. Many players today follow a rigorously supervised nutrition regime. They'd be crazy not to, considering what their bodies are worth if they can stay healthy and fit.

On a physical fitness scale from 1 to 10, players of my era would fall somewhere in the 4–5 range, compared to 8–9 among today's players.

I know. That's purely arbitrary. So let me put it another, even more scientific way: compared with today's ballplayers, we were a bunch of slobs.

2. The First-Year Player Draft

In 1964, the year I signed with the Yankees, I had about 15 other offers to pick from. Had I graduated from high school a year later, when the First-Year Player Draft went into effect, I would have had two choices: sign with the team that selected me in the draft, or go into another line of work.

Instead of narrowing my choice down to the Yankees or Dodgers, I'd have been picking between (say) the Washington Senators and Oklahoma Gas & Electric.

If I still wanted to play baseball rather than shinny up utility poles for a living, I could go to college and play ball and register for the draft again the following summer. But what hot-blooded young American baseball prospect wants to put his dream on hold to go off and take freshman English?

The First-Year Player Draft was put in place for two major reasons: to reduce the competitive advantage the richer clubs (Yankees, Dodgers, Cardinals, et al.) had, and to cut the size of signing bonuses.

The impact was immediate and dramatic on the latter. In 1965 the Kansas City A's had the first pick in the new draft and selected an outfielder, Rick Monday. His signing bonus: $104,000. The year before—as in, before the First-Year Player Draft—the Los Angeles Angels had to write a check for $205,000 to sign outfielder Rick Reichardt.

Since I was being wooed in the $10,000–20,000 range, the money wouldn't have mattered if I'd come out in 1965 rather than 1964. But not being able to sign with one of my top two choices, the Yankees or the Dodgers, that would have definitely mattered.

The impact of reducing the competitive advantage of rich teams wasn't so immediate; those teams already had plenty of talent in the pipeline. But it would be felt before long, as the Yankees would painfully discover.

3. The DH

You've already heard my thoughts on that subject—namely, that the DH has made for a much more entertaining game.

4. Media Coverage

Let's start with four little letters: ESPN. Ever hear of them? Well, when I broke into the big leagues, ESPN didn't exist. The Entertainment and Sports Programming Network wouldn't even be born for another 10 years.

Try imagining telecommunications today *without* the cell phone.

Now try imagining sports coverage today *without* ESPN.

But ESPN's just the tip of a very big iceberg that includes cable TV, talk radio, and the Internet. A very big iceberg that seems to just keep on growing.

The only component of sports media coverage that has shrunk over the last four decades has been newspapers. Most big league towns have lost at least one daily newspaper. And yet the pressure on players from the media has skyrocketed.

Back in my day, a player might sit down after a game and field questions from a dozen reporters and columnists, tops. That would be it in terms of his interaction with the media. Some guys didn't like even that, but I never dodged a reporter or a question. I figured talking with reporters was my best chance at getting my side of a story told.

Today, for every direct, one-on-one contact with a newspaper reporter, there's got to be a bazillion cases of something being written online or said on-air (sports talk radio's pretty much 24/7 these days) that makes its way into the larger conversation.

Star players today are gun-shy about the media. I can understand why. It probably gets old pretty fast to be asked for the 15th time "What did you mean when you said X-Y-Z?" and have to reply for the 15th time "I never said X-Y-Z."

So a lot of brand-name players adopt a strategy of duck-and-dodge. Personally, I don't think that's effective, but I was never subjected to the level of media coverage that today's ballplayers go through every day.

Three words sum up the earth shift in media coverage since I broke in: *More! More! More!*

5. Free Agency

Duh.

Free agency, of course, is the biggest change in baseball since 1969 by a wide margin. (Thank you again, Curt Flood.) But the single biggest change in the game *on the field*—how the game is actually played—since I broke in dwarfs all the rest and deserves special recognition.

And One More Thing . . .
Pitching, Pitching, Pitching

It's game two of the 2007 World Series, Red Sox vs. Rockies in Fenway Park. Top of the sixth inning, Sox up 2–1.

Sox starter Curt Schilling has been masterful for Boston, limiting Colorado to one earned run on three hits while walking one and striking out four. Schilling gets the first batter, Kaz Matsui, to pop to short, gives up a ground ball single to left to Matt Holliday, walks Todd Helton . . .

Time!

Sox manager Terry Francona walks briskly to the mound, says a word or two to his pitcher, pats him on the butt, raises his left hand to summon Hideki Okajima, and—*zap!*—Curt Schilling heads for the showers.

And your point, Professor Murcer?

The point is that back in 1969—even as recently as the early 1990s—a move like that would be absolutely, utterly, 100 percent unthinkable. Remove your starter, a right-handed stud like Schilling who's been pitching great, when he's got one out and a double play situation and is facing a right-handed batter, to bring in a lefty reliever, and in Fenway Park, to boot?

Preposterous!

Only today it's commonplace, strictly SOP.

How long a starting pitcher goes today is determined strictly by the number of pitches he's thrown. That limit varies from pitcher to pitcher, and it's constantly monitored and adjusted (say, if a pitcher has been a little gimpy). But in today's game, when your starter hits his limit, he's yanked, unless he's throwing a no-hitter or something.

As to the secondary point, lefty reliever to pitch to a righty batter in Fenway Park with a one-run lead in a World Series game—well, that does look a little odd, then or now. But you have to understand that Hideki Okajima is not just any lefty. In my book, he's the best Japanese import since the Lexus. In 2007, his first year in the majors, he gave up only 50 hits in 69 innings.

How good is that? Well, in 2007 Mariano Rivera—the best closer in baseball—gave up almost a hit an inning: 68 in $71\frac{1}{3}$ innings pitched. And in 2004, Mariano's best season, when he racked up 53 saves, he gave up 65 hits in $78\frac{2}{3}$ innings. But 50 hits in 69 innings? Unbelievable.

So how come Okajima got only a puny five saves in 2007? How come he didn't rack up 30–40?

One simple reason: closing games isn't his specialty.

Teams today have "situational relievers" whose specialty is to come in only at certain points of a game. You've got a guy who does the sixth and seventh when you're ahead. You've got arms you can bring in when you're behind a few runs and don't want to use up your best in a lost cause. You've got a setup man for the eighth inning. And you've got your closer to put the game away in the ninth.

In Boston, the 2007 closer was Jonathan Papelbon. In just his second year on the job, he was brilliant: 37 saves with a 1.85 ERA while allowing only 30 hits in $58\frac{1}{3}$ IP. But great as Papelbon was, a lot of people inside the game will tell you that Hideki Okajima was almost as important to Boston's championship season.

I'm one of them.

In today's game, the situational specialists between your starter and your closer determine whether you're still in the game, whether there's anything for your closer to close.

Back when I started out, your goal was to have your starter go all the way. He was one of the four best pitchers on your staff—we used four-man rotations then—and the longer he was out there on the mound, the better your chances were. If he was gone, it meant you were playing catch-up ball. If he was still pitching, it meant you had the lead. Not always, but most of the time.

Look at what's happened to two stats that used to be among the top measures of a pitcher's achievement: complete games and innings pitched.

COMPLETE GAMES

AMERICAN LEAGUE	NATIONAL LEAGUE
1969	
24 MEL STOTTLEMYRE	28 BOB GIBSON
2007	
7 ROY HALLADAY	4 BRANDON WEBB

INNINGS PITCHED

AMERICAN LEAGUE	NATIONAL LEAGUE
1969	
325 DENNY MCLAIN	325 $\frac{1}{3}$ GAYLORD PERRY
2007	
241 C. C. SABATHIA	236 $\frac{1}{3}$ BRANDON WEBB

Based on norms when I first came up—and which lasted well into the 1990s; CG toppers didn't go single digit until 2000—you'd look at that chart and figure that Halladay was a spot starter, not the staff ace. And you might surmise that Sabathia, with so few innings pitched, must have spent some time on the DL.

Based on today's norms, with pitch counts and situational

relievers and five-man rotations, the first two questions you'd ask would reflect the sea change in the way pitching staffs are deployed in today's game:

Why in the world did Toronto let their ace go nine innings so many times? Weren't they worried about burning him out?

Do You Think Bowie Kuhn Deserves to Be in the Hall of Fame?

No comment.

What About Marvin Miller?

No single individual has had a greater impact on the game of baseball over the last 40 years. The old redhead, Red Barber, put it even better 15 years ago: "Marvin Miller, along with Babe Ruth and Jackie Robinson, is one of the two or three most important men in baseball history."

He negotiated the first collective bargaining agreement between players and owners in 1968, and in the process got us the first increase in the annual major league minimum salary in *20 years*, all the way from $6,000 to $10,000. Four years later he got arbitration included in the Basic Agreement: before then, contract disputes between players and owners went to the commissioner for adjudication—and we all know whom the commissioner reports to. He spearheaded the move to wipe out baseball's reserve clause, which bound a player to a team for life, and win us free agency, which transformed the game. He led us through three strikes and two lockouts and maintained MLBPA solidarity through all those ordeals.

How to sum up his impact on baseball, from the players' point of view? That's easy. In his 16 years as executive director of the MLBPA, 1966–1982, the average player salary moved from $19,000 to $241,000.

So do I think he *deserves* to be in the Hall of Fame? You betcha.

Do I think he *will* be elected to the Hall? No.

Marvin came close in 2003 and 2007, falling just short of the 75 percent of the votes needed for election in the voting for executives. But then they revamped the electoral board, decreasing its size to 12 members and altering the owner-player mix: now 10 of the 12 electors are nonplayers. In the voting for the Class of 2008, he got just 3 votes, 6 shy of what he needed to get elected.

Jim Bouton, never at a loss for words, had a few choice ones concerning the issue:

> *Essentially, the decision for putting a union leader in the Hall of Fame was handed over to a bunch of executives and former executives. Marvin Miller kicked their butts and took power away from the baseball establishment—do you really think those people are going to vote him in? It's a joke . . . I blame the players. It's their Hall of Fame; it's their balls and bats that make the hall what it is. Where are the public outcries from Joe Morgan or Reggie Jackson, who was a player rep? Why don't these guys see that some of their own get on these committees? That's the least they owe Marvin Miller. Do they think they became millionaires because of the owners' generosity?*

I don't always agree with my old Yankee teammate. I sometimes find him a bit excessive. But in this case, I think he's right on the money.

Marvin Miller for the Hall of Fame!

What Did You Think About the Taco Bell Ads Coming from the Dugout During the 2007 World Series?

As far as I'm concerned, there's only one word to describe active players in the dugout shilling for Taco Bell in the middle of a World Series game: obscene.

I wasn't born yesterday. I know where the money comes from to pay for today's megabuck baseball. But in the dugout? With active players? In the middle of an inning? C'mon, let's draw a line *somewhere*. But you know what? I'm afraid it's going to get worse. I can see a conference at the mound, and an umpire strolling up to break it up, and the ump saying, "Let's break it up, guys. I'm starving, and what I really need is a Happy Meal."

Who'll Square Off in the 2008 World Series?

Let me dodge that question and tell you who I'd *like* to see in the 2008 World Series—my rotisserie league picks, if you will:

New York Yankees vs. Los Angeles Dodgers.

Joe vs. Joe.

Big Apple vs. La-La Land.

One of the greatest rivalries in baseball history, renewed.

And you know what else? I'd like to see a Yankee sweep.

I know, I know. The most exciting World Series over the last century have been seesaw seven-gamers, with the outcome not decided until the final inning of game seven.

That's great, if you're just looking for excitement, for thrills and chills and a ready source of fire for the Hot Stove League

But I'm looking for something else: revenge.

See, back in 1981, the one time I made it to the Fall Classic, the Dodgers beat the Yankees in six games. My one chance of a championship ring, and because of the Dodgers, the ring finger on my right hand is still naked.

So give me a sweep.

Sorry, Joe.

Go get 'em, Joe.

Each ball game can be a nail-biter. Start with a 2–1 pitchers' duel. Then a couple of 5–4 jobs, with one decided in the 11th inning. And finally a 13–12 free-for-all, with three homers a side, in game four.

But the headline I want to see?

Yankees Sweep Dodgers!

The Whole Baseball World Believes That the Yankees Made Joe Torre an Offer That They Knew He Would Refuse. Do You Agree?

No, I do not.

At the end of the 2007 season I—like most Yankee fans—was saddened to learn that my friend Joe Torre would not be returning as Yankee manager in 2008.

Was I that surprised? Can't say that I was, what with all the speculation of his firing cropping up almost daily during the team's truly horrendous early start. I mean, they were 14.5 games back of Boston at one point! Imagine having to come to the ball-park day after day only to watch that virtual All-Star team lose again *and* to sense—if not hear—grumblings from the front office, not to mention incessant variations on a single question from the media: "What's wrong?"

A lesser man might have folded up shop and gone home about mid-May, but Joe is a true professional in every sense of the word. I respect and admire him as a player, a manager, and a solid human being. I'll miss seeing that stoic face on the bench, and I'll miss those daily chats we shared in his office before the games—sometimes about baseball, sometimes about a new restaurant, but always flavorful, informative, and fun.

You have to understand that there are a couple of new brooms in Yankee Stadium. And Hank and Hal Steinbrenner couldn't stomach three straight first-round playoff losses and four in the last six years. They felt like they had to take dramatic action.

The Yankees didn't fire Joe. Yes, they proposed a cut in his base salary. Yes, they wanted to include incentive bonuses to a man who never needed them before to give his heart and soul to the team. And yes, they made it a one-year deal, not a three-year contract like the one he'd just finished.

But the contract the Yankees offered Joe would still have made him the highest-paid manager in baseball by a wide margin. I think the Yankees wanted Joe back. I do not believe they purpose-fully offered him a deal that they knew he would refuse.

Joe, who personifies dignity and self-respect, declined their offer, and subsequently accepted one from the Dodgers.

No reporter ever asked me to comment on all the hoopla that flooded the New York papers and sports talk shows following Joe's decision to leave. I wasn't privy to any of the high-level discussions that led to the position that the Yankees took—Hank and Hal Steinbrenner didn't consult with me.

Nor did I speak with Joe while all this was unrolling. He kept his own counsel, made his own call, and—so far as I know—never complained publicly about a single thing. I can guess what Joe said the minute the deal went down: "Let's move on."

And he has, leaving behind one heckuva legacy. In 12 seasons as manager, Joe took the Yankees into the postseason 12 times. Under him, they won six American League pennants and four World Championships. Looking at these numbers, it's hard to imagine that a front office would ever consider replacing the manager who put them up.

Speaking of legacies, the primary reason that the Yankees will continue to be the number-one franchise in sports, no matter who sits in the manager's office, is the legacy of one man: George Michael Steinbrenner III. Since 1973, the Boss has done everything humanly possible to bring Yankee fans a winner. Throughout his tenure, he has been totally, obsessively, utterly devoted to that single goal.

Like him or hate him, think what you will about his style and manner, nobody—*nobody*—can complain that Mr. Steinbrenner has ever been less than 100 percent dedicated to the pinstripes.

So now the torch in Yankee Stadium has been passed to another Joe—Joe Girardi. A recent Manager of the Year (2006, Florida Marlins), Joe is a good guy, a good baseball man, who has the skills and character to lead the Yankees along a historic path charted, most recently, by Joe Torre.

Will replacing one Joe with another Joe open the door to a disaster? Will the Yankees stumble and fall in 2008? Does this changing of the guard signal the beginning of a Third Great Depression similar to the one that engulfed the team after Mickey & Co. rode off into the sunset in the mid-to-late 1960s or the one that descended over Yankee Stadium after our 1981 World Series loss to the Dodgers?

Absolutely, positively not.

I believe Joe Girardi will take the reins with an easy transition and bring the final year of the "old" Yankee Stadium to a proud finish. More precisely, I'm predicting an AL pennant for the Yankees in 2008.

Otherwise, how am I going to get my Yankee sweep of the Dodgers in the 2008 World Series?

PLAY BALL!

*M*y goal is to throw out the first pitch in the new Yankee Stadium on Opening Day in April 2009—provided, of course, that they don't make me do it from third base.

Throwing out that first pitch on Opening Day would cap a wonderful life as a New York Yankee.

I played in the old Yankee Stadium.

I played in the new Yankee Stadium that emerged from the shell of the old one in 1976.

And in 2009, my goal is to throw a baseball in the *newest* Yankee Stadium, the third of my lifetime.

I've had a wonderful life.

Growing up, I was always a pretty good kid. Never broke any laws or spent a night in jail or got hit with a DUI. My folks kept a tight leash on me, laid down some pretty clear rules, and expected me to follow them. And I did.

My dad used to reward me—okay, bribe me—with a dollar bill if I got home by 10 P.M. on school nights. A buck could buy you three gallons of gas and a Dr Pepper, not exactly chump change. So I'd kiss Kay good night on her front porch at 9:58 P.M. and speed around the block in my old Chevy, and step through the Murcer front door at precisely 10 P.M.

I would imagine that I'm one of the few people lucky enough to say that all my boyhood dreams have come true. I played baseball for the New York Yankees. I married my high school sweetheart, my moral compass for life. I have two wonderful children and five wonderful grandchildren. I have a small army of good friends.

A wonderful life.

By the time this book hits the stores—on May 20, 2008, my 62nd birthday—I will be about 18 months into my new life.

My time with cancer has been quite a different life from the one I led and loved for the previous 40 years, first as a player and then as a broadcaster. The life in which my annual calendar began on March 1 with spring training, followed by seven months of regular-season baseball games, and then four months of R&R, which involved playing golf almost daily, riding my bike, working out, enjoying leisurely dinners, and watching my kids—and then my grandkids—grow up.

A wonderful life.

Then, about six months into 2007, Kay and I realized that I would not be returning to that life ever again. My life—our lives—had changed, irrevocably.

Change can be a tough pill to swallow, especially for me. Kay will tell you that I'm not known for my spontaneity. I like order. I like predictability. I like sticking to what I know, from my favorite rocker to my favorite pew at church. Familiarity breeds peace of mind.

Up until Christmas week 2006, I had been traveling along a very comfortable road. Very few bumps, none of them all that hard to negotiate. Then, out of nowhere, came three words: *malignant brain tumor.*

My initial response—I should say "our" initial response, because Kay and I have been drawn even closer together by those three little words—was methodical. Surgery. Therapy. Double Whammy trial. Monthly test. Repeat. (Except for the surgery part.)

But that was only the problem-solving part.

At a certain stage, it finally dawned on me; we all need to be a little smarter, a little more observant, and a little more introspective than we were in our youth. It shouldn't require a giant fly swatter from above to get our attention, to smack us down before we take an inventory of the life we are leading. But, in my case, it did: *malignant brain tumor.*

Midway through 2007, I realized I was seeing things more clearly.

I'm much more emotional now. I tear up more easily during the big and small moments, like returning to Yankee Stadium on Opening Day in 2007, or seeing my grandchildren blow out the candles on their birthday cakes, or watching a young soldier say goodbye to his girl at the airport, or taking in—as if for the first time—beautiful sunsets and skies lit by a full moon.

And though I've become something of a weeper, I find myself laughing as much as I ever did, if not more. Kay once told me when we were dating back in high school that as long as I continued to make her laugh, she'd stay with me forever. I don't think I have any worries on that score.

Another positive consequence of my *malignant brain tumor* has been an increase in self-awareness. I've jumped on the opportunity to hit the rewind button and review every event in my career. (Okay, maybe I have forwarded through a few frustrating moments against tough lefties.) But it has been a wonderful trip down memory lane. I had forgotten so many of the special encounters that baseball life allowed me to be part of.

Since my *malignant brain tumor* was removed, I've pulled out boxes of decades-old scrapbooks, filled with yellowed newsprint and photos reminding me of the many stops along the way in a rich, wonderful life.

We have revived connections with people and places that have always been in our hearts, but tucked away in the back.

Since my *malignant brain tumor* became public knowledge, I have heard from distant relatives, former teammates, old high school buddies and teachers, and people in public life whom I have met over the course of my wonderful life. They have bolstered the unwavering support extended to me by my immediate family and friends.

From the very start of a journey that began Christmas week 2006, Kay and I believe—we *know*—that we have been God-led.

And so we thank our God for illuminating the path, our family for taking our hands, and our friends and fans for cheering us along the way to a *new* wonderful life.